To the intrepid travelers who braved the khans and the Bolsheviks;

trekked across frozen steppes;

traversed the Kyzylkum and Karakum Deserts;

crossed the Pamirs, the Roof of the World;

and returned home to write about it.

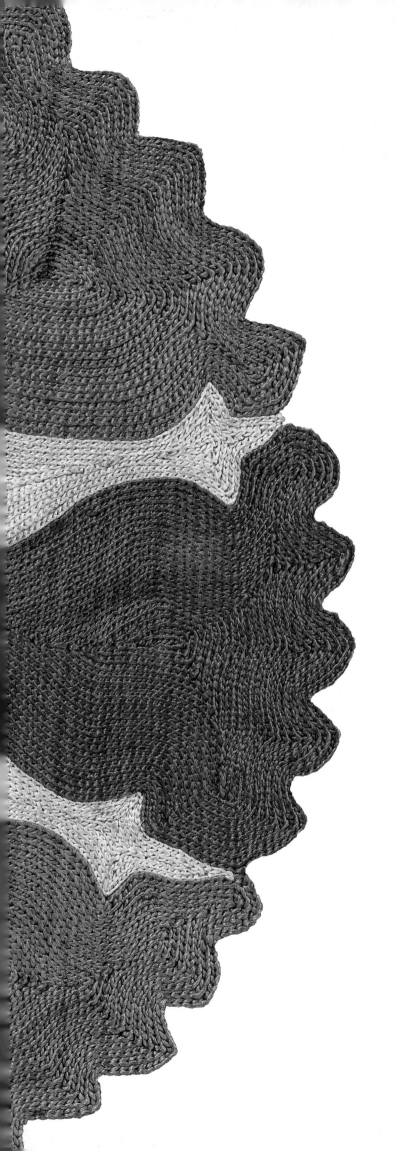

SILK
and
COTTON

TEXTILES
from the
CENTRAL ASIA
that was

~~~

Susan Meller

photographs by

Don Tuttle

with an essay by

Robert Kushner

Abrams, New York

CONTENTS

PREFACE

"Of a sudden one hears the muted sounds of bells far away. It is strange music, it creates an impression that is magical. It makes one sleepy. The sound gets more and more precise, finally it is very close. Like huge black ghosts, the camels appear out of the darkness; slowly, majestically, with dignity they move across the desert sands."
—Sven Hedin, letter to his family

For the past decade, I have traveled extensively through the Central Asia of the khans, the tsars, the Bolsheviks, and the Soviets. My guides spanned eight centuries. They were English, Russian, American, Swedish, Danish, Austrian, Swiss, Spanish, Italian, Hungarian, and Moroccan. They were explorers, adventurers, geologists, ethnographers, clergymen, merchants, journalists, diplomats, counter-revolutionaries, and spies. Indomitable travelers all, they endured brutal hardships and returned home to tell about them. These men and women are gone now, but their experiences and observations remain vividly alive in the books they left behind. Some had political and/or self-serving agendas, in particular those Russians and British engaged in the struggle for control over Central Asia in what came to be known as the "Great Game." Some were influenced by their ideological sympathies, for example pro-tsarist or pro-Bolshevik. But most took it upon themselves to record what they saw as accurately as they could, albeit through a personal lens. These are the people who have shaped my impressions of the Central Asia that was.

As I worked on this book, a phrase kept cropping up in my mind: "Nothing is as it seems." At times the process of creating *Silk and Cotton* was like an archaeological dig. Exciting finds, both textiles and tidbits of information, were uncovered, only to have other discoveries cast doubts. One expert's opinion contradicted another's. Like mirages on the shifting sands of the Takla Makan Desert, facts could be elusive. Central Asia, or Turkestan as it was formerly known, is a jigsaw puzzle with a million tiny, scattered pieces. I've gathered some of those pieces in this book and fitted them together into a small part of the whole, offering the reader a glimpse into an enigmatic place and its people. As that astute Hungarian Orientalist and traveler Arminius Vámbéry wrote in the preface to his book *Sketches of Central Asia* (1868), "The slightest notice of a country so

little known to us as Turkestan, which political questions will soon bring into the front of passing questions, will always have its uses."

Central Asian people lived their daily lives surrounded by textiles, most of their own making. Textiles defined practically every aspect of their traditional way of life, beginning with a young girl's dowry, through marriage, childbirth, old age, and death. There were *suzanis* for the marriage bed; niche covers; prayer mats; patchwork bedding quilts; camel trappings for a bridal procession; bags to hold tea, scissors, and mirrors; crib covers; lovingly embroidered children's hats; and robes of every color and pattern. Having spent many years as a textile designer, I was first attracted to the unusual patterns on the Russian-export cottons that lined many ikat robes. It was next to impossible to find just the cloth itself, so I began buying old robes simply for their printed linings. The collection grew until the time came to open the robes and give the long-hidden linings their due. *Russian Textiles: Printed Cloth for the Bazaars of Central Asia* was published by Abrams in 2007. As I became more immersed in the rich and varied textile culture of this region, it became impossible to focus only on linings—they were part of a much wider world—and so my collection expanded, and this book became the companion to *Russian Textiles*. With a few exceptions, the textiles illustrated in *Silk and Cotton* are drawn from my collection and, as such, reflect my personal taste. Rugs are not included as they are a world unto themselves; nor are other woolen items, such as tent bands and woven storage bags.

When writing about the broad spectrum of Central Asian textiles, one must invariably face the issue of transliteration. While Turkic and Persian dialects as well as Russian are still widely used, more than a century of Russian control has added further layers to the complexity. In many areas, the written language went from Arabic (prior to 1928) to Latin (1928–40) to Cyrillic (1940–91) and back to Latin (post independence). Spellings, translations, and pronunciations continue to evolve. Ascribing a name to a particular item is daunting. Take, for example, a hat: Not only does each broad ethnic group have their own generic word for "hat," each regional area or tribal subgroup has a term for its distinct style of hat, and as these styles vary, further descriptive terms come into play—all with multiple spellings. Because geographical names changed throughout history (depending on who

PAGE 1 **NIKOLAI GRIGORIEVICH KOTOV (1889–1968),** *THE TAQI-ZARGARON BAZAAR,* ***BUKHARA,*** 1933. Oil on board, 10 x 14.5". Author's collection.

The Taqi-Zargaron (jewelers' market) was built in the 16th century, and today the mud-brick vaulted dome still houses merchants "in mysterious recesses where rubies and emeralds and Circassian slaves once changed hands for fabulous prices."[1] On the far right of the painting is the Kalyan Minaret. One hundred fifty-eight feet high, it was the tallest freestanding building in the world at the time it was built in 1127. Kotov was an acclaimed Russian artist who spent a considerable time in Central Asia painting scenes of everyday life.

1 Fitzroy Maclean, *Back to Bokhara* (New York: Harper & Brothers, 1959), 116.

PAGES 2-3 **SUZANI (detail).** Bukhara, Uzbekistan, 3rd quarter, 19th c. Silk chain stitch on handwoven cotton.

PAGES 4-5 **MAN'S ROBE.** See page 43 for full description

was in power at the time) and spellings varied widely, I chose what appeared to be the most commonly used term prior to Central Asian independence in 1991.

I think of this book as a Central Asian album that introduces the reader to a broad range of silk and cotton textiles as well as to the people who made them. This is indeed such a vast and complex region that to do much more than introduce is not possible within the constraint of three hundred pages. To try and assign an attribution to every textile as to ethnic group, date, and place of origin is perhaps overly ambitious—actually, probably impossible. However, with pieces that were problematic, I chose to risk erring on the side of an educated opinion rather than offer no opinion at all. Whenever possible, I sought the input of other people well versed in Central Asian textiles. I also felt it important to put the textiles within their cultural-historical context. Period photographs by Russian photographers Max Penson and Sergei Prokudin-Gorskii; Western travelers such as Annette Meakin, Stephen Graham, and Edward Murray; explorer Sven Hedin; and photojournalists Maynard Owen Williams and John McCutcheon, among others, all give a sense of time and place. Each textile has its own integrity, and Don Tuttle's photographs do them justice. Some examples are particularly fine and showy, such as the early *suzanis*, but most are ordinary pieces made for everyday use. These are the textiles that were, and sometimes still are, part of the lives of the people of Central Asia.

—Susan Meller, 2013

Setting Forth on the Desert of Takla Makan, based on a sketch by Sven Hedin from "On the Roof of the World," *Harper's Magazine*, October 1898.

INTRODUCTION

"From the world that is, I want to go to that which was. From the West of today to the Orient of yesterday." —Countess Ida von Hahn-Hahn (1805–80), *Orientalische Briefe* (Letters from the Orient), 1844

"I don't want to live in the past, but I want to live in a present which is rooted in the past . . . the world is constructed for us by its history, and the constructors live on in their work." —Philip Glazebrook, *Journey to Khiva: A Writer's Search for Central Asia,* 1994

The heart of this book allows the reader a view of Central Asia through the prism of its everyday textiles and the people who made and used them. This introduction serves as a historical backdrop, setting the stage for the textiles themselves. Hundreds of different tribes ranged over an immense area of steppes, deserts, mountains, and oases. Their customs, languages, and ethnicities varied, yet for all of them, textiles were a vital part of everyday life. Clothing and household textiles were not simply practical necessities; they also were steeped in tradition, reflected pride in craftsmanship, and evoked aesthetic appreciation. They were objects of beauty that gave pleasure and magical protection to those who made and lived with them. The faded and tattered child's patchwork bib; the small, intricately embroidered baby hat; the moth-eaten tent hanging; the stained ikat robe—all of these pieces as well as the others illustrated in this book have survived because they were valued for far more than their monetary worth.

HISTORICAL OVERVIEW

The regions that now make up Central Asia have had many names throughout their long and complex history. To the ancients they were Khorezm, Sogdiana, Bactria, Margiana, Parthia, and Transoxiana. Under the Mongols, they were the Ulus of Chagatai. From the thirteenth century until the mid-nineteenth century the West referred to the entire area as Tartary. By 1865 Imperial Russia had gained enough control of Central Asia to declare it the Province of Turkestan. Henceforth, the region was known as Russian Turkestan or Western Turkestan—until the Bolsheviks came to power in 1917. Between 1924 and 1936 the Soviets divided Turkestan into five republics: Uzbekistan (1924), Turkmenistan (1924), Tajikistan (1929), Kyrgyzstan (1936), and Kazakhstan (1936). In 1991, after the dissolution of the Soviet Union, all five republics, colloquially referred to as the "Stans," became the independent countries that now make up Central Asia.

Historians have written volumes about Central Asia, from its ancient civilizations two thousand years ago to its recent independence in 1991. Franciscan friar William of Rubruck traveled through Central Asia from 1253 to 1255 and ambassador Ruy Gonzalez de Clavijo of Spain from 1403 to 1406. Emissaries of medieval kings, both men chronicled their trips to the courts of the great Mongol Khan Möngke and Timur-i-Leng (Tamerlane), respectively. From 1271 to 1295 Marco Polo voyaged from Venice to the court of Kublai Khan and back, and in 1325 Ibn Battuta, a Moroccan Berber, began the thirty-year odyssey that would take him through most of the known Islamic world and beyond. These two men traveled a total of ninety thousand miles and offered fascinating accounts of what they saw. Leaders of nineteenth- and early twentieth-century scientific expeditions, among them Sven Hedin and Ole Olufsen, charted the terrain and collected many ethnic artifacts; archaeologist Sir Aurel Stein uncovered lost civilizations; and ethnographers studied the customs of the region's many diverse peoples. Explorers, missionaries, British and Russian officers, diplomats, spies, and intrepid travelers such as Ella Maillart, Ella Christie, and Gustav Krist, all published accounts of their adventures. Contemporary social scientists study the effects of Russian/Soviet occupation; political scientists write about the expanding role of Central Asia in the world today; and collectors, dealers, artists, photographers, museums, and galleries mount exhibitions. Yet the majority of these perspectives are presented by non–Central Asians, and so, for the most part, it is through their lenses that the outside world sees Central Asia.

Perhaps the overall historical impression that readers will come away with is admiration for the Central Asian peoples' endurance and resilience. In the last century alone, millions of Central Asians died in the Civil War between the Bolshevik Red Army and the pro-tsarist White Army, and in the massive displacements and ensuing famine. Yet against this often dark and chaotic background, magnificent buildings with glazed tiles of turquoise, cobalt, and emerald green

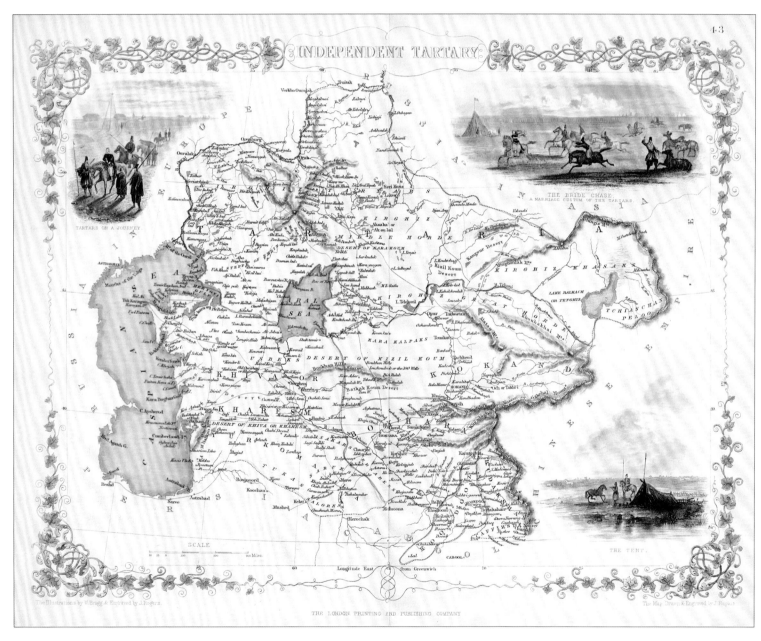

1. INDEPENDENT TARTARY. The London Printing and Publishing Company, 1851.
Central Asia was referred to as "Tartary" until the mid-19th century.

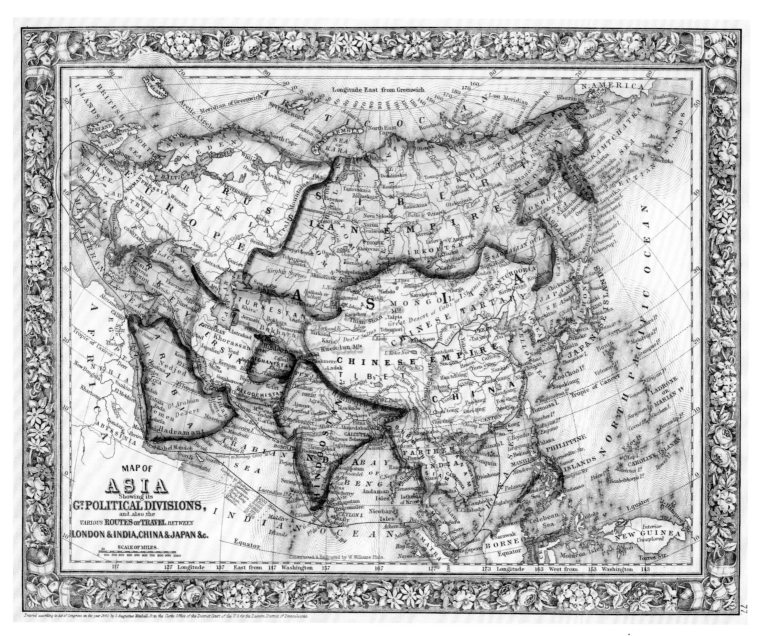

2. MAP OF ASIA. Augustus Mitchell, Jr., USA, 1860. At the time this map was created, Central Asia was called Turkestan, and Kazakhstan was firmly under Russian control. Within the next fifteen years, the Russians conquered the khanates of Kokand, Bukhara, and Khiva.

faience glowed like jewels; bazaars were crowded with merchants and shoppers in rainbow-colored robes; and women continued to embroider beautiful textiles.

WARLORDS OF OLD

For more than two thousand years Central Asia, strategically located between Russia to the north and west, China to the east, and Iran and Afghanistan to the south, has been invaded, conquered, and occupied by the armies of its neighbors. After the death of Muhammad in 632, the spread of Islam became the mandate of the ruling caliphs. The Arab conquest of Central Asia began in the mid-seventh century and was solidified by the Battle of Talas between the Muslim and Chinese

armies. This decisive battle established Muslim political, cultural, and religious dominance in the region.

The names of some of the greatest warlords in history are associated with this vast region: Alexander the Great, Cyrus the Great, Darius I, Darius III, Genghis Khan, Timur-i-Leng, and Babur. These conquerors brought mass destruction, but they also contributed to a rich heritage. Among the most infamous, Genghis Khan (c. 1162–1227) was born in Mongolia. He succeeded in uniting the many fractious Mongol tribes, and his armies (estimated to be between 150,000 and 200,000 horsemen strong) overran much of Central Asia, Afghanistan, Persia, China, the Caucasus, and Russia. Once the carnage was over and these lands came under the Mongol Empire's well-ordered sphere

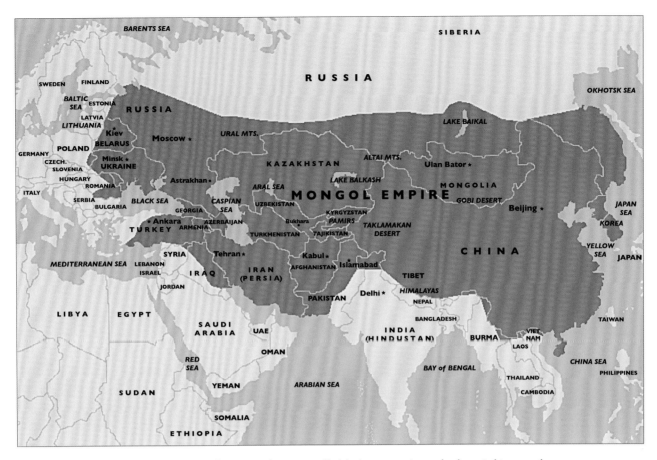

3. THE MONGOL EMPIRE. The empire at its height, c. 1279, when it controlled the largest contiguous land area in history and one-fifth of the world's population.

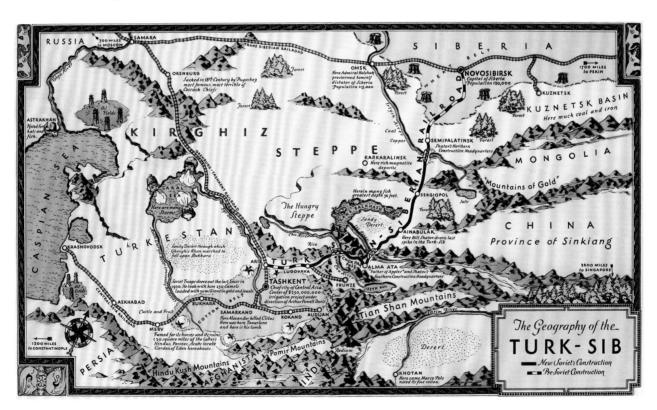

4. TURK-SIB MAP. *Fortune* magazine, 1930. The Turkestan-Siberian railroad was conceived in 1886. Work began in 1912, and it was finally completed in 1930 under Stalin's first Five-Year Plan.

5. AMIR TEMUR. Tashkent, Uzbekistan. This statue of Timur-i-Leng (Tamerlane) was erected in Tashkent's central square in 1993, the latest in a series of monuments that included General Konstantin Petrovich von Kaufman (1870), Free Workers (1917), the October Revolution's 10th anniversary (1927), Stalin (1947), and Karl Marx (1968).

of influence, travelers and caravans could pass safely along various established routes, which became known collectively as the Silk Road. Exchanges of commodities, technology, and ideas flowed until internal strife among Genghis Khan's descendants disrupted these overland passages, and they were replaced by faster sea routes. At its height, the Mongol Empire controlled approximately 16 percent of the earth's land area and an estimated one hundred million people—the largest contiguous empire in history.

Timur-i-Leng (1336–1405), also known as Timur the Lame or Tamerlane, was born in the town of Shakhrisabz (known then as Kesh) in what is now Uzbekistan, to the prince of a minor Turko-Mongol tribe. He had an insatiable lust for conquest and spent thirty-five years waging one victorious campaign after another. While he lived, his empire stretched from Georgia on the Black Sea to India, including much of Central Asia. He died at the age of sixty-nine while en route to attack China. Timur both destroyed and built on a grand scale. As ruler of one of the most powerful empires on Earth, he set out to create a befitting capital. Though he devastated cities such as Delhi and Baghdad, he spared the lives of their best artisans, whom he brought back to his homeland and its capital, Samarkand, where they helped construct magnificent buildings, including the Bibi Khanum

mosque and Gur-e Amir, his mausoleum. Captured Syrian and Persian textile weavers helped to make Samarkand a famous silk-weaving center. Today, Timur is considered a national hero in Uzbekistan, as is his descendant Babur (1483–1530), who was born to the ruler of the principality of Ferghana. Babur briefly captured and controlled Samarkand, but ultimately he was forced out by the Uzbeks in 1501, which brought the Timurid dynasty in Central Asia to an end. However, Babur went on to defeat the leaders of Afghanistan and India, thus setting the stage to become the founder of the Mughal Empire.

EMIRATE OF BUKHARA

Babur's loss of Samarkand to the Uzbek leader Shaybani Khan (a descendant of Genghis Khan) ushered in the one-hundred-year reign of the Shaybanid Empire, a prosperous and culturally significant period for the Uzbek people. Shaybani's grandfather, Abu al-Khayr (1412–68), had succeeded in unifying a large number of Uzbek tribes and their loyalty extended to his grandson, who was defeated and killed in battle in 1510. Twenty years later, the capital was moved from Samarkand to Bukhara (known as "Bukhara the Noble"), which became a center for the arts and education. The Shaybanid dynasty came to an end with the death of its ruler Abdullah Allah Khan II in 1598 and was replaced by the Janid (Astrakhanid) dynasty, which in turn was defeated in 1740 by Nadir Shah, the ruler of Persia, and made into a vassal state. After Nadir Shah's death in 1747, Muhammad Rahim, an Uzbek chief of the Manghit tribe, gained control of Bukhara, and by 1753 the Uzbek Manghit dynasty had begun its rise to power. In 1785 Shah Murad declared himself the first emir of Bukhara, which at that time included most of what is now Uzbekistan as well as part of Tajikistan. Shah Murad's descendants continued to rule until the Russians made the emirate a protectorate in 1868–73. By then it had been reduced to half its original size. The emirs were allowed to maintain control of their internal affairs until 1920, when the last emir, Alim Khan, was forced into exile by the Bolsheviks and the emirate was abolished. It officially became the Bukharan People's Soviet Republic and remained so until 1924, when it was incorporated into the newly formed Uzbek Soviet Socialist Republic.

KHANATE OF KOKAND

In 1709 a Shaybanid leader, Shahrukh, established a state in the Ferghana region, designating the town of Kokand his capital. By the time this city-state was officially declared the Khanate of Kokand in 1805, its territory had grown to include what is now eastern Uzbekistan, Tajikistan, Kyrgyzstan, and southern Kazakhstan. The khanate was wracked by internal instability and by attacks from Bukhara, and then, during the mid-nineteenth century, the Russian army began advancing from the northeast. By 1855 the Russians had firm control over Kazakhstan and had launched their campaigns against cities belonging to the Kokand khanate. One by one they fell—Bishkek, Tashkent, and Samarkand—until all of the khanate was under Russian control. In

1875 the besieged khan, Said Muhammed Khudayar, fled into exile. His son briefly succeeded him, but in 1876, after a prolonged rebellion, the Khanate of Kokand was officially abolished by the Russians and renamed the Ferghana Province of the Turkestan Governor-Generalship. After the Soviets created nation-states by establishing boundaries based along tenuous (and highly contentious) ethnic lines, the lands of the former khanate became part of the newly formed republics of Uzbekistan, Tajikistan, Kazakhstan, and Kyrgyzstan.

KHANATE OF KHIVA

The third Uzbek khanate was Khiva, part of a vast region historically known as Khwarezm (Khorezm). At its peak, it extended from the Aral Sea south into much of Persia and southeastward into Afghanistan. In 1379 Timur succeeded in adding this region to his growing empire, and his descendants retained control of it until the Shaybanid descendants of Genghis Khan's son Jöchi overthrew them. They ruled from 1511 to 1804 and, in turn, were followed by the Uzbek Kungrat dynasty. The Russians had their designs on Khiva as early as 1717, when Peter the Great sent in troops but was soundly defeated. Another attempt in 1839 also failed, but in 1872–73 the Russians finally defeated the Khivans and a peace treaty was signed, albeit with onerous terms for the khan. By then, the khanate had shrunk to a fraction of its original size. Unlike Bukhara and Kokand, which had sizeable Russian populations and well-developed trade, the tsarist government considered Khiva a backwater region and a thorn in its side. The surrounding area was populated by rebellious Turkmen tribes that fought fiercely against Russian and Khivan control. It was the last area of Turkestan to be completely conquered with the Russian capture of Merv in 1884. The khans, Muhammad Rahim and his son Isfandiyar, were allowed to remain as titular rulers and retained some autonomy in their internal affairs. After Isfandiyar's death in 1918, his son Sayid Abdullah had a tumultuous two years before he was forced to abdicate to pro-Bolshevik forces. The khanate was renamed the Khorezm People's Soviet Republic in 1920 and in 1924 it was officially incorporated into what is now the autonomous republic of Karakalpakstan and Khorezm province, both in Uzbekistan.

NOMADIC TRIBES

"Pastoral nomads have always fascinated the more earthbound peoples among whom they live." —Ida Nicolaisen, Editor's Preface to *Exploring Central Asia*, 2010

"Man must keep moving; for behold, sun, moon, stars, water, beast, bird, fish, all are in movement, it is but the dead and the earth that remain in their place!" —Kyrgyz nomad woman, from *Travels in Central Asia*, Arminius Vámbéry, 1864

Historically, the peoples of Central Asia have been broadly categorized as either nomadic or sedentary, and geography was

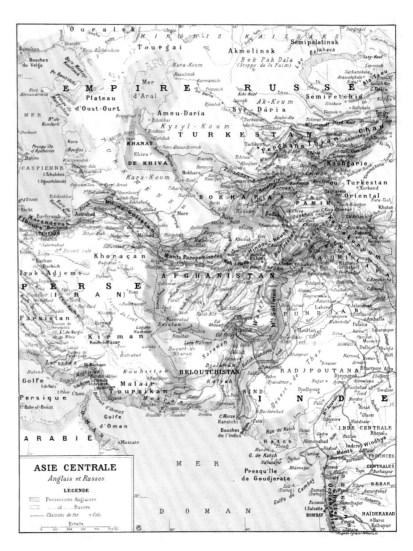

6. CENTRAL ASIA. *Atlas Larousse*, Paris, 1903. By the time this map was created, all of what is now Central Asia was part of the Russian Empire—called Russian Turkestan to distinguish it from Chinese Turkestan. The khanates of Khiva and Bukhara were still nominally independent.

largely a determining factor. Without irrigation, the windswept steppes, with their endless expanse of flat grasslands, were more conducive to supporting domesticated animals than agriculture. Large herds of fat-tailed sheep, goats, cattle, horses, and camels provided meat, fat, and milk, as well as the hides and wool needed to make clothing, felts, and carpets. Two-humped, shaggy Bactrian camels as well as horses and donkeys served as transport for riders and their possessions and provided dried dung for fuel. A large encampment (*aul*) of sixty tents and three hundred people could have as many as two thousand horses, one thousand camels, two thousand cattle, and ten thousand sheep and goats.[1]

Because their animals continually needed fresh pastureland, the people who kept them were continually on the move. Portable shelters (yurts)[2] and transportable household goods were a necessity. Kazakhs and Kyrgyz made extensive use of felt, mostly for floor and tent coverings, which the women made primarily from sheep wool. They also wove wool-pile carpets and tent bands. Silk floss and imported cloth were used to make large embroidered yurt hangings. Heavy coats, trousers, and hats of fur, sheepskin, leather, and felt were especially suited to the harsh winters and rugged nomadic lifestyle.

Although steppe populations were sparse compared to those of the settled villages and towns, the nomads' superb horsemanship, coupled with their archery skills (prior to the advent of firearms) and ease of mobility, gave them a decisive advantage when carrying out raids or warfare. They were also well positioned to provide pack animals and serve as guides to traveling caravans. Most of the steppe peoples of Central Asia were of Turko-Mongol origins and practiced forms of shamanism. Later the Silk Roads facilitated the introduction of Buddhism, Zoroastrianism, Manichaeism, Nestorian Christianity, and finally Islam. After the Arab conquests in the eighth century, Sunni Islam became the most widely adopted religion.

The Kazakh hordes were the first of the nomadic peoples to be subjugated by Imperial Russia's advances into Central Asia. During the eighteenth century, a line of forts and Cossack settlements was built along the northern Kazakh steppe bordering Russia. In order to distinguish between the words "Cossack" and "Kazakh," the Russians called the latter "Kirghiz" or "Kirghiz-Kaisaks." To further confuse matters, the people now known as Kyrgyz were called "Kara-Kirghiz." ("Kazakh" and "Kyrgyz" became the norm after the Soviets partitioned Turkestan into five republics.) In 1863 the Russians divided Kazakhstan into two districts: The northern and eastern regions were put under the administration of the Steppe District; the rest was made part of Russian Turkestan. During the latter part of the nineteenth century, Russian settlers began flooding into the fertile steppe lands of Kazakhstan. By 1917 there were nearly one million Russians in Kazakhstan, an estimated 30 percent of the population.

Traditional nomadic life was disrupted as Russian settlers took over grazing lands, erected fences, and, through irrigation, made use of the scarce water supplies. This situation intensified as railroads were built, revolution and civil war broke out, and the Soviets began collectivization. Between 1931 and 1934, Kazakh nomads lost a huge percentage of their herds due to forced collectivization, confiscation, and their own decision to slaughter their livestock rather than turn it over to Soviet authorities.[3] Food shortages became acute and practically no relief was sent from Russia. During this time, it is estimated that as many as 1.5 million Kazakhs died of starvation and epidemics, a majority of them nomadic herdsmen.[4]

South of the steppe and to the west were the drier, hotter regions around the Caspian and Aral Seas, in what are now Karakalpakstan (literally, "black hat land") and Turkmenistan. Hemmed in by two deserts, the Karakum (Black Sand) to the south and the Kyzylkum (Red Sand) to the east, the amount of arable land was limited. Most of the population in this region settled around the oasis towns of Khiva and Merv, leaving the rest of the lands to the seminomadic Karakalpaks and the numerous nomadic Turkmen tribes. Skilled horsemen, the Turkmen were notorious for their raiding parties (*alaman*), which preyed on caravans, hapless travelers, and small border settlements. These attacks not only netted livestock and other booty, but also slaves. The Turkmen captives were primarily Persian villagers and occasional Russian fishermen taken from the shores of the Caspian, while the Kazakhs tended to kidnap Russian soldiers and settlers on the Orenburg frontier. Some of the captured men, women, and children were ransomed and the rest either kept as slaves by their captors or sold in the bazaars of Khiva and Bukhara.[5] After the Russian conquest of Khiva in 1873, the khan was required to issue a proclamation abolishing slavery. (At the time, there were an estimated thirty thousand slaves, twenty-one of whom were Russian, the rest Persian.[6])

Turkmen women wove what were considered the finest wool-pile carpets, storage bags, and trappings. They also made intricately embroidered small bags, children's garments, robes, and hats for family use. While Turkmen women wove their own traditional cloth, the raw silk and cotton they used was obtained from settled neighbors—wool came from their own flocks of fat-tailed Karakul sheep. Each tribal group had a distinctive lexicon of patterns, handed down from generation to generation. In the latter half of the nineteenth century, however, political, social, and economic upheaval caused tribes to suffer large population and livestock losses, leaving a woman's carpet-weaving skill as many families' main asset. The need to produce more, and often larger rugs than were traditionally used in the yurt, with patterns and colors that appealed to outside markets, resulted in less refined weaving and a mixing of various tribal motifs.

The main Turkmen tribes in Turkmenistan were the Tekke (centered in the Merv and Akhal oases), Yomut (southern Caspian Sea region and the area near Khiva), Ersari (along the southern

7. KYRGYZ WOMAN AT LOOM. Tekes Valley, 1935. Wool tent bands were woven on narrow ground looms, and the bands were used to secure felt covers to the yurt framework. Photograph by Edward Murray.

banks of the Amu Darya River), Chodor (northern and southeastern Turkmenistan), and Saryk (southern Turkmenistan, near the Iranian and Afghan borders) with many smaller subtribes. Turkic people, they too became Sunni Muslims.

Far to the east, the lands that are now part of southern Tajikistan, southeastern Uzbekistan, and northern Afghanistan eventually became home to the fiercely independent Uzbek-Lakai and the more pastoral Kungrat tribes. Both tribes were originally part of the large Kipchak steppe confederation. They led seminomadic lives that depended on sheep and horse-raising, some agricultural crops, trade with oasis towns, and occasional raids for plunder. After the Soviets divided Turkestan into five republics, the Kungrat found themselves a majority ethnic group in what is now the Surkhandarya province of Uzbekistan. The Lakai, however, did not fare as well. Their homelands were incorporated into present-day Tajikistan, where they became a small, second-class minority. During the 1920s many joined the Basmachi movement, under the leadership of Ibrahim Beg, as guerrilla fighters against the Bolsheviks. By the early 1930s the Soviets had succeeded in putting down the rebels. Many fighters and their families were forced to flee into Afghanistan as a result, while others remained in Tajikistan, where most were settled on cotton collectives.

The women of both tribes were highly skilled embroiderers. Most textiles—embroidered decorative hangings (*ilgich*), storage bags of various sizes and shapes (*chai khalta, napramach, bugjama, aina khalta*), and cotton patchwork quilts (*caroq*)—were made as furnishings for their yurts or mud-brick houses. Lakai and Kungrat embroidered hangings display distinctive bold geometric shapes, swirling sun disks, and stylized scorpion motifs. Brightly colored and highly sought after in today's market, they were often stitched on a ground cloth of imported wool broadcloth, usually red or black.

The seminomadic Kyrgyz tribes inhabited the mountainous regions of the Altai, Tien Shan, Alai, and Pamir ranges, which run along the borders of China and Kazakhstan southwest into Kyrgyzstan and Tajikistan. During the harsh winter months they erected felt-covered yurts in the lowland valleys, where their herds of fat-tailed sheep, horses, cattle, and yaks could find forage. In early summer the women dismantled the yurts, and people and animals migrated to the lush, cool pasturelands of the high mountain plateaus.

Before the influx of imported cloth, Kyrgyz women made all of their families' clothing from local materials—leather and fur that they tanned themselves, and wool that was woven on narrow horizontal ground looms into strips that were later joined together. Camel hair was highly prized and woven into cloth called "*piazy*," which was used to make warm, weatherproof overcoats (*chepkin*). Felt made from sheep's wool was used for shepherds' capes, overcoats, and the distinctive white felt hats with upturned brims (*kalpak*) that are still worn today. Around the mid-1800s, when cultivated cotton could be bartered for, Kyrgyz women began to weave cotton cloth for their everyday clothes. Toward the latter part of the century, when factory-made plain

and printed cotton material from Russia became widely available, this practice more or less ended. In 1914 English journalist Stephen Graham observed in a small town in east Kazakhstan, ". . . the Kirghiz were extremely critical as to the quality of the cotton and the color and design. You could not palm off shoddy cotton on these people. It was their Sunday best as well as week-day . . . Its quality and appearance mattered."[7] Access to new materials such as silk and velvet, combined with more interaction with their settled Uzbek and Tajik neighbors, brought about a change in Kyrgyz traditional dress. Heavy woolen garments began to be replaced by padded silk ikat and striped silk/cotton *bekasab* robes (*chapan*) in the style of the nearest oasis towns, as well as Russian-style coats with a western cut (*beshmant*). Girls and women wore silk or cotton shifts with velvet vests. Married women continued to wear their tall white turbans.

Household textiles consisted of felt carpets, woven wool tent bands, various types of storage bags, quilts, and decorative hangings, such as *tush kiyiz*, the large dowry embroidery that a bride brought to her new home. A Kyrgyz family was proud of the fine needlework that decorated its yurt, garments, and animal trappings. Migrations were times to proclaim the family's status: Women wore their finest clothes, and horses and camels were equipped with their best harnesses and transport bags. Stephen Graham wrote, "Brides—girls of thirteen or fourteen—ride in extraordinary state in their midst, seated on palfreys [riding horses] with scarlet horsecloths, themselves clad in bright cottons . . . and ride with wonderful grace, as if conscious of being the treasure of the whole caravan."[8]

SEDENTARY PEOPLES

Ancient oasis cities such as Khiva, Bukhara, Samarkand, Tashkent, Kokand, and Ferghana were established in fertile flatlands sustained by the Amu Darya and Syr Darya Rivers (the legendary Oxus and Jaxartes, respectively) and the Zeravshan River. Over millennia, an extensive and complex irrigation system of canals was developed that diverted much of the rivers' water into fields and towns. When irrigated, the fertile loess soil was ideal for growing grain (wheat, barley, and rice), fruits (luscious melons, pomegranates, stone fruits, and grapes), vegetables, and cotton. Large herds of animals were no longer needed; a few cattle, sheep, goats, and chickens could help provide for a family. Everyone but the very poor had a few horses and donkeys—a transportation necessity.

Town life offered an alternative to an agricultural or nomadic lifestyle. One could survive as an artisan, merchant, street peddler, innkeeper, mullah, city official, or any of the myriad specialized niches that Central Asian urban society provided. Most of the residents were either Uzbek or Tajik, with smaller communities of Jews, Arabs, Hindus, Afghans, Armenians, and Gypsies. Originally members of nomadic Turkic tribes, many Uzbeks had settled into an agricultural or urban life by the late eighteenth century. By then the Uzbek khans were the rulers of the most powerful khanates in

Central Asia: Bukhara, Khiva, and Kokand. The other dominant ethnic group was the Tajiks. Of Persian ancestry, they are believed by some scholars to have moved north into Central Asia after the Arab conquest of Persia in the seventh century. The majority settled in the oasis towns where they and the Uzbeks engaged in many of the same occupations. The Pamiris, or so-called "Mountain Tajiks," lived in the mountainous regions of the Pamirs, known as the Roof of the World, primarily in what is now Tajikistan. Their villages (*kishlaks*) were scattered in the fertile valleys, where crops could be raised and small herds of goats, sheep, and cattle could graze. Most were members of the Shia Ismaili sect. Urban Tajiks and Uzbeks wore similar clothes and shared many of the same customs. Both were Sunni Muslims and lived as neighbors in the towns; however, they spoke different languages—Tajiks, a dialect of Farsi, and Uzbeks, a Turkic dialect.

During the nineteenth century, the Russians started broadly applying the term "Sart" to those people whom they deemed sedentary as opposed to nomadic, regardless of ethnicity. Later the term came to refer primarily to settled Uzbeks and Tajiks. The word's origins are unclear, and its definition and usage is hotly debated—both within and outside of Central Asia. Some thought it pejorative, others identified with it, and many simply shrugged it off as meaningless. Ole Olufsen wrote in his book, *The Emir of Bokhara and His Country*, published after his 1898–99 expedition, "Sart is said to be originally a nickname or term of abuse employed by the nomads against the sedentary people; now even sedentary Kirghiz in Turkestan are fond of calling themselves Sarts."[9] The term appears frequently on postcards and in literature from the period. However, under the Soviets, its use was phased out. Instead, all were encouraged to consider themselves members of their newly established republic—that is, Uzbek, Tajik, Kyrgyz, Kazakh, or Turkmen nationals, and, as such, loyal citizens of the USSR.

Settled and nomadic peoples relied on each other for certain goods. Their lives overlapped in the bazaars where Kyrgyz and Kazakhs could trade livestock, wool, and hides for such items as factory-made cloth, silk floss, tea, and metal cooking utensils. Turkmen found a ready market in the bazaars of Merv and Bukhara for their woven pile rugs, many of which were bought by carpet dealers and resold as "Bukhara" carpets. Prior to the Soviet era, almost all other textiles made for commerce were produced in the towns by skilled workers, either in small workshops or in their own homes. Block-printed cotton (*chit*) and woven fabrics such as *bekasab, alacha, banoras, shohi*, and ikat were all made according to a traditional distribution of labor among specialized guilds of male artisans. Embroidery was usually women's work, except for the highly esteemed gold embroideries (*zarduzi*) of Bukhara, which only men were permitted to sew. Embroidered skullcaps were among the few articles made by women specifically for sale. Of course, women in cities and villages also created textiles for their own household use,

including quilts (*kurpa*), wall hangings (*suzani, zardevor*), niche curtains (*kirpech*), and cradle covers (*beshikpush*). Locally produced and imported fabric could be readily purchased in the markets and sewn up either at home or by a professional seamstress. Ready-made robes, scarves, men's shirts and trousers, belts, turbans, and shoes were all available in the bazaar.

JEWISH COMMUNITY

It is thought that Jews may have settled in parts of Central Asia as early as the fifth and fourth centuries BCE, when a large part of that region was under Persian control and Jews could travel freely within the empire. The Silk Road was another route that facilitated their entry into Central Asia. Throughout the centuries that followed, Jewish emigrants, exiles, and those avoiding persecution—from Spain, Persia, the Middle East, Morocco, Europe, and Russia—found refuge in Central Asia. The majority settled in the cities of Bukhara, Samarkand, Tashkent, and Kokand. Collectively, they came to be known as the Bukharan Jews.

During the early sixteenth century, Uzbek tribes gained control of most of Central Asia, and they established laws that had a far-reaching effect on the Jewish population. Jews were subjected to onerous taxes that made it difficult for them to own land. As a result, many became local merchants, traders, currency changers, and lenders, as well as specialized workers in professions such as indigo textile-dyeing. Some profited from these activities and, in time, they came to control many of the caravans plying the routes to and from Russia. In 1833 Russia granted Bukharan Jews the right to trade at the important Russian fairs of Nizhny Novgorod and Orenburg, greatly enhancing their influence in the emirate. One of the most important export commodities carried by their caravans was raw cotton, and Russian factory-made cloth was one of the main imports.

Under the Islamic Uzbek rulers, Jews had to abide by certain laws. For instance, they were not allowed to secure their mandatory plain-colored robes with anything but a rope around the waist; they had to wear small black skullcaps edged with a narrow strip of fur; they were forbidden from riding on a horse or a donkey within the city; and they had to reside in their own *mahalla*, or quarter of the town. However, in the privacy of their own homes, Jewish families dressed much the same way as Muslim residents. Within the home, their women were not confined to separate quarters, they were not veiled, and they freely mingled with male members of the household. When venturing outside, however, they might don the *paranja* in order not to attract attention. More often than not, Jewish communities were able to maintain and worship in synagogues, although there were waves of anti-Semitism and forced conversion, particularly in the eighteenth and early nineteenth centuries.

In some ways, life improved for Bukharan Jews under Russian rule, and many prospered as a result. The tsars were more interested in maintaining and establishing trading partners in Central Asia

Бухара Еврейская школа № 1540   Ф. ОРДЭ л.

8. JEWISH SCHOOL. Bukhara, Uzbekistan, late 19th c. Photograph by F. Hordet. Hordet was a French photographer who took many photographs in Bukhara and Samarkand between 1885 and 1892. The four girls front and center are wearing ikat robes, and the two older girls, nose rings. The rest of the students wear robes of striped *alacha* and printed cotton.

(many of whom were Jewish) than controlling the individual's everyday life, and after the Russians signed a treaty with Bukhara in 1873, Bukharan Jews were given the right to own property and more freedom to settle where they wished. But this changed when the Soviets came to power. Laws and regulations actively discouraging religion were instituted. Synagogues and mosques were destroyed or turned into storage buildings and government offices. Rabbis and mullahs were persecuted. Private businesses were nationalized and craftsmen were forced to join cooperatives or work in factories. Under Stalin, anti-Semitism reared its head again, and Jewish professionals in Central Asia fell victim to his paranoia. Among those affected was Max Penson, whose photographs are included in this book.

Throughout the twentieth century, the Jewish population in Central Asia experienced dramatic shifts. During the 1920s and '30s, thousands of Jews left Central Asia for Palestine, yet from 1941–42 more than 152,000 documented Jewish evacuees, deportees, and refugees from advancing German troops arrived in Tashkent from other parts of the Soviet Union. Their registration cards still exist in the Uzbekistan Central State Archives in Tashkent.[10] Many Jews also went to other regions of Central Asia. Although a great number returned home after World War II, many chose to stay. Another exodus of the Jewish population began in the early 1970s, and it is estimated that between then and now, the total population of Central Asian Jews has dropped from between 30,000 and 35,000 to about 10,000. Most went to Israel or the United States, where they settled primarily in Queens, New York.

THE RUSSIANS

During the thirteenth and fourteenth centuries, the Russians were soundly defeated in battles with invading Mongols. In 1237–40, the Golden Horde, under Ghengis Khan's grandson Batu, gained control of much of Russia and the Ukraine. Many cities were destroyed, including Moscow, Vladimir, and Kiev. In 1381 Moscow was again sacked and burned by the Mongols. It was another hundred years before Ivan the Great freed Russia from Mongol dominance. Three hundred years later Imperial Russia turned the tables.

By 1717 Russia was powerful enough to begin a campaign into Central Asia; however, three hundred troops sent as part of Peter the Great's expedition were promptly slaughtered by the forces of the khan of Khiva. Turning temporarily away from Khiva, the Russians focused their attention on the Kazakh tribes. In 1735 the first fort was built in Orenburg, near the Russian/Kazakh border, and it was soon followed by more frontier posts. Orenburg served not only as a vital stronghold and a window into Central Asia, but also as the gateway into Russia used by thousands of caravans from the east. By the mid-eighteenth century the various Kazakh hordes had come under Russian protection (essentially as vassal states, albeit unruly

ones). Raids continued on caravans, and captured Russians were sold as slaves. Under the reign of Catherine the Great (from 1762 to 1796), Russian incursions were stepped up. More fortified posts were erected inside Kazakh territory, and Russian settlers began moving into the nomads' land. Between 1822 and 1848, Russia succeeded in defeating and officially "abolishing" the Kazakh hordes. By the time Tsar Alexander II emancipated the serfs in 1861, Kazakhstan was firmly under his control and thousands of Russian peasants began emigrating to the northern steppe. The conquest of Central Asia had begun in earnest.

During most of the nineteenth century, Imperial Russia vied with Great Britain for control of Central Asia. The British, unnerved by Russia's eastward advance, feared the Russians would gain control of Afghanistan and from there launch attacks into India. The Russians feared British incursions westward and wanted to make Central Asia their bulwark against them. And, of course, both wanted to expand their empires—an imperial competition that came to be known as the Great Game, or the Tournament of Shadows in Russia. The British eventually realized that they could not roll back the swift and unrelenting Russian march eastward, and in 1907 signed the Anglo-Russian Agreement. Boundaries were drawn up, and the classic period of the Great Game came to an end. In a mere twenty-two years, from 1862 to 1884, well-disciplined, well-armed Russian troops, under the command of seasoned and ambitious generals, rolled over the armies of the fractious khans, who were poorly armed with antiquated weapons. They succeeded in capturing all of Central Asia, henceforth known as Russian Turkestan. The tsarist Empire now faced the daunting task of ruling three million subjects of very different cultural and religious backgrounds than those of the Russian motherland, spread out over 1,500,000 square miles of rugged mountains, perilous deserts, and seemingly endless steppes.

The Russian government began by creating an administrative structure similar to that in other parts of the empire. The territory was divided into two large regions (*gubernya*), each with a governor-general, which in turn were subdivided into provinces (*oblast*), districts (*uezd*), and finally subdistricts (*volost*). The latter were generally left in the hands of local native people. Four Cossack regiments were employed to help support the regular army and police. For the most part, Russians and Central Asians lived their separate lives—the former in Russian-style towns that were established near the railroad depots miles outside of the native cities, or in the many agricultural settlements that sprung up in arid areas (thanks to Russian irrigation engineers). In time, however, the social, economic, and political tensions that arose in Russia also arose in Turkestan. Between 1905 and 1917, worker strikes, conscription rebellions, anti-colonial uprisings, and nationalist pro-independence movements were on the rise. In 1917 Tsar Nicholas II was overthrown and the Bolsheviks came to power.

9. IMPERIAL EMBLEM. Crest with the Imperial Russian double-headed eagle and Saint George slaying a dragon.

THE SOVIETS

*"We are for a fraternal union of all peoples . . .
we certainly don't want the peasant in Khiva
to live under the Khan of Khiva. . . ."*
—V. I. Lenin, Seventh Party Conference,
Moscow, April 1917[11]

*". . . a cultural problem cannot be solved as quickly as political and
military problems . . . By its very nature it requires a longer period;
and we must adapt ourselves to this longer period, plan our work
accordingly, and display the maximum of perseverance and method."*
—Lenin, "New Economic Policy," Report to the Second All-Russian
Congress of Political Education Departments, October 17, 1921[12]

The period from 1914 to 1923 was disastrous for the people of
Turkestan. World War I, the Russian Revolution, civil war between
the Red and White Armies, internal rebellions, and anti-Soviet
resistance by the Turkestan Basmachi movement resulted in a
tremendous population loss due to direct war casualties, widespread
famine, disease, and emigration. In addition, there was massive loss
of livestock, destruction of cotton-processing and other industrial
plants, and devastation of vital irrigation systems. By 1924 when the
Soviet government gained control of Turkestan, they found they had
inherited a colony whose output of cotton—its one cash crop—was
reduced to what it had been forty years earlier, when American cotton
was first introduced.

In response, the Soviets embarked on a campaign to rebuild
the infrastructure of Central Asia. During the 1920s and '30s,
railways were repaired and new rail lines laid, electric power
projects begun, major canals dug, irrigation improved, fields
replanted, and textile factories built—all using the manual labor
of hundreds of thousands of workers spurred on by a chorus of
propaganda rallies, films, and posters. Government-controlled
schools, hospitals, and regional healthcare clinics were built, as were
theaters, museums, and publishing houses. Boundaries based on
arbitrary ethnic lines were drawn up to form the basis of what were
to become five Soviet Socialist Republics (Uzbekistan, Kazakhstan,
Tajikistan, Kyrgyzstan, and Turkmenistan). Stalin's first Five-Year
Plan (1928–33) concentrated on both agricultural collectivization
and rapid industrialization. All land was nationalized, taking it out
of the hands of both small and large landowners. Central Asians,
including nomads and settled farmers, were assigned to collective
farms (*kolkhozy*), many of which grew only cotton. Draconian laws
governed each *kolkhoz*. Those who were collectivized had to turn over
their livestock to the state and were not permitted to leave without
special permission. Much of the collective's crop was confiscated by
Soviet authorities, ostensibly to supply resources to workers in the
cities who were doing their part in the great industrial leap forward.
The remainder was rationed to the *kolkhozniks*. It was in effect a

neo-serfdom. During 1932–33, the forced disruption in traditional
subsistence agriculture and nomadic pastoralism, drought, and
gross mismanagement of the collectives resulted in yet another
famine, especially in Kazakhstan, where at least 1,500,000 people are
estimated to have died. Many thousands more Central Asians fled to
Afghanistan, China, or Iran.

World War II brought more profound changes to the people of
Central Asia. Several million volunteers and conscripted men were
sent westward to fight alongside other Soviet troops, while hundreds
of thousands of Volga Germans, Poles, Crimean Tatars, Finns, peoples
from the Balkans and Caucasus, Koreans, and other ethnic groups
from the Soviet Union whom Stalin considered threats were deported
to Central Asia. Many thousands more came as evacuees, and still
others managed to escape as refugees from the advancing German
troops. Entire factories were disassembled and transported by rail
to Central Asia, along with their skilled workers and management.
Reassembled, they played an important role in the war effort. But
food, housing, and jobs were scarce. By the end of the war, tens of
thousands of displaced persons had died, as had an estimated 850,000
Central Asian soldiers and 720,000 civilians.[13] Central Asia had
become both a refuge and a cemetery.

COTTON (*PAKHTA*)

*"Cottons, handkerchiefs and cambrics, as is well known, are the great
forerunners of civilisation, the mute apostles of Western culture,
who spread blessings in their path, even though European arms and
military tactics occasionally accompany their footsteps."*
—Arminius Vámbéry, *Sketches of Central Asia*, 1868

11. TRANS-CASPIAN RAILWAY. Akhal Oasis region, Turkmenistan, c. 1918. Tekke
Turkmen and Russian soldiers. The railway ran from Krasnovodsk (now
Turkmenbashi) on the Caspian Sea to Andijan, in eastern Uzbekistan. Trains,
cars, and bicycles were sometimes referred to as *Shaitan araba* (devil carts).
Photograph by Maynard Owen Williams.

10. SOVIET STAR. Soviet five-pointed star with hammer and sickle.

12. CENTRAL ASIA. Present-day map of Central Asia.

Old World cultivation of cotton is believed to have begun in the Indus Valley region of northwest India and Pakistan as early as seven thousand years ago and spread from there into other parts of Asia. It is not known when cotton was first cultivated in Central Asia, although archaeologists have found evidence that it was being grown in Merv (a former oasis town in what is now Turkmenistan) from at least 500 CE, and most likely earlier. While cotton cultivation was know in Spain and Sicily by the ninth century, having been established by conquering Moors and Arabs respectively, medieval northern Europeans were only familiar with imported raw cotton. Not knowing its origins, they compared the fluffy white material to sheep's wool. A fantastic tale arose, spread by the fourteenth-century travelogue of a purported Englishman, Sir John Mandeville. He claimed that in Central Asia, cotton came from tiny lambs that grew on the ends of low-hanging tree branches. When hungry, they simply reached down and grazed on the grass below; when the grass was gone, they died and fell to the ground. These became known as the "Vegetable Lambs of Tartary." Interestingly, the German word for cotton is "*baumwolle*" or "tree wool," while the English word "cotton" is derived from the Arabic word "*qutn*," a term used by medieval Muslim-Arab traders.

During the years leading up to the full-scale tsarist invasion of Central Asia, economic as well as political factors came into play. Before the American Civil War (1861–65) most of Russia's cotton was imported from the American South, but after the Confederate ports were blockaded, that supply was cut off and a severe cotton famine resulted. Central Asia had been exporting an insignificant amount of raw cotton to Russia prior to this, but by 1862 Central Asia accounted for 40 percent of Russia's imported cotton.[14] Even after American cotton began flowing back into Russia, Central Asian cotton production continued to expand and ever-greater quantities were being shipped to Russian textile factories. Native cotton, however, was considered inferior because it was short-staple and manually cleaned, with considerable debris left in the bales. After five months on the caravan route from Tashkent to Orenburg, the outer layers of the bales were so damaged as to be unusable. By the 1880s the first governor-general of Turkestan, Konstantin Petrovich von Kaufman, had established seed plantations to grow imported American varieties of long-staple cotton. By the 1890s it had supplanted native cotton to a large degree. At the same time, Russia's textile industry was rapidly growing due to modernization and burgeoning domestic and foreign markets. In 1860 Russian cotton goods, particularly cotton cloth, made up 53 percent of the total value of Russia's exports to Central Asia.[15] Industrialists and merchants were doing an increasing amount of export business to Central Asia, particularly to Bukhara, where they had to compete with English imports. They began pressuring the tsar's ministers for not only more trade but also bodily protection.

Their wishes were soon granted as Russian troops gained control of one khanate after another, including Bukhara in 1868. In 1867 the first governor-general of Turkestan was appointed. Laws and tariffs were passed, effectively restricting competing goods from entering what had officially become Russian Turkestan. Imperial Russia now had a huge captive market for her factory-made cloth, particularly printed cottons, as well as a monopoly on all the raw cotton that the land could produce. Inexpensive, brightly patterned fabrics flooded the bazaars, making it increasingly difficult for local weavers and printers to compete. Agricultural land that once grew food crops and fodder was converted into cotton fields. Irrigation projects diverted water from the rivers and turned arid lands into productive cotton plantations. Cotton-ginning plants were established and railroads were built. By the turn of the century, American cotton ("white gold") had replaced almost all local varieties and most traditional grain crops. Trains carried cotton to the textile mills of Russia and returned with grain from Siberia. Turkestan had become a cotton-growing colony of Russia, her economy tied to a single crop and her staple food supply dependent on imported Russian grain.

After the Soviets came to power, Central Asian cotton production was given top priority. Uzbekistan, Turkmenistan, and Tajikistan (in that order) became the largest producers of raw cotton in the USSR. A thirsty and labor-intensive crop, cotton can have devastating ecological impact when it becomes a monoculture. As collective cotton quotas steadily increased, so too did the need for more cultivated land, more water, more fertilizers, and pesticides. Huge vertical textile plants were constructed to process the raw cotton, spin the thread, weave it into cloth, and even print it. The largest of these factories in Uzbekistan was the Tashkent Textile Combine, which opened in 1934. Originally called the J. V. Stalin Textile Combine, this vertical operation printed cotton cloth, including many faux-ikat patterns, for export to all of Central Asia. The enormous vertical Dushanbe Textile Combine was built in Tajikistan during the 1940s and also printed cotton cloth. In the ensuing years, another vertical cotton combine, called "50 Years of October," was constructed in southern Kyrgyzstan and still more factories were built in Bukhara ("10th of October"), Ferghana (Ferghana Textile Combine), and Namangan (Namangan Textile Combine). While these factories employed local people, the managerial and highly skilled jobs were mainly filled by ethnic Russians. After the collapse of the Soviet Union in 1991, most of these manufactories closed, and by the mid-1990s, Russia's textile industry was in a severe slump. It could no longer count on a guaranteed market and the Soviet government's artificially low fixed price on Central Asian cotton. The independent republics were now charging world-market prices and implementing their own cotton-industry policies.

13. TEXTILE WITH BOAR'S HEAD. Late 6th–early 8th c., Iran or Central Asia, Sogdiana. Tapestry weave; wool and linen, 20.7 x 25.2 cm. © The Cleveland Museum of Art, John L. Severance Fund 1950.509

SILK (*IPAK*)

If cotton was king, then silk was queen, and Central Asia has had a long relationship with both. Archaeological finds document that silk was being cultivated in China at least four thousand years ago, but its origins are revealed only in legends. Although the silk trade began in the second century BCE, the origin of silk remained a well-guarded Chinese secret until about 300 CE. Around that time, sericulture reached Japan by way of Korea, where it had long been established by the Chinese. According to legend, a Japanese military expedition to Korea succeeded in capturing four Chinese women experienced in sericulture, along with silkworm eggs. India also began silk cultivation around that time, and the practice eventually spread to Persia and the Middle East as well. Sericulture was brought to Europe by the Moors, who conquered Spain in the eighth century, and to Sicily by the Arabs in the ninth century. By the thirteenth century, Italy had become the most important producer of raw silk and woven textiles in the Western world, although Venetian traders still continued to bring in silk from the Orient. Whether silkworms arrived in Central Asia by way of a Chinese princess married to a Central Asian ruler who is said to have hidden the eggs in her elaborate headdress, or through other means lost in time, by the fourth century CE, Central Asia was also producing silk. The ancient kingdom of Sogdiana, which from the fifth to the eighth century comprised most of present-day Uzbekistan, including Bukhara

and Samarkand, was a major trading hub on the Silk Road and was renowned for its intricately woven figured silks. Sogdian patterns often depict pairs of confronted animals, such as boars, winged horses, stags, and lions, within repeating roundels. Some of these motifs were borrowed from the silks of Sassanian Persia, whose designs were also reflected in textiles from the Chinese T'ang dynasty (618–906). During the Timurid era (1370–1500), Samarkand once again became a center for finely woven patterned silks. Skilled textile artisans from distant parts of the empire came to Samarkand— some as captives and others willingly—where techniques and patterns were exchanged. Chinese, Persian, and Near Eastern motifs were woven into fine silk cloth that found its way to the courts and churches of Europe. Some of the few surviving examples of these Sogdian and Timurid textiles were discovered in the tombs of Italian noblemen and in the reliquaries of European churches. Luxurious patterned-silk fabrics from the Byzantine, Ottoman, and Mughal Empires also made their way westward. All these textiles in turn inspired other artisans, especially the silk-weavers of Italy, who incorporated the motifs into their figured cloth. Textile designs, too, traveled the Silk Road.

THE SILK ROAD

The name "Silk Roads" (*Seidenstrassen*) was coined in the late 1870s by Baron Ferdinand von Richthofen,[16] a German professor of geography, for the ancient trade routes that linked Asia and the West. The Silk Road, as it came to be known, flourished for about 1,500 years, until sea routes became well established in the sixteenth century (although camel-laden caravans would continue to ply the overland routes for another three hundred years). The Orient sent to the West not only silk, but also raw cotton and cotton textiles, furs, indigo, cochineal, spices, tea, rhubarb, sugar, precious gems, ivory, porcelain, rag paper, gunpowder, slaves—and in the fourteenth century, the bubonic plague. Conversely, the West sent coral, amber, linen and wool textiles, carpets, tapestries, wine, glass items, and metalware. Central Asia and China carried on a lively trade, with Central Asia supplying, among other things, prized horses and Bactrian camels for the emperor's stables, as well as melons and peaches for his table. Except for Marco Polo, few if any traders traveled the entire round trip from the Mediterranean Sea to China. Instead, merchants had their prescribed territories and trade was carried on in stages. By the time the final destination was reached, luxury items had passed through so many middlemen that the prices were exorbitant. Silk from China was among the most coveted items. In ancient Rome, every patrician woman wanted to clothe herself in it, and the resulting trade imbalance almost bankrupted the empire as vast amounts of Roman gold and silver wound up in the coffers of India and China.

Alexander the Great (356–323 BCE) is credited with first bridging the West and the East. His armies advanced deeply into regions

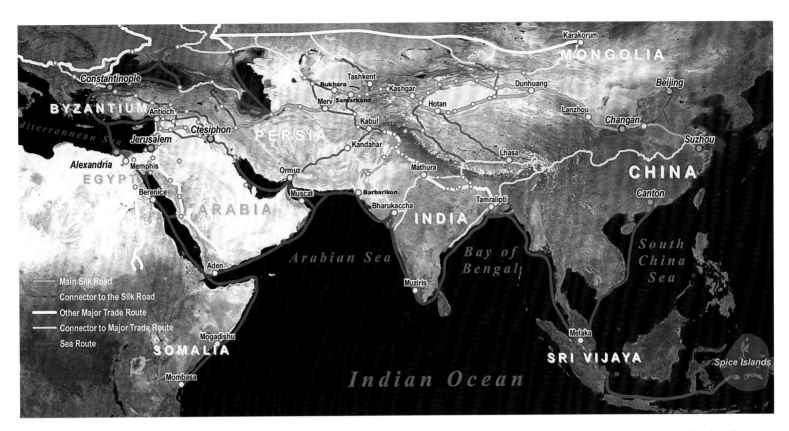

14. THE SILK ROAD AND ARAB SEA ROUTES (8TH–14TH CENTURIES). Source: Data adapted from Rob Harris. Cartography: Jean-Paul Rodrigue, Department of Global Studies and Geography, Hofstra University.

of Central Asia, known then as Transoxiana and Sogdiana, where he married Roxane, daughter of a Sogdian/Bactrian nobleman. Alexander encouraged his men to marry the native women and founded a Greek settlement in the Ferghana Valley, in what is now Khujand, Tajikistan. This stronghold became a major staging city on the northern Silk Road. After Alexander's death his empire began to fracture, but by then Greek culture had reached far across Asia. Only twelve years after his invasion of Central Asia, trade and ideas flowed freely between East and West.

During the thirteenth and fourteenth centuries, the Eurasian Silk Road flourished under what Western scholars have dubbed the Pax Mongolica (Mongol Peace). The Mongols encouraged trade, supported artisans, were tolerant of diverse religious beliefs, and upheld a unified system of government over their vast empire. They built garrisons and caravanserais along the routes to provide protection, shelter, and supplies. Special passports were issued to diplomats and officials, which enabled them to freely travel the length of the Silk Road. A mail system (Pony Express–style) was established, and paper currency was introduced—far lighter to transport than coins and bullion. The Pax Mongolica was what enabled Marco Polo, Friar William of Rubruck, Ibn Battuta, and Ruy Gonzalez de Clavijo to make their remarkable journeys and survive to write about them.[17]

15. SILKWORM AND MOTHS. Prang & Co., USA, 1895. Chromolithograph print. The small white moth is the domesticated silk moth, *Bombyx mori*. The caterpillar stage is at top left.

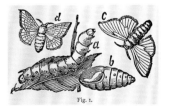

16. THE SILK MOTH. *Bombyx mori.* a. caterpillar; b. pupa; c. female moth; d. male moth. *Silk Dyeing, Printing, and Finishing*, G. H. Hurst. London, 1892.

SILK AND COTTON TODAY

In Central Asia, silk and cotton coexisted throughout the centuries and were an integral part of the region's culture and economy. But while cotton cultivation eventually developed into a complex, state-run agro-industry, with all its attendant societal and ecological issues, sericulture remained primarily a cottage industry, albeit under strict government control. It requires minimal investment and is not dependent on irrigation, chemicals, or large tracts of land. A family can raise thousands of silkworms in a relatively small space to bring in additional income. Government breeding stations supply the newly hatched larvae of the flightless domesticated silk moth (*Bombyx mori*), and the family cares for them until the final stage, when the cocoons are spun. Usually a room or several rooms in the home are turned over to the silkworms. Tables are set up with long trays to contain them, and the tiny caterpillars begin what will be four weeks of nonstop eating. This is a labor-intensive time for the host family: They must ensure that proper warmth, humidity, and ventilation are maintained, and gather and provide a plentiful supply of fresh mulberry leaves. (White mulberry trees are native to Central Asia and anyone engaged in raising silkworms usually has a generous supply nearby.) In about a month, the little silkworms grow into mature, three-inch, grayish-white caterpillars ready to spin their cocoons and attach themselves to the twigs and branches supplied by their host—a process that takes several days. Once this stage is complete, the farmers (usually the women of the family) gather the cocoons before the moths can emerge and damage the fibers. They carefully clean them of debris and take them to an official collection point to be weighed and sorted. Silkworm farmers are paid at the rate set by the government. Some moths are allowed to emerge, mate, and lay eggs, which are then kept in a cool place for future propagation. The rest of the cocoons are steamed in order to kill the pupae inside, then dried, stored, and sold in the market for export or domestic use. One continuous filament up to three thousand feet long can be unwound from a single undamaged cocoon, although in practice multiple filaments are reeled together to make the desired diameter of thread. Between two and three thousand cocoons (approximately twelve pounds) are required to make one pound of raw silk.

Central Asia remains a major producer and exporter of cotton, with Uzbekistan at this point in time among the top cotton-producing countries in the world (currently surpassed by China, India, the United States, and Brazil). To a lesser extent, cotton is also grown in Turkmenistan, Tajikistan, Kyrgyzstan, and Kazakhstan. While the governments of these Central Asian countries continue to try and increase the yield of their cotton fields, they face the ongoing problems resulting from decades of heavy pesticide and fertilizer use, lack of adequate water resources, and increasing salinization. In addition, more land is now being used for wheat cultivation to meet the needs of a rapidly growing population. The fluctuating global prices of raw cotton also dictate how much land is devoted to it.

17. MOUNTAIN OF COTTON. 1952. Aravan cotton-ginning plant, Kyrgyzstan/Uzbekistan border.

18. SORTING COTTON. Soviet collective farm, Turkmenistan, 1938. The two women on the left are wearing the traditional tall headdress of married women.

α Cotton Plant.

19. COTTON PLANT. Hand-colored engraving by Charlotte Mary Yunge, c. 1863. The flowers of the cotton plant first open a creamy white, then turn yellow. After a few days they wither and fall, leaving a small green pod—the cotton boll. When the boll matures, it splits open and the fluffy white cotton bursts forth.

Uzbekistan and Tajikistan face another issue: child labor. While the old-style Soviet *kolkhoz* with forced collectivization no longer exists, the Uzbek government implements compulsory labor at harvest time. Handpicking has proven more economical than mechanical harvesting. Schoolchildren, university students, teachers, and state employees are among those transported to the cotton fields, where they work on average two months, picking cotton bolls. Dormitory-style living arrangements are provided for those requiring it; rural children are generally transported to and from their homes each day. Every person is assigned a daily cotton quota and paid by the kilo (four to seven cents at recent rates). Tajikistan also relies heavily on child labor (much of its adult male workforce has sought higher-paying jobs in other countries), although the government has officially tried to prohibit it. Since children make up a sizeable part of the cotton-harvest labor force in both countries, it has aroused international concern.[18] Khans, tsars, and commissars have come and gone, but cotton is still king.

While sericulture still plays an active economic and cultural role in Central Asia, it contributes far less to the economy than cotton. All five Central Asian countries produce raw silk, but they lag far behind China and India. Figures vary, but recent ones put China at 80 percent of world raw-silk production, India at 16 percent, and Uzbekistan third at 1 to 3 percent. Central Asian sericulture at this point in time may find it difficult to expand as higher income–producing agricultural crops such as wheat and cotton displace mulberry tree plantations; markets in the former Soviet Union are lost; and cheaper synthetic fibers become readily available. This in turn affects the domestic silk textile industry, which also faces stiff competition, especially from China. Recognizing the value of maintaining their silk-weaving heritage, the governments of Uzbekistan, Tajikistan, and Turkmenistan have helped to support and encourage the production of traditional cloth such as ikat and *keteni*. The Uzbek government–sponsored showcase is the Yodgorlik Silk Factory in Marghilan, where visitors can watch the entire ikat-weaving process from cocoon to finished cloth. Smaller privately owned family workshops, primarily located in the Ferghana Valley region of Uzbekistan and Tajikistan, are also weaving ikat for domestic use and export. In Turkmenistan, the traditional silk fabric *keteni* is still woven by women on narrow handlooms. While most Uzbek women no longer wear the ubiquitous ikat smock-dress of the Soviet era, ikat is still considered the national fabric. However, in Turkmenistan, which has retained more of the traditional dress, women can still be seen wearing loose, ankle-length dresses made of *keteni*, perhaps with a robe of red, striped *alacha* thrown over their heads. UNESCO and international NGOs have also helped to support local artisans, as has the recent popularity of ikat in the world's fashion and home furnishing markets. It remains to be seen if this distinctive Central Asian cloth will become more than a passing trend and establish for itself an ongoing, well-deserved place in the international textile world.

1 J. W. Wardell, *In the Kirghiz Steppes* (London: The Galley Press, 1961), 100.

2 The Russians called all nomad domed wooden structures *yurta*. However, each ethnic group has its own terminology based on the felt coverings: Kazakh, *kiiz üy* (felt house); Kyrgyz, *boz üy* (gray house); Turkmen, *ak öy* (white house) or *kara öy* (black house).

3 In October 1929, 7.4 percent of the population of Kazakhstan was collectivized; by June 1933, that figure had risen to 95 percent. See Martha Brill Olcott, *The Kazakhs* (Stanford, CA: Hoover Institution Press, 1987), Appendix 5.

4 A booklet extolling Lenin states in a matter-of-fact manner: "Collectivization put an end to the nomadic way of life, which hampered agricultural development of a considerable part of the Central Asian population." The "agricultural development" the author is referring to was cotton production. See B. Lunin, *Lenin and the Peoples of the East* (Moscow: Novosti Press Agency Publishing House, 1970), 66.

5 Nikolay Murav'yov, *Journey to Khiva through the Turkoman Country* (Moscow: Avgust Semyon Printing House, 1822; London: Oguz Press, 1977), 77. In 1821–22 a twenty-four-year-old Russian envoy to Khiva was readying his equipment for the return journey. As he was about to clean a double-barreled gun that had been repaired there by a Russian slave, he found a slip of paper in one of the barrels. On it was written in Russian: "We venture to inform your Honor that there are over three thousand Russian slaves in this place, who have to suffer unheard misery from labour, cold, hunger, etc. Have pity on our unhappy situation and reveal it to the Emperor. In gratitude we shall pray to God for your Honor's welfare." (At this time Murav'yov also reported about thirty thousand Persian slaves in Khiva.)

In 1840 the English lieutenant Richmond Shakespear succeeded in his mission to convince the khan to release any Russians held in captivity, ostensibly to forestall a tsarist attack on Khiva. According to his account, he left the city with all 416 Russian slaves and safely returned them to Russian soil, thereby depriving the tsar of his pretext for invading Khiva. Might these numbers (and accounts) be skewed to reflect the interests of each player in the Great Game?

6 Emil Schmidt, *The Russian Expedition to Khiva in 1873* (Calcutta: Foreign Department Press, 1876. Nabu facsimile), 122–23.

7 Stephen Graham, *Through Russian Central Asia* (New York: The Macmillan Company, 1916), 224.

8 Ibid., 131.

9 Ole Olufsen, *The Emir of Bokhara and His Country* (London: William Heinemann, 1911; Elibron Classics, 2005), 284.

10 Peter Landé, "Jewish Refugees in Tashkent," www.jewishgen.org/databases/Holocaust/0136_uzbek.html.

11 Quoted in Seymour Becker, *Russia's Protectorates in Central Asia: Bukhara and Khiva, 1865–1924* (Cambridge: Harvard University Press, 1968), 262.

12 V. I. Lenin, "New Economic Policy" (report to the Second All-Russian Congress of Political Education Departments, October 17, 1921), www.marxists.org/archive/lenin/works/1921/oct/17.htm.

13 Vadim Erlikman, *Poteri Narodonaseleniia v XX Veke: Spravochnik* [Population losses in the 20th century: Handbook] (Moscow, 2004), 23–35.

14 Becker, *Russia's Protectorates in Central Asia*, 22.

15 Ibid., 21.

16 Von Richthofen was the professor and mentor of Swedish explorer Sven Hedin and the uncle of World War I flying ace the Red Baron.

17 For detailed lists of caravan routes, see Arminius Vámbéry, *Travels in Central Asia* (London: John Murray, 1864; Elibron Classics, 2005), Chapter 21.

18 Based on a survey of the 2006 cotton harvest in Uzbekistan, about 2.4 million children between the ages of ten and fifteen were recruited to work in the fields, picking an estimated 40 to 50 percent of the total harvest. Conditions have not improved in subsequent years. Information from "What Has Changed?: Progress in Eliminating the Use of Child Forced Labour in the Cotton Harvests of Uzbekistan and Tajikistan," an in-depth report by the School of Oriental and African Studies, University of London, November 2010.

THE GREAT GAME

1.

These are portraits of some of the key people in what came to be known as the Great Game, or the Tournament of Shadows, between Imperial Russia and the British Empire over who would gain supremacy in Central Asia. Played out over most of the nineteenth century, it was ultimately the Russian tsars who reigned supreme. Today, a new Great Game is being waged in the region, with many more players and higher stakes. Oil, natural gas, and rare metals have usurped King Cotton. As Peter Hopkirk, author of *The Great Game*, wrote, "But one thing seems certain. Central Asia, for good or for ill, is back once more in the thick of the news, and looks like [it's] staying there for a long time to come."[1]

---

1 Peter Hopkirk, *The Great Game: The Struggle for Empire in Central Asia* (New York: Kodansha America, 1994), xviii.

1. QUEEN VICTORIA (1819–1901). Steel engraving, c. 1870. Queen Victoria reigned from 1837 until her death in 1901. In 1876 she was given the additional title of Empress of India, so as not to be overshadowed by Russian Emperor Alexander II.

2. KING GEORGE V (1865–1936) **and TSAR NICHOLAS II** (1868–1918). c. 1913. First cousins, King George V reigned from 1910 until his death, and Tsar Nicholas II reigned from 1894 until he abdicated in 1917. Nicholas was executed by the Bolsheviks in 1918.

3. ORENBURG COSSACKS. Russian period postcard, c. 1914. The Orenburg Cossacks played key roles in the expansion of Russia into Central Asia. In 1735 they constructed the first fortress at Orenburg near the border of the Kazakh steppe. Skilled riders, one of the Cossacks in this photograph could not resist showing off with a headstand atop his horse.

4. KONSTANTIN PETROVICH VON KAUFMAN (1818–82). c. 1870. Von Kaufman was the first governor-general of Turkestan, a position he held from 1867 until his death in 1882. He waged victorious campaigns against the emirate of Bukhara and the khanates of Kokand and Khiva. Photograph from the Turkestan Album.

5. SAYID ABDUL AHAD (1859–1911). 1899. Sayid Ahad was the emir of Bukhara from 1885 until his death. He was succeeded by his son, Alim Khan (fig. 9).

6. "SAVE ME FROM MY FRIENDS!" *Punch* magazine, Nov. 30, 1878. Abdur Rahman (1844–1901), the emir of Afghanistan, was "wooed" by his Russian and British neighbors. Ultimately, he favored the British.

7. MUHAMMAD KHUDAYAR KHAN. c. 1833–1918. Notorious for his tyranny, Muhammad Khudayar Khan was deposed several times—his fourth and last reign was from 1866 to 1875, when he was forced to flee once again. He was succeeded briefly by his son, the last khan of Kokand.

2.

8. ISFANDIYAR JURJI BAHADUR KHAN (1873–1918). 1911. Isfandiyar Khan reigned over the khanate of Khiva from 1910 until his death in 1918. He was succeeded by his son, Sayid Abdullah (reigned 1918–20), who became the last khan of Khiva. Photograph by Prokudin-Gorskii.

9. EMIR SAYID MIR MOHAMMED ALIM KHAN (1880–1944). 1911. The last emir of the emirate of Bukhara, Alim Khan reigned from 1911 until 1920, when he was forced to flee to Afghanistan. Photograph by Prokudin-Gorskii.

3.

4.

5.

"SAVE ME FROM MY FRIENDS!"

6.

7.

8.

9.

THE PHOTOGRAPHERS

The archival photographs in this book are drawn primarily from the *Turkestanskii Al'bom* (Turkestan Album) and the color photographs of Sergei Mikhailovich Prokudin-Gorskii, both housed in the Library of Congress; period postcards; photographs from early travelers' narratives and magazines; and the family archives of the photojournalist Max Penson.

In 1872 the first governor-general of Turkestan, Konstantin Petrovich von Kaufman (1818–82), commissioned an extensive photographic survey of all the lands under his control: the khanates of Khiva, Kokand, and Bukhara. The project was intended to provide Tsar Alexander II with images of practically every aspect of daily life in his new territories. The esteemed Orientalist Alexander Kuhn (1840–88) was chosen to head the expedition. He and his staff compiled a staggering number of photographs (approximately 1,200 are included in the albums), all taken in the field with glass-plate negatives—not an easy task when one is dealing with sensitive emulsions in extreme heat, cold, and dust. The Turkestan Album is divided into four parts: Archaeological, Ethnographical, Trades, and Historical. The six large leather-bound albums contain albumen photographic prints covering Islamic architecture, portraits of different indigenous peoples, artisans and merchants in the bazaars, and the various military units serving in Turkestan.

Between 1909 and 1915, Russian photographer Sergei Prokudin-Gorskii (1863–1944) followed in the tradition of recording the Imperial Empire. He had developed a process of color photography in which three rapid shots of the same scene were taken, each through a separate red, green, and blue filter, onto a three-by-nine-inch glass plate. The images could be viewed when projected onto a screen. The colors were remarkably true to life and so impressed Tsar Nicholas II that he agreed to provide Prokudin-Gorskii with a specially equipped railroad car for his long journey throughout the Russian empire. In 1911 Prokudin-Gorskii arrived in Central Asia, where he took numerous black-and-white as well as color photographs of the diverse population, from the last emir of Bukhara to prisoners in the jails. Unfortunately, he was unable to complete his survey: The execution of the tsar forced him to flee Russia in 1918 with his family and some two thousand of his glass negatives, most of which are now housed in the Library of Congress. The color photographs by Prokudin-Gorskii that appear in this book were reproduced digitally by the Library of Congress from his original glass-plate negatives.

Prior to the Bolshevik revolution, photo-postcards were the most widely disseminated images of Central Asia. The earliest cards date to the late 1800s, but the majority were printed between the turn of the century and 1917. Often companies simply reproduced earlier images; others used photos taken by professional photographers such as the Frenchman F. Hordet, who took many photos in Bukhara and Samarkand between 1885 and 1892; by local photographers, some of whom had small commercial studios; and by amateurs who seemed to think anything Central Asian would make a fitting postcard. However, the very mundane nature of these latter images often imparts an appealing candor to them—such as the scruffy street cur that just happened to wander into the frame and becomes the unintended focal point . . . forever.

Late nineteenth- and early twentieth-century scientists, explorers, anthropologists, authors, and adventurers who traveled to Central Asia often returned home with photographs, artifacts, and tales to write about. Samuel M. Dudin (1863–1929), an extraordinary Russian, was all of the above—and more. Between 1893 and 1915 he traveled extensively throughout Central Asia, spending years compiling photographs and collecting artifacts for Russian institutions. Swedish explorer Sven Hedin (1865–1952) was one of the most prolific, as was Danish explorer Ole Olufsen (1865–1929). The Englishwoman Annette M. B. Meakin (1876–1959) traveled through Central Asia in 1896 (solo) and again in 1902 (with her mother) "for purposes of personal observation." Her book *In Russian Turkestan* includes sixteen of her photographs and provides a rare woman's perspective. American journalist William Eleroy Curtis's book *Turkestan: The Heart of Asia* covers his 1910 trip and includes many Kodak photographs taken four years earlier by John Tinney McCutcheon (1870–1949), a Pulitzer Prize–winning political cartoonist and foreign journalist for the *Chicago Herald*. *National Geographic* magazine's first field man, Maynard Owen Williams (1888–1963), went to Central Asia in 1918 and sent back hundreds of fragile glass-plate negatives. (A process of

1. **MAX PENSON** (1893–1959). Portrait, c. 1930s.

2. **SERGEI MIKHAILOVICH PROKUDIN-GORSKII** (1863–1943). Portrait, c. 1905–15. "Beside the Karolitskhali River," Georgia

3. **SVEN HEDIN** (1865–1962). Portrait, c. 1899.

coating glass-plate negatives in a fine layer of potato-starch grains was invented by the French Lumière brothers, who began marketing their Autochrome Lumière photographic plates in 1907, revolutionizing color photography.) Another contributor to *National Geographic* was Edward Murray (1909–85), a young American teaching at Roberts College in Istanbul. In the summer of 1935, he decided to accept the invitation from several of his Central Asian students to visit their cousin, a Kyrgyz chieftain. Setting off alone on horseback from Kuldja, a city in western China, he rode into the Tekes Valley, where he knew the Kyrgyz nomads were summering on one of the high plateaus. His account of that visit is illustrated with many of his photographs, poignant memories of a way of life that was rapidly disappearing.

MAX PENSON

Max Penson was born in 1893 into a Russian-Jewish family from a small town in what is now Belarus. In 1914 he emigrated to Uzbekistan with his parents and sister in order to escape the pogroms that had flared up once again in Russia. Settling in Kokand, and later Tashkent, Penson was teaching art at local schools when he was given his first camera in 1921 as an award for his work.[1] Self-taught, by 1926 he had become a photojournalist for *Pravda Vostoka* (Truth of the East), Uzbekistan's largest newspaper. For the next twenty-three years, Penson, a prolific and dedicated photographer (more than forty thousand of his prints and negatives survive), provided an unparalleled photo-reportage of the modernization of Uzbekistan.[2] Many of his photos were picked up by TASS, the official photograph agency of the Soviet Union, and distributed throughout the USSR. One of his best-known images, "Uzbek Madonna,"[3] won the Grand Prix at the 1937 Paris World Exposition.

Despite his ongoing important and highly successful role in documenting how Soviet ideology had permeated Central Asian life, Penson could not escape the long arm of Stalin. Once again, he fell victim to anti-Semitic purges. In 1949 his photojournalist's license was revoked by Stalin's secret police. Unable to earn a living, he became increasingly despondent and erratic until his death in 1959.

Max Penson has finally been recognized as one of the finest Socialist Realism photographers of the Soviet era. He was one of the very few photographers of his time who actually lived in Uzbekistan, spoke the language, and was well acquainted with the country and its people. While many of his images reflect the tough, angular aesthetics of Constructivism—often with the worker as icon—his portraits of Uzbek family life are tender, sympathetic views seldom captured during this period of radical Sovietization. Socialist Realism photography was the main medium used by the Bolsheviks to spread their message, and there is no doubt that Penson's job was to show an idealized view of Uzbek life under the Soviets. But propaganda aside, he succeeded in showing universal emotions that anyone who looked at his images could relate to: joyful children, a mother's love, families sharing a meal. Max Penson's photographs transcend the ideology in which he was inexorably caught up.

1 Max Penson's first camera utilized glass negatives. According to a family member, in 1928 he obtained a fine Leica camera that used 35mm film. It appears that Penson continued to use both methods, at least through the 1920s and into the 1930s.

2 The famous Russian cinematographer Sergei Eisenstein met Penson in 1940, when both were documenting the construction of the Ferghana Canal. Eisenstein said, "There cannot be many masters left who choose a specific terrain for their work, dedicate themselves completely to it, and make it an integrated part of their personal destiny." From the journal *Sovetskoye Foto* (Soviet Journal), 1940.

3 A very similar photograph by Penson, "A Mother and Child," appears on page 147 of this book.

THE ARTISTS

When Russian artists first arrived in Central Asia, they found fertile ground for inspiration. Although some had come as campaign artists with the tsar's troops, or later as soldiers and evacuees from two world wars, they were nevertheless seduced by the clear turquoise skies and the kaleidoscope of colors and patterns. Some chose to stay in Central Asia and became instrumental in establishing schools of fine art, where both Russian and national artists had the opportunity to study with them. In this vibrant and extremely creative atmosphere, young artists were free to explore different styles. However, as Soviet doctrine became more entrenched under Stalin, and as the only recognized "legitimate" art was Socialist Realism, the state condemned and banned impressionist and avant-garde works. It would take decades for the paintings of many of the Central Asian and Russian artists of this period to be seen and appreciated.

The Nukus Museum in Karakalpakstan, Uzbekistan, houses one of the world's finest collections of Russian avant-garde art, as well as local textiles and artifacts—all assembled by one extraordinary man, the Russian artist and collector Igor Savitsky (1915–84). His is an incredible story, beautifully told in the documentary film *Desert of Forbidden Art*. The works of two artists represented in this museum are illustrated here: Aleksey Isupov (1889–1957) and Robert Falk (1886–1958). Isupov came to Central Asia in 1915 as a conscript in the Russian army during World War I. A graduate of the Moscow School of Painting, he remained in Tashkent and Samarkand until 1921. His painting *Tea-House* (fig. 1) reflects his early training as an icon painter. Falk and Savitsky were among the artists evacuated from Russia during World War II. Falk was a founding member of the Jack of Diamonds, a group of artists who greatly admired the works of Paul Gauguin, Henri Matisse, and particularly Paul Cézanne. Falk's early paintings show a strong Cubist influence, grounds for the Bolsheviks to condemn them as "decadent bourgeois art." His works languished until he was recognized posthumously as one of Russia's great avant-garde artists (fig. 2).

The much-acclaimed Russian realist artist Vasily Vereshchagin (1842–1904) had a Turkmen grandmother, a heritage of which he was proud. Vereshchagin saw firsthand the horrors of war in Central Asia. While accompanying General von Kaufman's army in Turkestan, he was caught up in the 1868 siege of Samarkand. Already an accomplished painter, he relied on his many sketches to create a series of paintings so accurate and powerful that they served as a photo-reportage of Russia's newly won territory. Widely displayed in Russia and Europe, both applauded and condemned, they gave many Russian people their first look into Central Asia. While Vereshchagin's battle scenes depict the savagery of both sides in gruesome detail, his paintings of local people, including *Dervishes in Festive Dress* (fig. 5), are so finely executed that the patchwork fabrics on their robes are clearly recognizable as block-printed cotton *chit*. One Russian paisley fabric even shows the partial stamp of the manufacturer, "Antonov L. Koky—"

Some artists incorporated Central Asian textiles as decorative backdrops for portraits or props in still lifes. In his painting *Portrait of E. V. Meyerhold* (fig. 4), Russian Socialist Realism artist and founding member of the Jack of Diamonds Petr Konchalovsky (1876–1956) enlarged an Uzbek *suzani* to outsized proportions, evocative of an Orientalist stage set. While exuberant in color and pattern, this painting is a sad reminder of the Stalin-era purge of Vsevolod Emilevich Meyerhold, considered one of the most innovative theatrical directors of the twentieth century and a central figure in the Russian avant-garde. Shortly after he posed for this painting, Meyerhold was arrested by the Soviet secret police and executed in 1940. Konchalovsky went on to embrace Socialist Realism, and in 1942, he was awarded the Stalin Premium of the First Degree State prize in the arts.

The French Fauvist Henri Manguin (1874–1949) was a close friend of Matisse. Both artists made frequent use of richly patterned textiles in their paintings. *Still Life with Cyclamens* (fig. 3) features an Uzbek *suzani* draped across the table—the fabric itself a Fauvist-like work of art.

Contemporary artist Robert Kushner is one of the founders of the Pattern and Decoration movement (c. 1975–1985) whose artists explored the "esthetic role of beauty and utilitarianism; the intersection of high and low cultures; the appropriation of tribal, outsider, or Third World cultural motifs; and the consideration

1.

2.

4.

of crafts and traditional 'women's work,'"[1] or in Kushner's words, "Decoration has always had its own agenda, the sincere and unabashed offering of pleasure and solace." His paintings are in the permanent collections of major museums around the world. Kushner's cross-cultural borrowings, in particular Central Asian textiles and Japanese screen paintings, infuse his work with color, pattern, and shades of exoticism. *Twelve Red Emperors* (see fig. 2, pages 34–35) from his Silk Road exhibit at the DC Moore Gallery in New York (2009) pays homage to the tulip, which grew wild in Central Asia, was domesticated by the Turks, and eventually gave rise to "tulip mania" in Holland. The tulips in this painting intermingle with the motifs of an Uzbek *suzani*. As the art critic Donald Kuspit wrote in 2007, "Robert Kushner is arguably the most significant decorative artist working today . . . his art goes against the prevailing trend toward the anti- or nonaesthetic, which takes revenge on life. He chooses instead to affirm the wonder of existence."[2] Robert Kushner is the author of the following essay, "Suzani Sonata."

1 Michael Duncan, *Robert Kushner: Wild Gardens* (San Francisco: Pomegranate, 2006), 9.

2 Donald Kuspit, "Robert Kushner," *Artforum*, summer 2007.

3.

5.

SUZANI SONATA

In and out. Positive, negative. Curlicue, zigzag, circle. Throughout my career as an artist, as well as my admittedly self-indulgent tendencies of looking at decorative sources from around the world, I have been most strongly attracted to drawn (as opposed to woven or tessellated) traditions of visual decorative expression. Woven designs are a wonder. But since I am a painter/drawer and not a weaver, I like to employ found images that originated with the drawn line.

The strict building-block character of Caucasian and Turkish kilims was my first love. However, as a studio artist, not averse to borrowing from other traditions, kilims presented an unexpected problem. Their strength lay in their adherence to and innovation within the woven grid. To replicate these woven grids with brush and paint diffuses their power and majesty. To me, painting a weaving looks like just that—a weak repetition of something that has already been done better on a loom.

When I discovered eighteenth-century dress silks, I was in heaven, particularly with the subset known as "bizarre" silks (1695–1720). These luxurious brocades are a sophisticated, urban consumer item. New designs were created and woven annually to please the tastes of Europe's uppermost class. Since the woven grid was so small, the woven contours of the forms neatly replicated the original shapes in the larger-scale hand-drawn maquettes. The strangeness of these drawn-then-woven motifs offered me endless curvaceous and fresh opportunities to explore.

And then there was my long love affair with Japanese textiles and screens . . .

But now, later in my artistic life, I have come around to the grandly barbaric majesty of Central Asian *suzanis*. Each *suzani*'s genesis starts with lines drawn on a textile substrate. Often an inexplicably unembroidered area reveals these original pencil directives. Given their drawn, rather than gridded, origins, *suzanis* became perfect candidates for my own decorative explorations. *Suzanis* have enormous sophistication without the fussy coyness of French rococo elegance and good taste. They are earthy, vital, energetic: designed to wow you, seduce you with a hammer—not a fan and a powdered wig. They seem to arise from the earth. Am I romanticizing? Even so, whether these images trace their origins over the millennia to Zoroastrian sun discs, Sassanian garlands, or even older sources, their ancientness is palpable. They radiate vitality and aggressive energy.

Suzanis were not always well known, not even to "schmattephiles" like myself. I was confronted by my first great *suzani* in 1974, in an off-the-beaten-track monument in Iran. I still remember seeing it languorously draped over a wall in the Sufi shrine of Bayazid al-Bistami in Bistam—huge magenta rosettes, green-and-black snaking vines, the entire embroidery slung like a cloak that the mystic dropped when returning from the bazaar. I had no notion of what I was looking at, but I tried to memorize its components. Back in the studio, I tried to paint my memories of that textile as best I could. Shortly thereafter, I worked as a kilim restorer for Artweave Gallery, an innovative textile gallery in New York that specialized in nineteenth-century *suzanis* and ikat silks. There, I could study magnificent examples of impeccable early *suzanis* that had been embroidered with vegetable-dyed silk on hand-loomed cotton grounds. In 2007 the *suzani* game was reignited when I discovered the power of more recent examples while traveling in Turkey. Many of the carpet sellers I encountered, short on Turkish embroideries, would show us twentieth-century Central Asian embroideries, hoping that the naïve tourists would not notice the difference between the words "Turkoman" and "Turkish."

I had been unfamiliar with these more recent manifestations, yet somehow they spoke to me more directly than the rarefied, bankable specimens that I had previously studied. I was less intimidated by them than I was by their ancestors; they seemed more plucky, quirky, up-to-date—and more usable in my work. New dye colors and image sources were freely combined with tradition. And unlike their museum-piece antecedents, I could afford them! On my return from that trip, I began collecting late twentieth-century *suzanis* in earnest, mostly via the miracle of the Internet. There was always a thrill when, after buying a new *suzani* online, a tightly packed, cloth-wrapped bundle from Tashkent arrived, secured with string and sealing wax, asking to be opened, assessed, and admired.

Certain questions of studio practice arose as to how to incorporate this rambunctious energy into my work, and after some experimentation I arrived at a direct solution. I photographed the embroidery and printed the image on clear acetate that I projected via an overhead projector onto my painting. I could project the image at any scale, trace the lines with conté crayon or pencil, and begin to manipulate the image in many different ways. I omitted sections, filled in the positive or the negative, painted in color, or gilded the motif in a wide variety of metal leafs. Each time I made one decision, another was suggested . . . and another.

I try to create a balance of gilded and painted areas, open expanses, and densely filled passages—all the while maintaining a balance between my own drawn floral images and the abstracted motifs of the embroideries. The *suzani* designs give me well-considered, preexisting motifs, both odd and classicized, ancient and strangely modern. I have learned from the scale relationships of the different elements and, particularly, from the interaction of positive to negative forms. I might use an entire design to activate a background, leaving the flower nearly devoured by its energetic field, or only a fragment of the overall motif to pep up an uneventful passage. Most often, I start by chalking the *suzani* design over the entire background of the canvas, and then I add a large grid over this expanse. From this beginning, I start to treat the different segments of the grid individually. In one area I might gild the design elements in gold leaf, perhaps a neighboring area in silver, but this time filling in only the negative forms. In another section I can pit painted red oil glazes against blue, and so on. The final composition bounces and crackles with the energy of these disjunctive curves and zigzags but remains somehow unified as the eye connects the various segments and repeated elements of the overall *suzani* motif. If I have worked well, the drawn lines of my flowers create the illusion of volume enclosed by the lines of the petals and leaves, while the *suzani* passages lay out an expansive, flattened, opulent field.

One can always bring up the critique that I am not Uzbek; nor am I a weaver/embroider; nor am I a woman. Consequently, am I indulging in an aestheticized form of cultural poaching? Perhaps some will feel this way, but the process of replication is more nuanced

1. SUZANI. Samarkand, Uzbekistan, 2nd quarter, 20th c. Silk couching stitch on cotton. Robert Kushner calls this piece "Old Faithful," and he has worked its motifs into many of his paintings. 64 x 57"

2. ROBERT KUSHNER, *TWELVE RED EMPERORS*, 2008. Oil, acrylic, gold leaf, silver leaf, and copper leaf on canvas, 72 x 108". Private collection. Courtesy DC Moore Gallery, New York.

than this. Decoration is by its nature a rather conservative kind of art form. Motifs are admired, copied, varied to meet specific needs, copied again, changed to reflect disparate temperaments, and so they evolve over time. Yet designs remain distinct and fall into identifiable families, in this case the extended family of *suzanis*. It is a glacially slow process compared to our Western avant-garde notion of sweeping out the cobwebs of the old with the broom of modernism. Consequently when I (or anyone else) re-creates one of these designs, we are actually making it again, creating it anew. This re-creation is more than a rote appropriation of a *suzani* motif; it is a process of respect. Keeping this attitude in mind aligns me with the generations of women, stitching their hearts out to make their individual and exquisite expressions of pride and passage. Each time I think I have used up the recombinant possibilities at hand, either a new *suzani* design reaches me, demanding to be explored, or a new way to hybridize these divergent forms emerges. For now, *suzanis* and I are good friends, and we intend to remain that way.

—Robert Kushner, 2012

1

ADULT CLOTHING

"Everybody wears a coat like a rainbow. The poor made them of cotton prints and the rich of silk brocades . . . No matter how humble or hungry a man may be, and even if he have [sic] but a single garment, that is made of the most brilliantly colored material he can find."
—William Eleroy Curtis, *Turkestan: The Heart of Asia*, 1911

Throughout the nineteenth and early twentieth centuries, traditional articles of Central Asian clothing remained basically unchanged. The classic T-shaped outer robe (generically called a *chapan, khalat*, or *don*) was worn by both nomadic and settled peoples. The sleeves were very long in order to conceal the hands, both as custom dictated and for protection in cold weather. For winter warmth the robes were padded with a thick layer of cotton batting ("cotton wool") and quilted; for summer, they were either lightly padded or lined without batting. The edges of most robes had trimming known regionally as *sheroza, zeh*, or *jiyak*—not only for decorative effect, but also to prevent evil spirits from gaining access. Some trims were woven first on narrow tablet looms or embroidered on strips of cloth, and then applied. Others were simultaneously woven and attached directly onto the robe's edges by two women using their fingers to manipulate the warp threads, while a third woman used a needle to insert the weft through the edges of the robe. This complicated and ingenious method is called warp-twining loop manipulation[1] (see figs. 6–9, page 105).

Except for the distinctly feminine *munisak* (see fig. 1, page 44 and fig. 1, page 54), men's and women's robes looked similar. However, men's robes had a narrow stand-up collar and sometimes a simple tie closure (see fig. 6, page 55), while women's robes had no collar or attached closure. There were regional preferences in fabrics and colors as well as variations in cut. In Bukhara, which was considered the "Paris of Turkestan," the well-to-do flaunted layers of brightly colored, boldly patterned silk robes, usually generously styled in order to show off expensive ikats and fine embroidery. And it was de rigueur that the robes emit the distinct sound of crisp rustling silk to presage the wearer's arrival. Swedish explorer Ole Olufsen remarked about the *divanbegi* of Bukhara, ". . . he had become a real mountain of rustling silk, so that he was hardly able to sit down."[2] The Hungarian traveler Arminius Vámbéry had this to say about the robe bazaar in Bukhara: "It was always an object of great delight to me to see the seller [buyer] parading up and down a few paces in the new *chapan*, to ascertain whether it gave out the orthodox [rustling] tone."[3] In Khiva, residents dressed more conservatively, preferring highly glazed *alacha* with dark narrow stripes. The khan of Khiva (see fig. 8, page 27) posed for his portrait wearing such a robe, while the emir of Bukhara donned his finest imported silk brocade (see fig. 9, page 27).

In addition to the ubiquitous *chapan*, nomadic tribes wore their own traditional garments. Among the most distinctive Kyrgyz clothes were the women's elaborate turbanlike headdresses (*ileki* and *elechek*) and embroidered apron-style skirts (*beldemchi*), and the men's white felt hats (*kalpak*), heavy sheepskin coats (*ton*), and embroidered buckskin trousers (*sayma shym*). Turkmen women wove narrow-striped red cloth (*gyrmyzy donlyk*) for men's robes and a silk cloth (*keteni*) for their own long, shiftlike dresses (*koynek*). Women's and young children's garments were intricately embroidered, while the men's robes (*gyrmyzy don*) bore little embellishment, if any at all. Turkmen men were rarely seen without their tall, shaggy sheepskin hats (*telpek*). Like the carpets they wove, each Turkmen tribe had its own lexicon of motifs, which resulted in a wide variety of patterns and stitches on clothing, hats, and household textiles. Karakalpak women's traditional dress included the cloaklike *aq jegde* and the *kiymeshek* (an exquisitely embroidered cowl and cloaklike garment). Kazakh women wore a less ornate version of the *kiymeshek*. By the 1930s Russian velvet had become widely available, and women from all areas of Central Asia could be seen wearing sleeveless velvet waistcoats over their shifts.

It was considered an honor to receive a robe as a gift. While a man might give one to a special servant, it was customary to present one (or more) to a wealthy person or important official when calling on him. Emirs and *begs* bestowed robes of honor on members of their courts, dignitaries, and foreigners they deemed worthy—the more expensive the robe, the higher the honor. Robes were also used to repay a service rendered or to ensure loyalty. Olufsen wrote, ". . . I received an endless number of caftans, with the advantage that I could again use them as presents either for other *begs* or for my servants."[4]

Urban Uzbeks and Tajiks dressed in similar clothes. While at home, women wore long shifts (*kuylak* or *kurta*) under their full-length outer robes, called *kaltacha* in Bukhara and Samarkand; *munisak* in Tashkent and the Ferghana region; and *misak* in Khorezm. Loose trousers (*lozim* or *shalwars*) with a drawstring top that rested on the hips were worn as underwear beneath the shifts or chemises. The bottom cuffs peeked out and were often embroidered, which added to the overall effect. Indoors, both men and women wore boots of soft leather or velvet, often beautifully embroidered, which they covered with wooden galoshes (or rubber galoshes in Soviet times) when they went outdoors. In warm weather, children usually went barefoot.

Men also wore baggy trousers (*ishton*). These were similar in cut to a woman's, but instead of printed cotton or silk ikat, they were usually made of white homespun cotton (*buz*), or factory-made plain cotton cloth. Tunic-style shirts (also called *kuylak* or *kurta*) of the same material were worn over them and a large square scarf or sash (*belbog*), which was tied or twisted around the waist, added a dash of color. Wealthy men might wear beautifully embroidered deerskin pants on special occasions. In summer, a man might wear a lightweight robe (*yahktak*) similar to a *chapan*, but unpadded and often unlined. Men also secured their inner robe with a *belbog* (the outer was usually left open to show off the layers underneath). If a man was an important official or very wealthy, he wore a wide belt of velvet-covered leather or embroidered silk (*kamarband*) adorned

with silver or gilt buckles and disks. As none of these garments had pockets, small bags (*khalta*) for holding personal items were tucked into the sashes or hung from a belt. Under the Uzbek khans, a Jewish man was not allowed to use either a *belbog* or a belt in public—a length of cord had to suffice.

When urban women and girls (starting at about age nine) ventured outside their homes, they wore a *paranja*, a long cloaklike garment that draped over the head and enveloped the body. Long false sleeves were fastened in the back. Women hid their faces behind a stiff black veil (*chachvan, chasband, chedra*) that reached to their waists. This garment was hand-woven from black horsehair and sold in the bazaar. Women would cut it to the desired length and add a border of black sateen or velvet. While Westerners were usually appalled by the sight of these shrouded women (in her book *Turkestan Solo*, 1935, the Swiss traveler Ella Maillart described them as "walking upright coffins"), the *paranja* itself could be very attractive. Wealthy women had them made from costly silk velvets, brocades, and occasionally ikat. Many *paranjas* are found with alterations to the length. This may point to a standardization of size, a hand-me-down, the natural growth of a young girl, or all three. Elaborate tassels, trimming, and embroidery embellished the front, back, and false sleeves. Practically all *paranjas* were lined with Russian printed cotton in the gayest of patterns and colors—as if the woman inside moved in a hidden world strewn with exotic flowers.

After the Soviets consolidated their control over Central Asia, some people began to wear Western-style clothing, primarily in the cities. The real turning point, however, came after World War II. By the 1950s most women were no longer veiled, and by the 1970s knee-length ikat dresses had become the vogue (older and more conservative women wore them longer, together with ikat pants). Textile factories in Uzbekistan, Tajikistan, and Kyrgyzstan were producing an endless array of ikats, woven as well as printed ones, on silk, cotton, and polyester. It seemed that every female wore dresses made from ikat—at home, at work, in the streets, and in the bazaars. With the dissolution of the Soviet Union in 1991, most of the factories closed, and imported, garish floral prints on shiny synthetics replaced the once ubiquitous ikats.

---

1 For detailed descriptions of this process, see Kate Fitz Gibbon and Andrew Hale, *Uzbek Embroidery in the Nomadic Tradition: The Jack A. and Aviva Robinson Collection* (Minneapolis: Minneapolis Institute of Art, 2007) and David and Sue Richardson, *Qaraqalpaqs of the Aral Delta* (Munich: Prestel Verlag, 2012).

2 Ole Olufsen, *The Emir of Bokhara and His Country* (London: William Heinemann, 1911; Elibron Classics, 2005), 469. The *divanbegi* was second only to the emir.

3 Arminius Vámbéry, *Travels in Central Asia* (London: John Murray, 1864; Elibron Classics, 2005), 172.

4 Olufsen, *The Emir of Bokhara and His Country*, 471.

1.

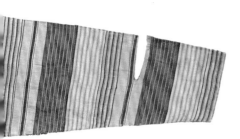

BEKASAB ROBES

Bekasab (*bekasam*), also called *alacha*, is a heavyweight, handwoven, multicolored striped fabric. It was produced in vast quantities in Uzbekistan, where it was called *bekasab* in the Tashkent and Ferghana regions and *alacha* in the rest of the country. *Bekasab* was woven with a silk warp and cotton weft, while *alacha* might also be made entirely of cotton.[1] The surface of the cloth was usually polished to a high sheen, a process that also created a moiré effect. Another characteristic was a fine horizontal ribbing. Robes of this fabric were worn by everyone—from khans to the common man, woman, and child.

Today most *bekasab* is machine-woven and lacks the heft, polish, and moiré of the handwoven material. Yet it still retains the bright variegated stripes that evoked a rainbow to so many nineteenth- and early twentieth-century travelers.

1 In order to avoid confusion, where applicable, the term "*bekasab*" will be used for silk warp/cotton weft striped cloth and "*alacha*" for all-cotton striped cloth.

1. WOMAN'S ROBE.[2] Uzbekistan, 3rd quarter, 19th c. *Bekasab*; block-printed, local handwoven cotton cloth (*chit*) lining; Russian block-printed cotton facing. 52" length; 52" cuff to cuff

2 This robe is shown inside-out in Susan Meller, *Russian Textiles: Printed Cloth for the Bazaars of Central Asia* (New York: Abrams, 2007), 190.

2. ROBE. Uzbekistan, 3rd quarter, 19th c. *Bekasab* (see fig. 6, page 264 for detail); *chit* lining; *adras* ikat and handwoven striped facing. 53" length; 70" cuff to cuff

2.

1.

2.

3.

BEKASAB ROBES

By the 1920s Central Asian robes reflected the influence of Western styles. Sleeves were cut narrower and often attached at the shoulders in such a way that the robe no longer had the classic T-shape. Curved necklines with a collar and loop-and-button closure at the base came into vogue. Sometimes shallow pockets were added. Despite these modifications, *bekasab* continued to be widely used and woven in an endless variety of vibrant stripes.

1. MAN'S ROBE. Uzbekistan, 2nd quarter, 20th c. *Bekasab*; printed-cotton lining; applied handwoven trim. 46" length; 69" cuff to cuff

2, 4, 5. MEN'S ROBES. Uzbekistan, 2nd quarter, 20th c. *Bekasab*; printed-cotton linings. (fig. 2) 45" length; 65" cuff to cuff; (fig. 4) 46" length; 63" cuff to cuff; (fig. 5) 48" length; 70" cuff to cuff

3. MAN'S ROBE. Uzbekistan, 2nd quarter, 20th c. *Bekasab*; machine-woven striped-cotton lining; inside breast pocket. 43" length; 64" cuff to cuff (see fig. 8, page 265 for detail)

4.

5.

BEKASAB/ALACHA ROBES

According to the Uzbek textile scholar Sayora Mahkamova,[3] there were regional color preferences in *bekasab/alacha* stripes. In and around Ferghana, shades of green, blue, and purple predominated, while in Bukhara, Khorezm, and the surrounding areas (where the term "*alacha*" was used), warmer colors such as red, pink, violet, and yellow were favored. The weavers gave the various stripes descriptive names that reflected their color combinations and layouts, for example, *para-pasha* (fly wings) and *kora kosh* (black eyebrows).

In 1925 two American women visited Bukhara and wrote about the robes of male passersby: "Bright Baghdad stripes [*alacha*] are perhaps the most general, but all kinds of gay chintz and cretonne patterns are popular . . . A very favorite pattern was enormous and violently pink roses and green leaves on a black background . . . worn not only by the younger set, but by elderly men whose sobriety of demeanor was in amusing contrast to their gay and fantastic garments."[4]

3 Sayora Mahkamova, *Old Silk Costumes of Uzbekistan* (Moscow: Tair Tairov, 2010), 30–31.

4 Helen Calista Wilson and Elsie Reed Mitchell, *Vagabonding at Fifty: From Siberia to Turkestan* (New York: Coward McCann, 1928), 299.

4.

1. **WOMAN'S ROBE.** Uzbekistan, early 20th c. *Bekasab*; applied handwoven trim; Russian printed-cotton lining; Russian machine-woven striped-cotton facings. 48" length; 54" cuff to cuff (see fig. 5, page 264 for detail)

2. **MAN'S ROBE.** Uzbekistan, 2nd quarter, 20th c. *Bekasab*; machine-woven plain-weave cotton lining; inside breast pocket. 49" length; 63" cuff to cuff

3. **WOMAN'S ROBE.** Khorezm, Uzbekistan, late 19th c. Quilted-cotton *alacha*; loop-manipulation silk trim; Russian printed-cotton lining. 47" length; 48" cuff to cuff

4. *MADRASSAH* **STUDENTS.** Samarkand, Uzbekistan, 1911. The seated man wears a Russian printed-cotton robe; the other man is wearing a *bekasab* robe. Photo by Sergei Prokudin-Gorskii

5. **MAN'S ROBE.** Samarkand, Uzbekistan, early 20th c. *Bekasab*; loop-manipulation silk trim; Russian printed-cotton lining; silk-satin striped facing. This mustard-and-black-striped *bekasab* was given the poetic name "Musk and Saffron." 53" length; 85" cuff to cuff

5.

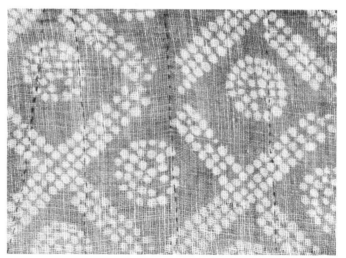

4.

5.

ALACHA WOMEN'S ROBES

These robes were entirely handmade and likely worn by elderly rural women in southern Uzbekistan. In these examples, the outer striped cloth, called *alacha* in this region, was woven with a cotton warp and weft. The narrow trim along the edges of the robes was embroidered directly onto the robe in fine chain stitch, called *yurma*. The dyes are natural, with indigo predominating.

It is rare to find robes such as these since they were usually worn until no longer serviceable—and in any case, unlike ikat robes, they were not considered special enough to preserve. (The cut of fig. 1, with the gathering under the arms and wide, flared skirt, is a humbler version of the ikat robe shown in fig. 1 on page 54.)

1–3. ROBE (and details). Southeast Uzbekistan, 3rd quarter, 19th c. Cotton *alacha*; embroidered trim; local block-printed cotton-cloth (*chit*) lining; *alacha* facing. (fig. 1) 46" length; 65" cuff to cuff; (fig. 2) 5.5 x 11"; (fig. 3) 5.5 x 12"

4, 6. ROBE (and detail). Southeast Uzbekistan, 3rd quarter, 19th c. Cotton *alacha*; embroidered trim; handwoven striped cotton lining. (fig. 4) 5 x 7.5"; (fig. 6) 44" length; 63" cuff to cuff

5, 7. ROBE (and detail). Southeast Uzbekistan, 3rd quarter, 19th c. Cotton *alacha*; embroidered trim; handwoven cotton lining. (fig. 5) 3.5 x 6.5"; (fig. 7) 44" length; 53" cuff to cuff

6.

7.

1.

2.

3.

KHOREZM ROBES

The khanate of Khiva was in far western Turkestan in a part of Central Asia also known as Khorezm (Khwarezm), which was the historic homeland of nomadic Turkmen and Uzbek tribes. After the Soviets created new boundaries, the area became part of Turkmenistan, Kazakhstan, and the Karakalpak region of Uzbekistan.

Khorezm robes were straight-cut, generally with dense vertical quilting (*kavik*) that was usually machine-stitched. They were trimmed with a red braid (*jiyak*) that was woven directly onto the robe by a process called loop manipulation. Highly polished, all-cotton *alacha* was a favorite material, as was silk warp/cotton weft *adras* ikat. According to research by David and Sue Richardson (*Qaraqalpaqs of the Aral Delta*), Khiva produced both kinds of fabrics, although the ikat patterns were generally limited to a few simplified versions of Bukharan ikats, such as fig. 3.

1. WOMAN'S IKAT ROBE. Possibly Karakalpak, late 19th c. *Shohi* ikat with tree of life, pomegranate, amulet, and ram's horn motifs; loop-manipulation silk trim; Russian printed-cotton lining; *adras* ikat facing. 48" length; 46" cuff to cuff

2, 5. WOMAN'S IKAT ROBE (and detail). Khorezm, late 19th c. *Adras* ikat; loop-manipulation silk trim; Russian printed-cotton lining and facing (lining is made from scarf material). (fig. 2) 50" length; 53" cuff to cuff; (fig. 5) 5.5 x 4.5"

3. WOMAN'S IKAT ROBE. Possibly Karakalpak, late 19th c. *Adras* ikat, probably woven in Khiva; loop-manipulation silk trim; Russian Turkey-red printed-cotton lining; *adras* ikat and Russian machine-woven striped-cotton facing. 48" length; 47" cuff to cuff

4. KHIVA. Engraving, 1895. The walled oasis city of Khiva was the capital of Khorezm and the seat of the khan of Khiva.

6. WOMAN'S *ALACHA* ROBE. Khorezm, late 19th c. *Alacha*; loop-manipulation silk trim; Russian printed-cotton lining; *adras* ikat and *alacha* facing. 51" length; 56" cuff to cuff

7. WOMAN'S *ALACHA* ROBE. Khorezm, late 19th c. *Alacha*; loop-manipulation silk trim; Russian printed-cotton lining; Russian machine-woven striped-cotton facing. 44" length; 47" cuff to cuff

4.

5.

6.

7.

TURKMEN WOMEN'S GARMENTS

Turkmen women's traditional everyday wear consisted of a long, usually red, handwoven silk (*keteni*) dress (*koynek*); pants (*balak*) with a drawstring waist and narrow embroidered cuffs (see fig. 5, page 98); and an elaborately embroidered robe (*kurte*) made of solid-color or red, striped, hand-loomed silk (usually worn over the tall headdress as in figs. 6 and 8). A distinctive type of lacing (or ladder) stitch, called *kesdi* (see figs. 7 and 8, page 103), can be found on many Turkmen embroideries.

1⁵, 3, 4. ROBES (and detail). Tekke Turkmen, c. 1930s. Handwoven silk; silk lacing stitch (*kesdi*); loop-manipulation silk trim; Russian printed-cotton linings; *alacha* facings. This type of robe was generally worn on top of the woman's headdress. (fig. 1) 44" length; 62" cuff to cuff; (fig. 3) 44" length; 60" cuff to cuff; (fig. 4) lining of fig. 3; 7 x 7"

5 The printed lining of this robe is shown in Meller, *Russian Textiles*, 142.

2. DRESS (*koynek*). Tekke, 2nd quarter, 20th c. Handwoven silk (*keteni*); silk embroidery; loop-manipulation silk trim around neckline; plain cotton facing. Wide yellow selvedges were traditional features of these dresses. 48" length; 53" cuff to cuff

5. *CHYRPY*. Tekke, c. 1900. Handwoven silk; lacing stitch; silk fringe; local block-printed cotton lining. A *chyrpy* was reserved for special ceremonies and worn over a headdress, with its long false sleeves fastened together and hanging down the back. Tulips (*lolagul*) were the main motifs on these intricately embroidered robes. A yellow *chyrpy* is said to have been worn by married women of middle age. 60 x 44"

6. THE TURKMEN BEAUTY. 2nd quarter, 20th c. A young Tekke woman wears an engraved-and-gilded silver headdress set with carnelians. A velvet robe is draped on top of it. She holds the end of a silk scarf in her mouth in order to partially conceal her face. Photograph by Max Penson.

7. PRINTED CLOTH. Probably Russian, c. 1930s. Printed cotton. Backing of a Turkmen camel trapping. This is the same fabric pattern as the one seen lining the woman's robe in fig. 8. 2 x 3"

8. TURKMEN WOMEN. Merv, Turkmenistan, 1935. Turkmen *kolkhoz* women in traditional dress. Multiple scarves create the headdress with a robe, such as those in figs. 1 and 3, draped over it. Photograph by Professor Gregor Grabar.

5.

6.

7.

8.

1.

2.

TURKMEN MEN'S ROBES

For the most part, Turkmen women wove their own cloth. Silk and cotton were obtained from the bazaars, as were dyes such as cochineal and indigo. Sheep wool and camel hair usually came from their own animals. Lining fabrics were mainly local block-printed cotton or imported factory-printed Russian cotton. Men wore robes made from *alacha* or striped red *gyrmyzy donlyk* over a long white tunic (*koynek*), pants, and a tall sheepskin hat (*telpek*). Well-off men wore warm overcoats made from camel wool (*chekmen*).

In 1925 the Soviet Union created the Turkmen SSR with the boundaries of modern-day Turkmenistan. By the 1930s freedom of movement was restricted and the Turkmen tribes were collectivized. Though many Turkmen fled to Afghanistan and Iran, most continued to live in Turkmenistan.

1. ROBE. 2nd half, 20th c. Handwoven plain-weave silk; green wool gussets with silk lacing stitch; loop-manipulation silk trim; block-printed *chit* lining; handwoven check facing. 45" length; 62" cuff to cuff

2. ROBE (*chekmen*). 1st half, 20th c. Handwoven camel-hair overcoat; applied small wool triangles; loop-manipulation silk trim; *alacha* facing. 45" length; 64" cuff to cuff

3. A TURKMEN SKIPPER WITH HIS DESERT SHIP. Merv, Turkmenistan, 1919. His cargo consists of two bales of fabrics. Photograph by Maynard Owen Williams.

4. ROBE (*gyrmyzy don*). 3rd quarter, 20th c. Lacing stitch; loop-manipulation silk trim; machine-printed cotton lining; silk ikat facing. A traditional Turkmen robe worn by men and women (women usually wore it on top of their heads). 46" length; 74" cuff to cuff

5. TURKMEN MEN. 1911. These men, standing in front of a yurt, are wearing traditional red robes and sheepskin hats. Photograph by Prokudin-Gorskii.

3.

4.

5.

1.

2.

3.

MEN'S ROBES

Warm, plain wool outer robes (figs. 1, 4, 6) were cut very full with long sleeves. They could be worn over several other robes for protection against the elements or the ever-present mud and dust. Thick, handwoven outer robes made from undyed sheep's wool or camel hair were called *chekmen*. The example shown in fig. 6, made of imported felted-wool broadcloth, appears to have been cut from the end pieces of a length of cloth. The lot numbers evident on both front flaps were machine-stitched by the British or Russian textile manufacturer. We can only guess at why the robe-maker let them remain—thrift, or perhaps prestige?

1. **MAN'S OUTER ROBE** (*chekmen*). Uzbekistan, c. 1930s. Handwoven camel hair; loop-manipulation silk trim; Russian machine-woven stripes and printed-cotton facings; unlined. 49" length; 78" cuff to cuff

2, 3. **MAN'S ROBE (and detail).** Probably Uzbek, late 19th c. Silk warp/cotton weft stripe; loop-manipulation silk trim; Russian printed-cotton lining and facing. (fig. 2) 50" length; 80" cuff to cuff; (fig. 3) 9.5 x 7"

4. **MAN IN CAMEL-HAIR COAT** (*chekmen*). Samarkand, Uzbekistan, 1911. Photograph by Prokudin-Gorskii.

5, 6. **MAN'S OUTER ROBE (and detail).** Probably Uzbek, last third, 19th c. Imported wool broadcloth; loop-manipulation silk trim; probably Russian printed-cotton lining; *adras* ikat facing. (fig. 5) 9.5 x 7"; (fig. 6) 56" length; 95" cuff to cuff

4.

5.

6.

1.

2.

3.

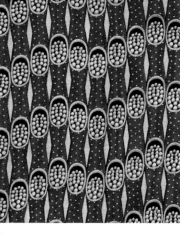

4.

ADRAS IKAT ROBES

Adras is a heavy, plain-weave fabric, often ikat, with a dense silk warp and cotton weft. It was usually polished to a high sheen. "*Ikat*" is a Malay-Indonesian word that is widely used to refer to the ikat pattern, the cloth, and the process of making it. However, in Central Asia, the word "*abr*" ("cloud" in Persian) refers to ikat design and cloth, and "*abrbandi*" to the ikat-weaving technique. Most nineteenth-century ikat was produced in Bukhara and the Ferghana Valley. By the early 1920s, due to economic reasons and Soviet policies, the time-consuming production of *adras* ikat ceased.

1, 2. WOMAN'S ROBE (and detail). Bukhara, Uzbekistan, last quarter, 19th c. *Adras* ikat with ram's horn motif; Russian printed-cotton lining; *adras* ikat facing. This type of women's robe with gathering (*chucha*) under the armpits, a narrow waist, and a full skirt was called a *munisak*. By the early twentieth century it was no longer in style, yet elderly women kept a few to cover their burial litter. (fig. 1) 50" length; 68" cuff to cuff; (fig. 2) 14 x 12.5"

3, 4. WOMAN'S ROBE (and detail). Uzbekistan, late 19th c. *Adras* ikat with ram's horn motif; loop-manipulation silk trim; Russian printed-cotton lining; Russian printed-cotton and *bekasab* facing. (fig. 3) 48" length; 48" cuff to cuff; (fig. 4) 6.5 x 6"

5. WOMAN'S ROBE. Uzbekistan, late 19th c. *Adras* ikat; loop-manipulation silk trim; Russian printed-cotton lining (see fig. 4, page 288 for detail); *adras* ikat facing. 47" length; 62" cuff to cuff

6. MAN'S ROBE. Uzbekistan, 1st half, 20th c. *Bekasab* stripe with ikat; applied handwoven trim; printed-cotton lining. This elegant fabric has it all—lustrous hand, moiré, *bekasab* stripes, and dashes of ikat. 52" length; 76" cuff to cuff

5.

6.

1.

2.

3.

SHOHI IKAT ROBES

Shohi (also *shahi*, *shaii*, *shoii*, and *kanous*) is an all-silk, plain-weave cloth. *Shohi* ikat was usually woven with a red or black weft and looked slightly iridescent. It was popular for robes and continued to be handwoven into the 1920s. *Shohi* robes made a rustling noise when worn, which contributed to their appeal. Before a man purchased a new *shohi* robe, he would make sure that it made the desired sound. Bukhara and the Ferghana Valley were the centers of *shohi* ikat production.

1. WOMAN'S ROBE. Bukhara, Uzbekistan, late 19th–early 20th c. *Shohi* ikat; loop-manipulation silk trim with cross-stitching; Russian printed-cotton lining; Russian printed striped-cotton facing. 51" length; 61" cuff to cuff

2. ROBE. Bukhara, late 19th–early 20th c. *Shohi* ikat with pomegranate and *bodum* (almond) motifs; applied handwoven trim; Russian printed-cotton lining; *adras* ikat facing. 49" length; 48" cuff to cuff

3. WOMAN'S ROBE.[6] Bukhara, late 19th c. *Shohi* ikat with amulet, ram's horn, and pomegranate-flower motifs; loop-manipulation silk trim with cross-stitching; machine embroidery; Russian printed-cotton lining; *adras* ikat facing. 46" length; 63" cuff to cuff

4, 6. TAJIK WOMAN'S ROBE (back and front). Ferghana Valley, last third, 19th c. *Shohi* ikat; loop-manipulation silk trim; Russian block-printed cotton lining; *adras* ikat and Russian machine-woven striped-cotton facings. Dark ikat robes of this type were traditionally worn at funerals. 51" length; 64" cuff to cuff

5. "KOKAND SARTS." c. 1910, Russian period postcard. The woman on the left is wearing an outfit that appears to be made from silk brocade; the girl on the right is wearing an ikat robe.

6 The lining of this robe is shown in Meller, *Russian Textiles*, 98–99.

4.

5.

6.

1.

2.

3.

SHOHI ROBES

Solid-color all-silk *shohi* robes, such as the two on this spread, tend to appear less often in shops and museum collections than their showier counterparts. But open them up and a richly patterned world is revealed, one with beautiful imported cotton prints framed by tantalizing strips of ikats.

1. WOMAN'S ROBE. Uzbekistan, last third, 19th c. All-silk, loop-manipulation silk trim; probably Russian printed-cotton lining; *adras* ikat and machine-woven striped-cotton facing. 50" length; 55" cuff to cuff

2, 3. ROBE (and detail). Uzbekistan, last third, 19th c. All-silk, loop-manipulation silk trim; Russian printed-cotton lining; *adras* ikat and machine-woven striped-cotton facing. (fig. 2) 51" length; 62" cuff to cuff; (fig. 3) 8.5 x 6"

4, 5. WOMAN'S ROBE (and detail). Uzbekistan, 2nd quarter, 20th c. Plain-weave, all-silk, woven stripe; printed-cotton lining. This robe has a decidedly Western cut, with its full collar, side pockets, narrow waist, and A-line flare. (fig. 4) 11 x 10"; (fig. 5) 50" length; 55" cuff to cuff

4.

5.

1.

2.   3.

SATIN-WEAVE ROBES

The term "*atlas*" refers to a satin-weave fabric, generally with a silk warp and weft. *Khanatlas* is a higher-grade *atlas*. "*Yakruya*" is a term also used for a silk warp/cotton weft satin-weave cloth. These fabrics have a very soft hand and highly glossy appearance. They were frequently woven with multicolored stripes or ikat patterns and were popular for robes.

1. WOMAN'S IKAT ROBE. Bukhara, Uzbekistan, c. 1900. Silk warp/cotton weft; machine-embroidered cotton trim; Russian printed-cotton lining. 49" length; 64" cuff to cuff

2, 3. WOMAN'S IKAT ROBE (and detail). Uzbekistan, 3rd quarter, 19th c. Silk warp/silk weft; loop-manipulation silk trim; Russian block-printed cotton lining; *adras* ikat facing. (fig. 2) 52" length; 55" cuff to cuff; (fig. 3) 18 x 10"

4. ROBE. Uzbekistan, c. 1900. Silk warp/cotton weft; loop-manipulation silk trim; plain-cotton lining; *adras* ikat facing. 60" length; 52" cuff to cuff

5. MAN'S ROBE. Uzbekistan, 1st third, 20th c. Silk warp/cotton weft; plain-cotton lining; striped-silk facing. 50" length; 71" cuff to cuff

4.

5.

ATLAS IKAT ROBES

Satin-weave, all-silk *atlas* ikat is woven on a four-harness loom, while *khanatlas*, a higher-grade *atlas*, is woven on an eight-harness loom. The weft threads are usually dyed red or black to make them blend in better with the warp threads and impart richer color to the fabric (as the wefts are slightly visible on the surface of the cloth). The ikat pattern shows clearly only on the right side. All the robes on pages 62–65 are woven with red silk wefts.

Robes such as these and the ones shown on the following two pages were particularly popular with women in the southern provinces of Uzbekistan.

1, 2. WOMAN'S ROBE (back and front). Kashkadarya, Uzbekistan, mid-20th c. *Atlas* ikat; applied handwoven trim; probably Russian machine-printed cotton lining and facing.[7] 51" length; 72" cuff to cuff

3. WOMAN'S ROBE. Uzbekistan, 3rd quarter, 20th c. *Atlas* ikat; Uzbek printed-cotton lining. 50" length; 71" cuff to cuff

4. WOMAN'S ROBE. Uzbekistan, 3rd quarter, 20th c. *Atlas* ikat; printed-cotton lining. 48" length; 75" cuff to cuff

7 Two other colorings of this popular printed cloth are shown in Meller, *Russian Textiles*, 116 and 117.

3.

4.

1.

2.

3.

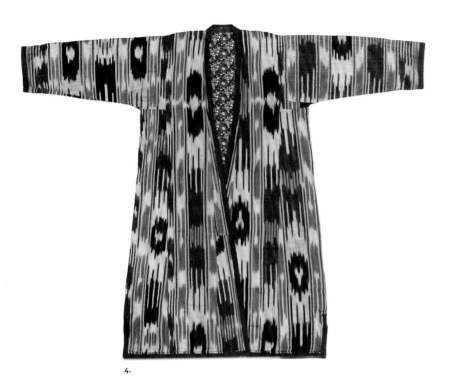

4.

ATLAS IKAT ROBES

During the Soviet era, small hand-weaving ikat workshops were organized into workers' co-ops (artels). Even these artels were mostly phased out after the large textile combines began manufacturing *atlas* ikat. *Shohi, adras,* and *yakruya* ikat ceased being woven, while factory production of *atlas* and *khanatlas* ikat continued in ever-increasing quantities from the 1960s until the demise of the Soviet Union in 1991. Today, most ikat is either *atlas* or *khanatlas* and made, at least in part, by machine.

1, 2, 4. WOMEN'S ROBES (and detail). Kashkadarya, Uzbekistan, 3rd quarter, 20th c. *Atlas* ikat; cloth trim; Russian or Uzbek printed-cotton linings and facings. (fig. 1) 46" length; 63" cuff to cuff; (fig. 2) 10 x 9"; (fig. 4) 48" length; 61" cuff to cuff

3. WOMAN'S ROBE. Uzbekistan, 3rd quarter, 20th c. *Atlas* ikat; applied handwoven trim; Russian or Uzbek printed-cotton lining with sweet peas and carnations; machine-woven striped-cotton facing. 48" length; 61" cuff to cuff

5, 6. WOMAN'S ROBE (and detail). Uzbekistan, 3rd quarter, 20th c. *Atlas* ikat; cloth trim; probably Uzbek printed-cotton lining and facing. (fig. 5) 12 x 11"; (fig. 6) 48" length; 74" cuff to cuff

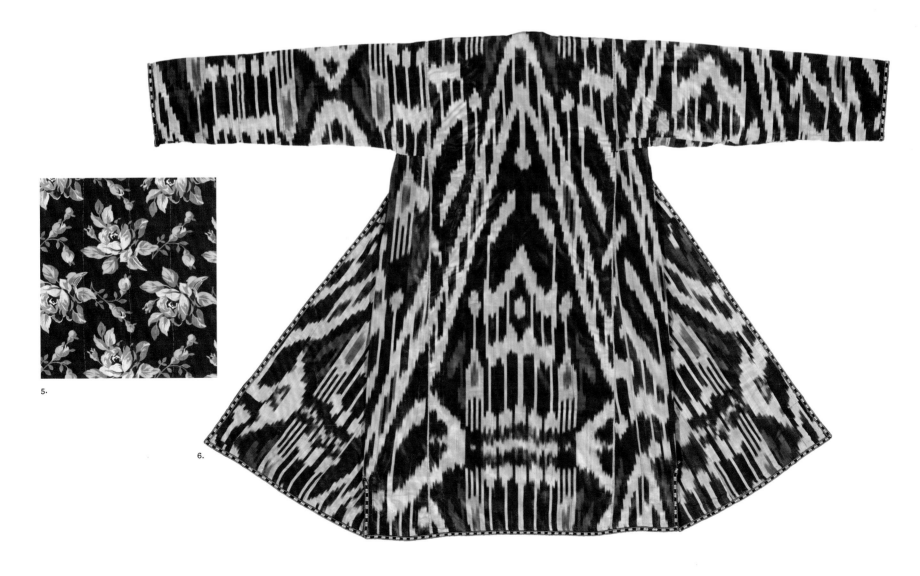

5.

6.

1.

2.

3.

4.

5.

VELVET ROBES

Russian factory-made silk or cotton velvet was a popular material for robes, vests, and skullcaps; however, a silk velvet robe would have been a luxury item. Some silk velvets were embossed with subtle motifs, such as the checkerboard pattern shown in fig. 3.

1, 2. WOMAN'S ROBE (and detail). Samarkand, Uzbekistan, c. 1900. Silk velvet; applied handwoven trim; Russian printed-cotton lining; *adras* ikat facing. (fig. 1) 53" length; 59" cuff to cuff; (fig. 2) 16 x 14"

3, 4. WOMAN'S ROBE (and detail). Samarkand, c. 1900. Silk-embossed velvet; applied handwoven trim; Russian printed, art nouveau cotton lining; *atlas* ikat facing. (fig. 3) 45" length; 65" cuff to cuff; (fig. 4) 16 x 13"

5, 6. MAN'S ROBE (and detail). Uzbekistan, early 20th c. Silk velvet; applied handwoven trim; Russian printed-cotton lining; *bekasab* facing. (fig. 5) 35" length; 48" cuff to cuff; (fig. 6) 12.5 x 10"

7, 8. WOMAN'S ROBE (and detail). Samarkand, early 20th c. Silk velvet; applied handwoven trim, Russian printed-cotton-jacquard lining; *bekasab* facing. (fig. 7) 13 x 10.5"; (fig. 8) 47" length; 55" cuff to cuff

6.

7.

8.

1.

2.

VELVET ROBES

Many nineteenth- and early twentieth-century women's velvet robes were unadorned, except for trimming around the edges. However, velvet robes made for special occasions, especially weddings, could be heavily embroidered. Bukharan robes with elaborate gold embroidery (*zarduzi*) are called *zarchapan*. The example shown in fig. 3 was a Jewish ceremonial robe.

1. WOMAN'S ROBE. Uzbekistan, c. 1910. Silk velvet; applied woven trim; Russian printed-cotton lining; *adras* ikat and Russian machine-woven striped-cotton facing. 53" length; 66" cuff to cuff

2. *KALANDARS* (dervishes). Samarkand, Uzbekistan, 1911. The man in the turban, who does not appear to be a *kalandar*, wears a *bekasab* robe over a printed-cotton robe. The print on the inner robe is the same as the lining print shown in fig. 1. Photograph by Prokudin-Gorskii.

3. JEWISH MAN'S ROBE. Bukhara, Uzbekistan, last third, 20th c. Cotton velvet; gold thread and Lurex hand embroidery with menorah and Star of David motifs; sequins; plain cotton lining. Bukhara was the center of Jewish life in Central Asia. 47" length; 61" cuff to cuff

4, 5. MAN'S ROBE (front and back). Bukhara, 3rd quarter, 20th c. Silk velvet; hand-embroidered with gold thread and Lurex; sequins; plain cotton lining. 49" length; 68" cuff to cuff

3.

5.

4.

1.

BROCADE ROBES

In 1821 a young Russian officer was sent on a mission to Khiva. He was received by the khan and presented with an "embroidered turban . . . [that] was tied on my head, whilst my waist was bound round with a rich Indian girdle, into which a silver-sheathed dagger was stuck, and a robe with short sleeves made of Russian brocade thrown over my shoulders."[8]

By the 1880s Russia controlled all of Central Asia, and most imported cloth found in the local bazaars was manufactured in Russia, including costly silk brocades and velvets. In Uzbekistan, imported European and Russian fabric in general was referred to as *farangi*. Imported Russian brocade was called *parcha*. Today, brocade is known as *kundal*.

8 Murav'yov, *Journey to Khiva*, 73.

1. MAN'S ROBE. Bukhara, Uzbekistan, 1st quarter, 20th c. Russian silk brocade with gold-wrapped threads; Russian printed-cotton lining. This lavish robe was probably worn by a well-off urban man at his marriage ceremony. 49" length; 72" cuff to cuff

2. WOMAN'S ROBE. Uzbekistan, early 20th c. Russian silk brocade with gold- and silver-wrapped threads; woven trim; Russian printed-cotton lining. The cut of this urban robe shows a distinct Western influence, with its turn-down collar, fitted waist, and flared fullness. 42" length, 60" cuff to cuff

2.

1.

BROCADE ROBES

Figured silks were imported, mainly from Russia, India, and China. They were produced on hand-operated drawlooms or mechanized jacquard looms. Under the tsars, Russian mills manufactured large quantities of silk brocade for both the church and the upper classes. However, under the Soviets, wagonloads of appropriated church vestments were shipped to artels in Central Asia, where they were recycled into skullcaps (see footnote 3, page 135). Figured silks with a distinct ecclesiastical look can occasionally be seen on Central Asian robes. Robes may also have been fashioned from these priestly garments and from yard goods no longer saleable in the Soviet Union. Some brocaded patterns are similar to French florals (fig. 1), while silks from Kashgar in western China, called *Kashkartovar*,[9] often have Chinese motifs (see fig. 5, page 85).

9 Naphisa Sodikova, *National Uzbek Clothes* (Tashkent, 2003), 128, fig. 19.

1. **ROBE.**[10] Uzbekistan, late 19th c. Imported silk brocade; cloth trim; Russian printed-cotton lining. 48" length; 65" cuff to cuff

10 A robe made of similar fabric from Ole Olufsen's late nineteenth-century expedition is shown in Esther Fihl, *Exploring Central Asia: From the Steppes to the High Pamirs* (Seattle: University of Washington Press, 2010), 1:127.

2. *KUSH-BEGGI.* Minister of the Interior, Bukhara, Uzbekistan, 1911. Second only to the emir, this man displays all the accoutrements of his very high rank—an imported silk-brocade robe, gilt-and-enameled belt and saber, and a chest full of medals. Photograph by Prokudin-Gorskii.

3, 4. **WOMAN'S ROBE (and detail).** Uzbekistan, last third, 19th c. Imported silk brocade; loop-manipulation silk trim; Russian printed-cotton lining; woven striped-silk facing. (fig. 3) 11 x 8"; (fig. 4) 49" length; 64" cuff to cuff

2.

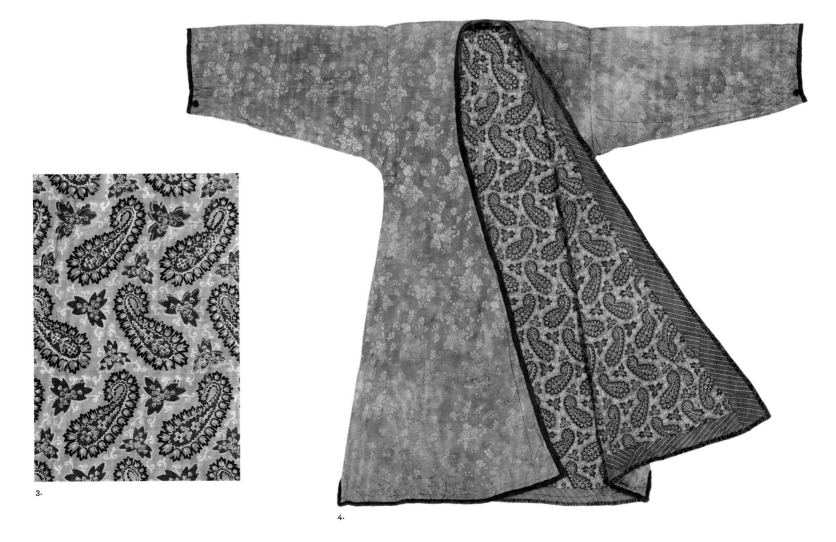

3.

4.

1.

2.

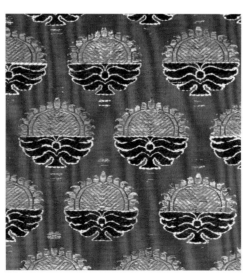

3.

4.

BROCADE ROBES

The figured-silk motifs on these robes have a decidedly Indian look. In fact the brocade fabric shown in fig. 6 (the earliest robe in this book) was handwoven in India no later than the mid-nineteenth century.[11] The other robe was also made from imported silk brocade, but the cloth was probably factory-woven in Russia. (Russian mills exported excellent imitations of Indian brocades.)

The printed cotton lining shown in fig. 2 was block-printed on a plain-weave handwoven cotton. It too may well have been imported from India.

11 A silk brocade with very similar motifs is illustrated in Kokyo Hatanaka, *Textile Arts of India* (San Francisco: Chronicle Books, 1996), 217.

1, 5. MAN'S ROBE (and detail).[12] Probably Uzbekistan, late 19th c. Imported silk-satin brocade; cloth trim; Russian printed-cotton lining. (fig. 1) 49" length; 60"cuff to cuff; (fig. 5) 8 x 7"

12 The lining pattern is shown in Meller, *Russian Textiles*, 94.

2, 3, 4, 6. MAN'S ROBE (and details). Probably Uzbekistan, mid-19th c. Indian handwoven silk brocade with gold- and silver-wrapped thread (note that two slightly different brocades were used); loop-manipulation silk trim in two shades of indigo; block-printed cotton lining; finely woven, striped-ikat facing (probably Indian). (fig. 2) 4 x 3.5"; (fig. 3) 8.5 x 6.5"; (fig. 4) 7.5 x 6"; (fig. 6) 52" length; 86" cuff to cuff

5.

6.

1.

2.

3.

4.

5.

PRINTED ROBES

By the 1820s Russian printed chintz and calicos were being exported in quantity to the markets of Central Asia. As the nineteenth century progressed and Russia gained more and more control over Turkestan, laws were enacted to ban competing European goods, particularly British textiles. By the 1860s and '70s, Russian cloth, especially factory-printed cotton, was the most prevalent material in all the Central Asian bazaars. Inexpensive, brightly colored, and comfortable to wear, it quickly became popular with the local people—for both the outside and the lining of their robes.

1–3. WOMAN'S ROBE (and details). Uzbekistan, 3rd quarter, 19th c. Russian block-printed cotton; loop-manipulation silk trim; Uzbek block-printed cotton lining; *alacha* and roller-printed cotton facing. Factory-printed cotton did not wear as well as yarn-dyed local cloths such as *bekasab*. It faded in the sun and often ran when washed. Relatively inexpensive to begin with, printed robes were either discarded or recycled into other textile items when they were no longer wearable. This is a rare example, in perfect condition, of what was once a very common garment. (fig. 1) 18.5 x 14"; (fig. 2) 3.5 x 3"; (fig. 3) 51" length; 61" cuff to cuff

4, 5. PRINTED ROBE (and detail). Uzbekistan, c. 1900. Russian machine-printed cotton with carnations; cotton cloth trim; Russian printed-cotton lining. (fig. 4) 11 x 8"; (fig. 5) 48" length; 58" cuff to cuff

6. PRINTED ROBE. Boysun, southern Uzbekistan, c. 1960s. Uzbek machine-printed cotton; applied handwoven trim; cotton lining; printed-cotton facing. This printed-stripe pattern is a less costly imitation of a woven stripe. 46" length; 65" cuff to cuff

7. PRINTED ROBE. Probably Uzbekistan, early 20th c. Probably Russian machine-printed cotton; cloth trim; cotton lining. 49" length; 66" cuff to cuff

6.

7.

1.

2.

PRINTED ROBES

The 1920s through 1940s were a difficult time, due to political, economic, and social upheavals, and World War II. Printed cloth was available, but not nearly in the quantity and variety found earlier.

After recovering from the war, Soviet-operated textile mills in Russia, Uzbekistan, Tajikistan, and Kyrgyzstan began printing cloth again. In the Central Asian combines, the machinery and technical expertise was supplied by the Russians—perhaps many of the textile designs were as well. (It can be difficult to tell if a print from this time was produced in a Russian or Central Asian factory.)

While few printed robes from the nineteenth and early twentieth centuries still exist, many can be found dating from the 1960s through the 1980s, particularly examples from the southern provinces of Uzbekistan. These later robes tended to be made from cotton printed in Uzbek factories.

1. WOMAN'S ROBE. Southern Uzbekistan, c. 1960s–70s. Probably Uzbek machine-printed cotton with poppies; applied handwoven trim; handwoven cotton lining (*buz*); printed-cotton facing. 42" length; 58" cuff to cuff

2, 4, 5. WOMAN'S ROBES (and detail). Southern Uzbekistan, c. 1960s–70s. Russian or Uzbek machine-printed cotton (figs. 2 and 4 feature the same print in different colorings); applied handwoven trim; machine-printed cotton linings and facings. (figs. 2, 4) 42" length; 56" cuff to cuff; (fig. 5) 11 x 8"

3. WOMAN'S *KUYLAK*. Uzbekistan, mid-20th c. Russian or Uzbek machine-printed cotton; machine-embroidered trim; unlined. A *kuylak* was a generously cut tunic- or smocklike garment. 46" length; 74" cuff to cuff

3.

4.

5.

1.

2.

0.

EMBROIDERED GARMENTS

Elaborately embroidered garments were usually reserved for festivities. Women generally embroidered their own clothes, which also enabled them to show off their sewing skills. The two dresses (*chakan*) shown here were made in southern Tajikistan and worn by Tajik women for special occasions. The green wedding robe from southern Uzbekistan was entirely machine-embroidered—no mean feat.

1, 2. WOMAN'S WEDDING ROBE (front and back). Kashkadarya, Uzbekistan, c. 1960s–70s. Satin-weave silk; silk and cotton machine-embroidery; rickrack; applied machine-embroidered cotton trim; printed-cotton lining. 42" length; 52" cuff to cuff

3, 4. WOMEN'S DRESSES (*chakan*). Kuylab, Tajikistan, c. 1960s–70s. White plain-weave cotton; red silk; silk embroidery; unlined. (fig. 3) 37" length; 47" cuff to cuff; (fig. 4) 41" length; 58" cuff to cuff

4.

Типы Ташкента.   Сартянка.
Types de Taschkent.   Femme sarte.

1.

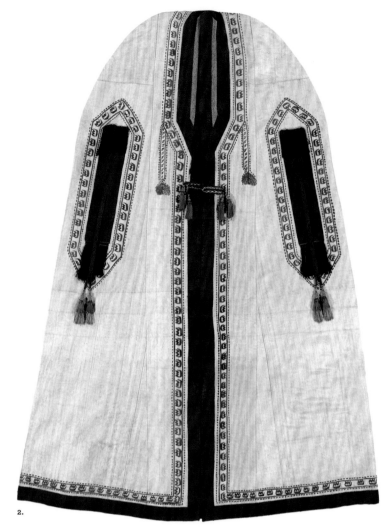

2.

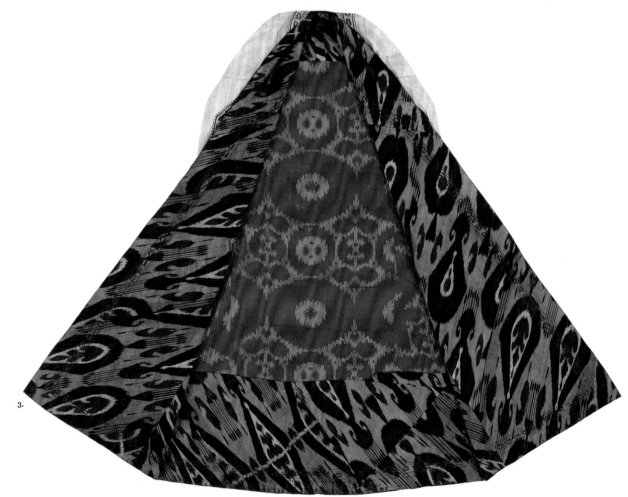

3.

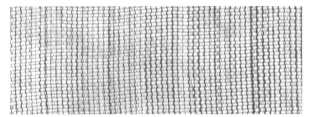

4.

5.

6.

PARANJAS

The *paranja* was a capelike garment with long false sleeves that were fastened together and hung down the length of the back. Draped over a woman's head, it enveloped her completely. It was worn with a stiff, black, waist-long veil (*chachvan*), which was woven out of horsehair and totally concealed her face. Beginning in the 1870s, urban women and girls as young as nine wore the *paranja* and veil whenever they left their homes. The *paranja* was typically made from *banoras*—a handwoven gray, green, or blue silk warp/cotton weft cloth with fine black pinstripes that sometimes had a subtle moiré finish. Paired with the *chachvan*, it served its purpose well—as American journalist J. A. MacGahan wrote while in Khiva in 1874, "Nothing but men's faces for weeks and months, until you long for the sight of a woman's face, as you do for green grass and flowers in the desert."

1. **"SART WOMAN."** Tashkent, Uzbekistan, c. 1910. Russian period postcard. In pre-Soviet days, "sart" was the term Russia applied to the settled peoples of Central Asia (as opposed to nomadic ones). The woman in this studio portrait wears a *paranja* similar to the one shown in fig. 2, with a *chachvan* thrown back over her head.

2, 3. *PARANJA* (front and lining). Tashkent, c. 1900. *Banoras*; silk hand-embroidery; applied handwoven, silk trim; silk tassels; Russian printed faux-ikat cotton lining; *adras* ikat facing. Silvery-gray *banoras* cloth such as this was called *para-pasha* (fly wings). 60" length; 44" width closed; 78" width open

4, 5. *BANORAS* (details). Uzbekistan, c. 1910. Silk warp/cotton weft handwoven cloth; details of figs. 2 and 7 (front). 5 x 2.5"

6. **BUKHARAN WOMEN WEARING THE PARANJA.** Uzbekistan, c. 1924. Photograph by Gustav Krist.

7. *PARANJA* (lining). Jizzak region, Uzbekistan, c. 1900. *Banoras*; silk hand-embroidery; loop manipulation silk trim with cross-stitching; elaborate silk tassels with glass beads; glass buttons (see fig. 5, page 104 for detail); Russian printed-cotton lining; *adras* ikat and Russian striped-cotton facing. 39" length; 55" width closed; 79" width open

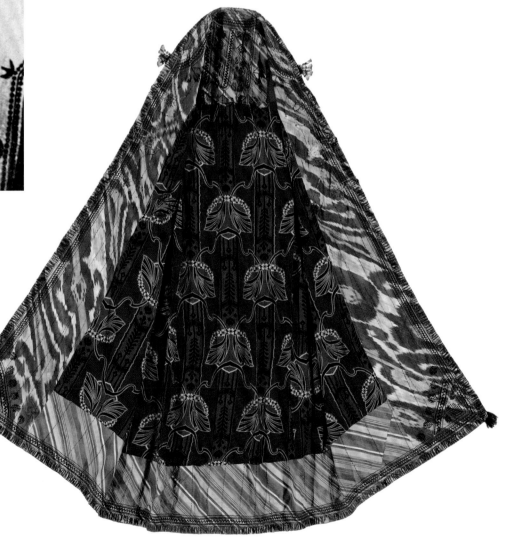

7.

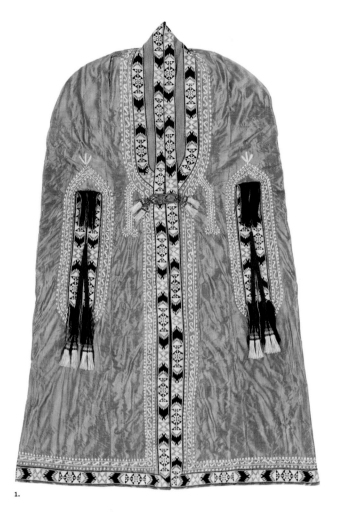

1.

2.

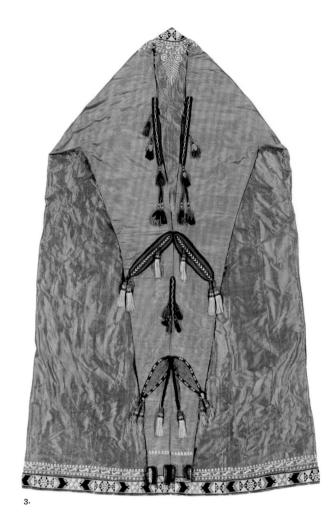

3.

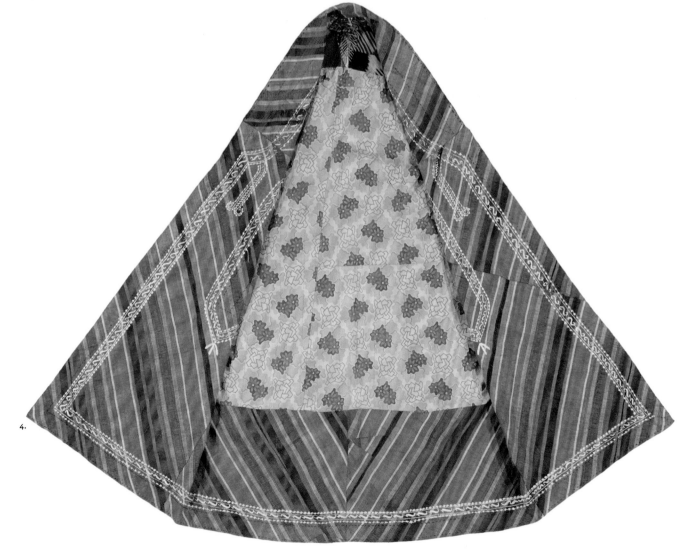

4.

5.

PARANJAS

A *paranja* could be quite a luxurious garment, especially when made from imported silk velvet or silk brocade and ornamented with elaborate trimmings. These costly *paranjas* were often made to order by seamstresses. Yet even an outwardly plain *paranja* usually hid a colorful Russian printed lining.

1–4. PARANJA (front, trim, back, and lining). Uzbekistan, early 20th c. *Banoras* with pronounced moiré; silk hand-embroidery; applied handwoven and cross-stitched silk trim; silk tassels; Russian printed-cotton lining; *bekasab* facing. (figs. 1, 3, 4) 52" length; 37" width closed; 73" width open; (fig. 2) trim detail; 10 x 1.25"

5. PARANJA. Uzbekistan, early 20th c. Chinese silk damask; silk hand-embroidery; applied handwoven and cross-stitched silk trim; silk tassels; *adras* ikat lining. 59" length; 46" width closed; 93" width open

6, 7. PARANJA. Uzbekistan, c. 1900. Russian embossed silk velvet; silk hand-embroidery; applied handwoven and cross-stitched silk trim; silk tassels; Russian printed faux-ikat cotton lining; *atlas* ikat facing. 61" length; 43" width closed; 89" width open

6.

7.

1.

2.

3.

JELAKS

While similar in appearance to a *paranja*, a *jelak* was much shorter and was never intended to conceal. It was worn on top of a rural woman's headdress and draped like a shawl over the head and shoulders, with false sleeves hanging in back. The hem was deliberately left unfinished in the belief that by so doing a woman could bear many children.[13]

13 Binafsha Nodir, *San'at* magazine (Academy of Arts, Uzbekistan), issue 2, 2005.

1. **BOYSUN FESTIVAL.** Boysun, Uzbekistan, 2005. Boysun Bahori was a folklore festival held each year from 2001 to 2005 in the Boysun region of Surkhandarya province in southern Uzbekistan. Performers dressed in traditional costume. The women in this photo are wearing *jelaks* on top of their headdresses.

2, 3. **JELAK** (back and front). Southern Uzbekistan, mid-20th c. or earlier. Handwoven cotton *boz* with narrow gray stripes; silk hand-embroidery; applied handwoven trim; unlined. 39" length; 27" width closed; 62" width open

4. **JELAK.** Southern Uzbekistan, mid-20th c. Machine-woven striped cotton; silk hand-embroidery; applied handwoven trim with cross-stitching; unlined. This jelak includes many protective motifs (including ram's horn and triangles). 36" length; 29" width closed; 60" width open

4.

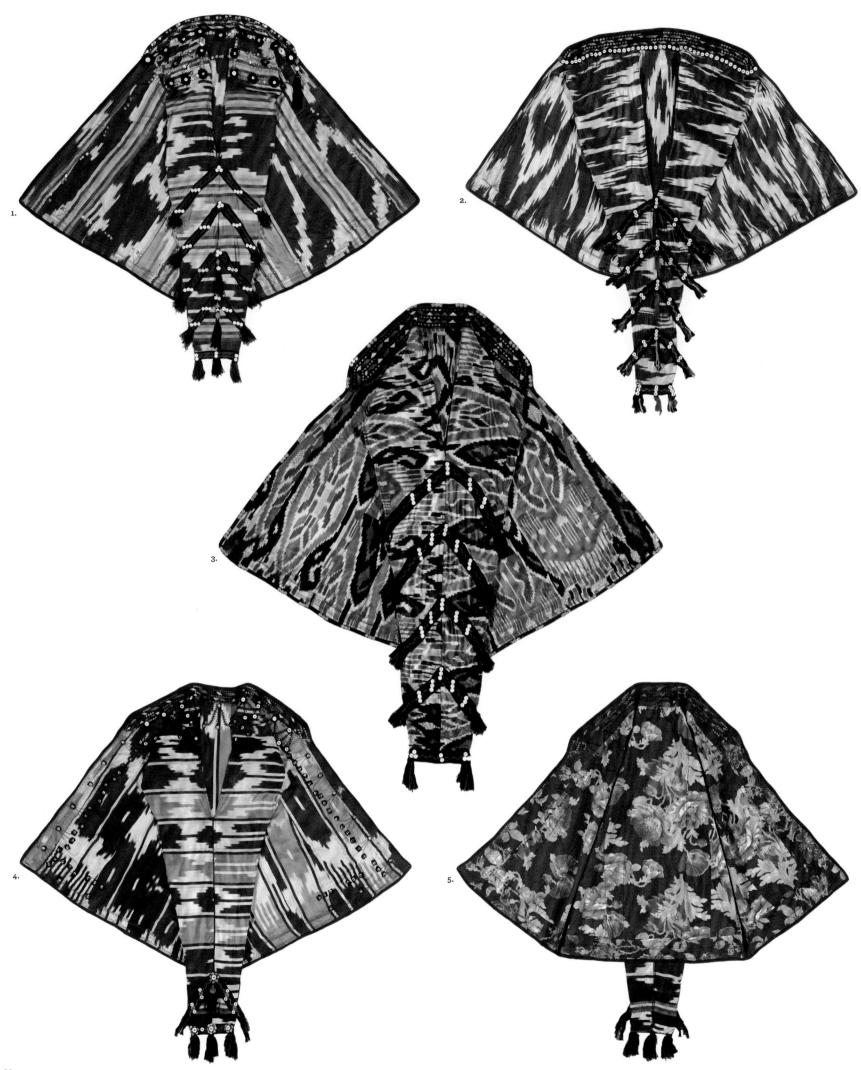

JELAKS

Very short, capelike *jelaks* such as these date from the 1960s to the 1970s and were popular in the Jizzak region and rural areas around Samarkand. Like the longer *jelaks* on pages 86–87, they were worn by Tajik women as headdresses, with the long false sleeves joined behind. Ikat, both woven and printed, and solid red cloth were the preferred materials. They were ornamented with many pearl or white glass buttons, braid, tassels, and cross-stitching along the top.

1, 2, 4, 5. *JELAKS.* Jizzak/Samarkand area, c. 1960s–70s. *Atlas* ikat; cross-stitch embroidery; machine-embroidery along edges; black cloth binding; handwoven trim on sleeves; pearl buttons; sequins; printed-cotton linings and facings. (fig. 1) 35" length; (figs. 2 and 4) 32" length; (fig. 5) lining of fig. 4; all lengths are from top to hem

3. *JELAK.* Jizzak area, c. 1960s–70s. Silk printed faux-ikat; cross-stitch embroidery; machine-embroidery along edges; black cloth binding; handwoven trim on sleeves; pearl buttons; sequins; printed faux-ikat cotton facing. 32" length

6, 7. *JELAK.* Jizzak area, c. 1960s. Plain-weave cotton; cross-stitch embroidery; white machine-embroidery: black cloth binding; handwoven trim on sleeves; pearl and glass buttons; printed cotton facing. 30" length

6.

7.

KARAKALPAK

The Karakalpak people (literally, "black hat," after their traditional tall, shaggy, sheepskin hats) live in far western Uzbekistan in an autonomous republic that was once part of the Khorezm khanate. In 1924–25 the Soviets partitioned off an area of mostly desert (and the shrinking Aral Sea) and declared it Karakalpakstan.

It was the unique costume and exquisite embroidery of the Karakalpak women that initially attracted the Russian artist Igor Savitsky to that remote area. Settling there in the mid-1950s, he began to amass his incredible collection of Karakalpak folk art, textiles, and Russian avant-garde art, now housed in the Nukus Museum.[14]

14 For in-depth information and images of Karakalpak textiles and culture, see David and Sue Richardson, *Qaraqalpaqs of the Aral Delta* (Munich: Prestel, 2012). See also the documentary film *Desert of Forbidden Art.*

1–4. *QIZIL KIYMESHEKS* (and details). Karakalpakstan, c. 1900. Silk lacing and chain stitch on imported red- and black-wool broadcloth (*ushiga*); loop-manipulation trim; *adras* ikat; silk fringe; Russian printed-cotton cap and border. Believed to have protective powers, a *qizil* (red) *kiymeshek* was worn by a young bride at her wedding and, later, on special occasions. It covered her head and shoulders with her face framed by the U-shaped opening. A long ikat panel, bordered by embroidery and fringe, trailed down the back. A soft attached cap covered her head and was hidden by an elaborate turban. The ikat panel is missing from the *aldi* section shown in fig. 4. (fig. 1) 55 x 50"; (fig. 2) 2.5 x 3.5"; (fig. 3) 3.5 x 3.5"; (fig. 4) 19 x 31"

5, 6. *AQ JEGDE* (and detail). Karakalpakstan, early 20th c. Factory-made cotton; fine silk cross-stitching on handwoven cotton panel; *adras* ikat gussets; loop-manipulation trim; Russian striped-cotton facing; unlined. The *jegde* was worn cloaklike over a woman's turban and served to partially conceal her when she went outside. Like a *paranja*, the long false sleeves were fastened in back. This garment was worn only on formal and festive occasions. (fig. 5) 11 x 4"; (fig. 6) 44" length; 83" cuff to cuff

5.

6.

1.

2.

3.

IKAT DRESSES (*Kuylak*)

Women's and girls' dresses called *kuylak* (Uzbek) or *kurta* (Tajik) took several forms. Smocklike ones with spread collars (figs. 1, 2) became popular as everyday wear during the Soviet era. They were most often made of *atlas* ikat and had a more Western cut. The classic T-shaped ones (figs. 5, 6) were unlined and often worn underneath a woman's robe. They were cut full with long, wide sleeves and could be layered in such a way that the cuffs, which were sometimes elaborately embroidered, would show below the sleeves of the outer robe.

Large-scale ikat patterns, such as those shown in figs. 5 and 6 and similar to those that the women are wearing in fig. 4, were popular in the 1930s and '40s.

1, 2. *KUYLAKS.* Uzbekistan, c. 1960s. *Atlas* ikat; unlined; cotton facings. (fig. 1) 44" length; (fig. 2) 48" length

3. MUSLIM FAMILY. Uzbekistan, c. 1930–40s. Photograph by Max Penson.

4. THREE GIRLS. Stalin Street, Tashkent, Uzbekistan, c. 1930s. Photograph by Max Penson.

5. *KUYLAK.* Uzbekistan, c. 1930s. Silk *shohi* ikat; machine-embroidery around neckline and hem; unlined. 48" length; 66" cuff to cuff

6. *KUYLAK.* Uzbekistan, c. 1940–50s. Silk *shohi* ikat; unlined; yellow selvedges. 46" length; 59" cuff to cuff

4.

5.

6.

1.

2.

3.

4.

5.

6.

FAUX-IKAT DRESSES (*Kuylak*)

In the early 1960s the Tashkent Textile Combine began printing faux-ikat patterns. Other factories in Uzbekistan and Tajikistan followed, printing ikat patterns on cotton, silk, and synthetics. It was often difficult to tell a real ikat from a printed one. Cheaper than woven ikat, but just as colorful, they continued to be produced in a great variety of designs until the dissolution of the Soviet Union in 1991. Shortly after, the combines shut down.

1, 6. *KUYLAKS.* Uzbekistan or Tajikistan, c. 1970s–80s. Machine-printed silk; cotton facings; unlined. (fig. 1) 45" length; (fig. 6) 41" length

2. *KUYLAK.* Ashkhabad, Turkmenistan, c. 1970s–80s. Machine-printed synthetic fabric; machine-printed cotton facing; unlined; factory label attached. 44" length

3, 7. *KUYLAKS.* Uzbekistan or Tajikistan, c. 1970s. Machine-printed silk satin; unlined; home-sewn. (fig. 3) 41" length; 61" cuff to cuff; (fig. 7) 44" length; 70" cuff to cuff

4, 5. *KUYLAKS.* Uzbekistan or Tajikistan, c. 1970s–80s. Machine-printed silk satin; printed cotton facings; unlined. (fig. 4) 44" length; (fig. 5) 42" length

7.

1.

2.

3.

4.

IKAT CHEMISES

Short-sleeved unlined ikat chemises such as these were favorite summer clothes during the 1970s through the 1990s. A stroll through the bazaar on a hot summer's day would evoke the rainbow metaphors of long-ago travelers.

The term *"atlas"* refers to a silk warp/silk weft satin-weave fabric. *Khanatlas* is a higher-quality *atlas*. Most *atlas* ikat was produced in large textile combines in Uzbekistan and Tajikistan until the end of the Soviet era.

1, 2, 5. CHEMISES. Uzbekistan, c. 1970s–80s. *Khanatlas*; machine-printed facings; unlined. The black-and-white ikat pattern was called "Night Beauty." (fig. 1) 48" length; (fig. 2) 39" length; (fig. 5) 42" length

3. FASHION PHOTO. Uzbekistan, 1975. Women modeling the latest "national dress" for an Uzbek fashion magazine.

4. CHEMISE. Uzbekistan, c. 1970s–80s. *Khanatlas*; printed-cotton facing; unlined; home-sewn. 42" length

6. CHEMISE and TROUSERS. Uzbekistan, c. 1990s. *Khanatlas* silk and Lurex machine-embroidery; cotton facing; unlined. Traditionally, dresses were worn with long pants (*lozim*), often mismatched, that peeked out from under the hem. 46 " length (chemise only)

7. CHEMISE. Uzbekistan, c. 1990s. *Khanatlas*; cotton facing; unlined. Elaborate ikats such as figs. 6 and 7 might have been produced in small artisan workshops, which began to be reestablished after independence. 50" length

5.

6.

7.

1.

2.

4.

3.

5.

6.

WOMEN'S TROUSERS (*Lozim*)

Under their dresses, women and girls wore loose-fitting trousers—called *lozim* (Uzbek), *shalwars* (Tajik), *balak* (Turkmen), or *ichtan* (Kyrgyz, Karakalpak)—with a drawstring top that rested on the hips. The narrow cuffs were usually embellished with embroidery or some sort of applied trimming. The upper part was made from a less expensive fabric. Nineteenth- and early twentieth-century pants were voluminous; later styles had a slimmer cut, though they were still roomy. Trousers were generally worn from babyhood through old age.

1. TROUSERS. Uzbekistan, c. 1930s. *Shohi* ikat; printed cotton above; unlined. 35" length

2. WOMEN'S CLOTHING. Samarkand, Uzbekistan 1871–72. The woman on the left is wearing at-home clothes—ikat *kuylaks* with *lozim*; the other is wearing street garb—a long robe, *lozim*, *paranja*, and *chachvan* (horsehair veil) thrown back over her head. Photograph from the Turkestan Album.

3, 4. TROUSERS (and detail). Uzbekistan, late 19th–early 20th c. *Shohi* ikat; Russian printed-cotton; applied handwoven silk trim; unlined. (fig. 3) 40" length; (fig. 4) 3.5 x 4"

5. PAIR OF TROUSER (*BALAK*) CUFFS. Yomut Turkmen, 3rd quarter, 20th c. Silk chain stitch; handwoven silk stripes; black braid trim; printed-cotton lining. When trousers could no longer be worn, the embroidered cuffs were often cut off and reused on another pair of pants. 5" ankle opening; 12" and 16" lengths as shown

6. TROUSERS. Uzbekistan, c. 1980s–90s. Uzbek printed silk satin with cotton-boll motifs; unlined. 38" length

7. TROUSERS. Uzbekistan, c. 1970s–80s. Pleated *khanatlas* ikat; printed cotton; machine-made Lurex trim, unlined. 37" length

8. TROUSERS. Uzbekistan, c. 1960s. Cotton velvet; printed cotton; hand-embroidered with gold and silver metallic thread; sequins; partially lined. 32" length

7.

8.

1.

Типы аллайскихъ киргизокъ.

2.

KYRGYZ

Traditionally, Kyrgyz nomads wore clothes made from handwoven sheep or camel wool, animal hides, furs, and felt. During the latter part of the nineteenth century, Uzbek silk fabrics and imported Russian cotton and velvet cloth were widely used. Women favored cotton for their long tunic-style dresses (*koynok*) and their pantaloon-style trousers (*ichtan*) worn under them. Men wore shorter white cotton tunics (*koynok, djegde*) and baggy trousers (*ichtan*). Both wore Uzbek-style robes (*chapan*), often bought in the bazaars. The women had elaborate turbanlike headdresses (*elechek* or *ileki*) made of fine white cotton and the men, peaked white felt hats (*kalpak*). Fur, sheepskin, heavy hand-loomed wool cloth, and felt were all used to make winter clothing.

1. *BELDEMCHI.* Central Asia, 2nd quarter, 20th c. Silk lacing stitch on velvet; ikat panels; red cotton trim; Russian printed-cotton lining. This apronlike skirt was worn by a woman over her tunic dress (with the open side in front) to celebrate the birth of her first child. Later she would wear it on festive occasions. 25 x 69"

2. **"KIRGHIZ TYPES."** Central Asia, early 20th c. Russian period postcard. Group of six married women in traditional headdresses and *chapans*, two unmarried girls in headscarves, and a small boy.

3. **MILKING SHEEP.** Tekes Valley, Central Asia, c. 1935. Fat-tailed sheep (called *dumba*) such as these are the most common breed in Central Asia. Their tails can yield as much as ten pounds of prized fat, and their pelts, the famed Astrakhan fur. A nomad family's well-being depended on their flocks of sheep. The woman shown here is wearing a fleece-lined sheepskin coat (*ton*). Photograph by Edward Murray.

4. **KIRGHIZ WOMEN.** Central Asia, 1898. The women shown here are wearing ikat robes and the traditional headdress of married women from northern Kyrgyzstan. Called an *elechek*, this turban was made from a long length of narrow white cloth that was wrapped around a plain cap. Photograph by Sven Hedin.

3.

4.

1.

2.

3.

4.

COLLAR TRIM

Uzbek and Tajik women's dresses and Turkmen women's robes were often decorated with a wide embroidered band around the neckline that usually extended partly down the front of the garment. When the clothing wore out, this band might be removed and reused on another dress or robe—or saved because of its beautiful workmanship. The Uzbek term for this part of the garment is "*peshkurta.*"

1, 3. *PESHKURTA* **(and detail).** Central Asia, c. 1930s. Extremely fine silk hand-embroidery; Russian kopek coins (1925–37); backed with Russian machine-printed cotton. (fig. 1) 35 x 4"; (fig. 3) 8.5 x 4"

2, 4. *PESHKURTA* **(and detail).** Uzbekistan, 1st half, 20th c. Silk cross-stitch (*iroki*) and chain stitch (*yurma*) embroidery. (fig. 2) 32 x 3"; (fig. 4) 13 x 3"

5–8. COLLAR BANDS (and details). Tekke Turkmen, 1st half, 20th c. Silk lacing stitch (*kesdi*) on handwoven silk base cloth. (fig. 5) 42 x 4"; (fig. 6) 45 x 3.5"; (figs. 7, 8) 3 x 1.25"

7.

8.

5.　　6.

1.

2.

3.

4.

5.

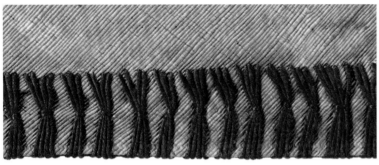

6.

7.

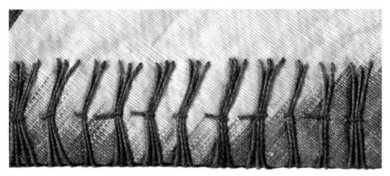

8.

TASSELS and TRIMMING

Tassels and trimming were integral parts of costumes and household textiles. Not only did they embellish, they also provided protection from evil spirits, who feared becoming entangled in the tassels. Glass beads, shiny metal bits, and buttons all added their protective powers. Evil spirits were thought to gain access to a person through the openings of their clothes, so trimming was sewn around all the edges as a preventative measure. Regional terms for trim are "*jiyak*" (Tashkent), "*zeh*" (Bukhara), and "*sheroza*" (Surkhandarya).

1. **DECORATIVE TASSELS.** Uzbekistan, c. 1960s–80s. Handmade silk tassels with glass and metal beads, cotton braid. 12 x 7" as shown

2. **HAIR PLAITS and TASSELS.** Uzbekistan, 1st half, 20th c. Handmade with silk, glass beads, and brass caps. Annette Meakin, a traveler to Russian Turkestan, observed in her 1903 book *In Russian Turkestan* that unmarried girls wore their hair in many long braids. One "had fifty-five long plaits" where "a little below the waist they merged into false ones of black silk, each of which terminated at the ankle in a tassel of coloured glass beads." 9 x 8" as shown

3. **PENDANT TASSELS.** Uzbekistan, c. 1960s–80s. Handmade silk tassels with glass beads; silk cross-stitch embroidery. 23 x 2.5"

4. *PARANJA* **TASSELS.** Uzbekistan, c. 1900. Handmade silk tassels with glass beads and silver clay or plaster beads; loop-manipulation silk trim along the edge of the *paranja*. 8 x 7" as shown

5. *PARANJA* **TASSELS.** Uzbekistan, c. 1900. Handmade silk tassels with glass beads; brass caps; glass buttons; eternal knots; handwoven silk trim with cross-stitching. 10.5 x 9" as shown

6, 7. **ROBE TRIM (front and back).** Uzbekistan, late 1800s. Loop-manipulation silk trim. The reverse side (fig. 7) shows how the warp threads appear when this technique is used. 1.5 x 3" as shown

8, 9. **ROBE TRIM (front and back).** Uzbekistan, late 1800s. Loop-manipulation silk trim. 1.5 x 3" as shown

10. *PARANJA* **TRIM.** Uzbekistan, late 1800s. Handwoven silk trim with cross-stitching. 3 x 7" as shown

11. *PARANJA* **TRIM.** Uzbekistan, late 1800s. Handwoven silk trim. 1.5 x 5" as shown

12. *ADRAS* **IKAT ROBE TRIM.** Uzbekistan, late 1800s. Chain-stitched silk trim. 1.5 x 4" as shown

9.

11.

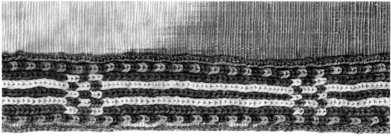

12.

10.

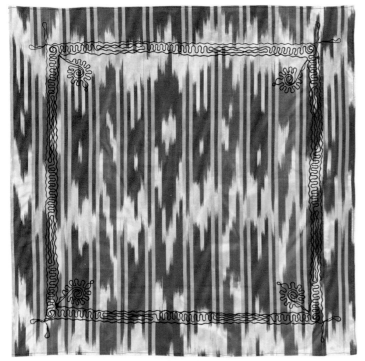

1.

2.

3.

4.

SASHES (*Belbog*)

A man's robe and tunic-style shirt were fastened with a colorful sash (*belbog, belbew, belbo'o*) that looked like a large scarf. This piece of fabric might either be simply folded into a triangle and tied around the waist (figs. 3, 5) or elaborately wrapped (fig. 4). Often embroidered around the edges, it was an essential part of a man's dress. A girl's dowry included *belbogs* to give as gifts to her future husband and his male relatives. Since traditional clothing had no pockets, the *belbog* also served as a convenient place to store personal objects. Instead of *belbogs*, court officials and the very wealthy wore wide leather or velvet belts embellished with elaborate silver plaques. Women did not as a rule wear belts.

1. *BELBOG.* Uzbekistan, last quarter, 20th c. Artificial silk ikat; machine-embroidery. 34 x 34"

2. *BELBOG.* Tashkent, Uzbekistan, 2nd quarter, 20th c. Silk *shohi*; silk hand-embroidery. Similar to *belbog* worn by the barber (fig. 5). 29 x 30"

3. "SAMARKAND SARTS." Samarkand, Uzbekistan, 1911. Photograph by Prokudin-Gorskii.

4. "STANDING SART MAN." Uzbekistan, early 20th c. The multitude of sashes around this man's *bekasab* robe appears to be more of a fashion statement than functional. Photograph by Samuel Dudin.

5. BARBER. Tashkent, c. 1930s. Many Muslim men followed custom and had their heads shaved by the local street barbers. A skullcap, usually worn under a turban, always covered their bare heads. Photograph by Max Penson.

6. FOLDED *BELBOG.* Tashkent, Uzbekistan, 2nd quarter, 20th c. Silk *shohi*; silk hand-embroidery. 52 x 48"

6.

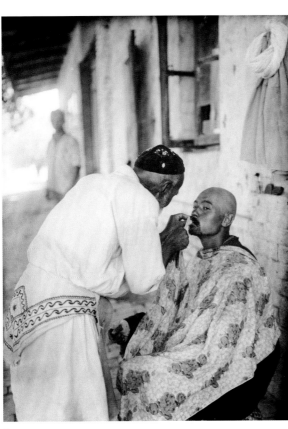

5.

1.

2.

3.

4.

5.

SCARVES Central Asia

Large silk *rumols* (figs. 1, 2) were, and still are, popular with Turkmen women, who wear them as a combination everyday head covering and shawl. *Kulrumols* (fig. 5) are part of traditional Uzbek (in the Samarkand area) and Tajik wedding ceremonies: The bride carries one folded into a triangle over her right arm and uses it to partially hide her face during her ritual bow to guests (*Kelin Salom*).

1, 2. SCARVES. Samarkand, Uzbekistan, c. 1930s. Handwoven silk with a very soft hand; hand-printed by a complicated method utilizing cardboard stencils and tie-dyeing. 58 x 58"

3. AT WORK. Uzbekistan, c. 1930s. Drying tie-dyed scarves after printing. Photograph by Max Penson.

4. SCARF. Uzbekistan, c. 1930s. Tie-dyed, very fine handwoven silk. 41 x 39"

5. WEDDING *RUMOL*. Uzbekistan, 3rd–4th quarter, 20th c. Gold embroidery on silk velvet; Lurex and gold-wrapped threads; glass beads and spangles; brass caps and bells; cross-stitch trim; red cloth backing. Pairs of birds are symbols of mutual happiness. 22 x 22"

8. *NOWRUZ* GIRLS. Urgut, Uzbekistan, 1997. *Nowruz* (*Navruz*) is the joyous celebration of the New Year, of spring rebirth. It begins on March 21 and lasts a month. Originating thousands of years ago in Persia, it is now celebrated throughout Central Asia. It is a time when recent brides greet the community and are welcomed into the new cycle of life.

6.

1.

SCARVES Russia

Along with the flood of Russian printed-cotton yard goods came printed-cotton scarves. Each scarf ran selvedge to selvedge along the bolt of cloth and a scarf would be cut off (literally along the dotted line) when purchased.[15] Turkey-red patterns were very popular and often show up as lining material inside robes.

15 For more Russian Turkey-red scarves, see pages 50–51 of Meller, *Russian Textiles*.

1. RUSSIAN SCARF. Exported to Uzbekistan, early 20th c. Russian Turkey-red roller-printed cotton scarf. A border of *shohi* ikat was added later. Machine-embroidered silk trim; printed-cotton backing. 43 x 43"

2, 3. RUSSIAN SCARF (and detail). Exported to Uzbekistan, 1st quarter, 20th c. Russian roller-printed cotton scarf. (fig. 2) name of the manufacturer printed on the scarf: "F. R. Zubov, Aleksandrov." (fig. 3) 38 x 40"

2.

3.

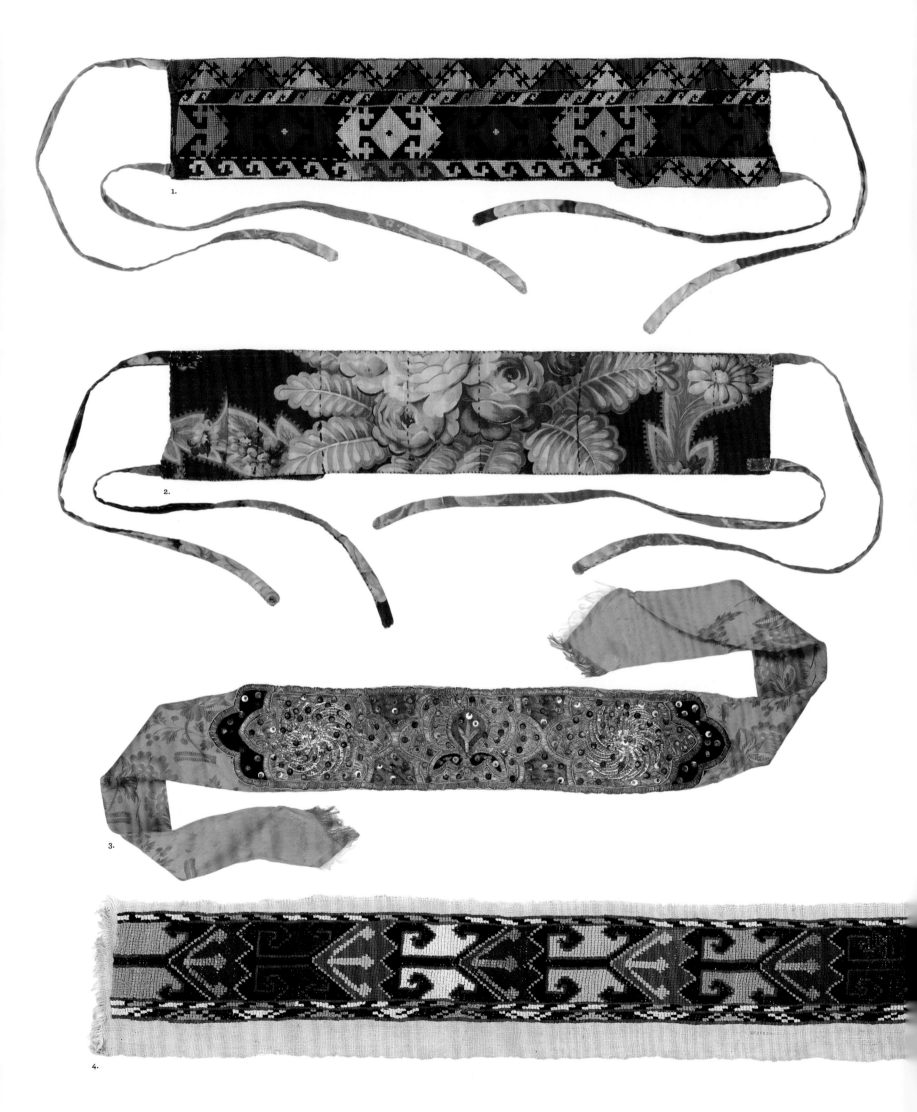

BANDS

The short bands (figs. 1, 2, 3, 6) were worn as headbands. Fig. 5 shows a decorative band probably used as trimming on a woman's garment; fig. 4 may also be decorative trimming, or an unfinished belt. The patterns and fine cross-stitch embroidery illustrated in figs. 1, 4, and 5 are characteristic of the Uzbek-Lakai tribe. Gold embroidered headbands (*peshanabands*) were worn by the ladies of Bukhara.

1, 2. HEADBAND (front and back). Lakai, early 20th c. Silk cross-stitch embroidery on cotton; triangular *tumar* (amulet) motifs; backed with Russian printed cotton. 3 x 16" (minus ties)

3. WOMAN'S HEADBAND (*peshanaband*). Bukhara, Uzbekistan, 2nd half, 20th c. Metallic gold and silver embroidery with metal spangles and glass beads; silk-velvet inserts; silk-jacquard backing and ties. 4.5 x 56" as shown

4. BAND. Probably Lakai, 2nd quarter, 20th c. Silk cross-stitch on cotton; unlined. 2.5 x 42" (embroidery only)

5. BAND. Probably Lakai, early 20th c. Silk cross-stitch on cotton; unlined. 2.5 x 51"

6. WOMAN'S HEADBAND (*peshanaband*). Bukhara, 2nd half, 20th c. Two peacocks; metallic gold and silver embroidery with spangles on silk velvet; silk-jacquard backing. 4 x 16" (without ties)

5.

6.

2

CHILDREN'S CLOTHING

"The children are especially attractive . . . They wear little gowns of the same pattern and material as their fathers and imitate them in demeanour as well as in dress." —William Eleroy Curtis, *Turkestan: The Heart of Asia,* 1911

"The nomads have great love for children and will play with them by the hour. Even the richest Beg is considered poor if he has no children, while the poorest servant gains much respect if he has many children playing around his yurt." —Edward Murray, "With the Nomads in Central Asia," *National Geographic,* 1936

Since young children were thought to attract the attention of the Evil Eye, their mothers sewed protective amulets onto their clothes and caps. Small cloth triangles (*doga, tumar*), which sometimes contained verses from the Koran or bits of salt or coal, were widely used to ward off evil spirits (*jinns*). Kyrgyz children often sported owl feathers, considered a powerful talisman, on top of their hats. Patchwork (*caroq*) clothing was not just a thrifty way to recycle scraps of cloth—all the little pieces were believed to confuse malevolent forces and scare them away. The Evil Eye was known to be notoriously jealous, and beautiful children were especially at risk. Therefore, it was considered dangerous to compliment a baby or young child for fear doing so would attract the Evil One's attention.

Turkmen mothers made special protective garments for their young children—poncholike *kurtes* and small bibs (*kirliks*). These were believed to have magical powers, and Turkmen children wore them until about the age of five. All Central Asian children, even babies, wore embroidered skullcaps, usually made by their mothers. Uzbek and Tajik boys began wearing turbans over their caps at between ten and twelve years of age.

By age seven or eight, children dressed basically the same as adults. Girls would wear a shift dress with pantaloon-style trousers, and boys, a long tunic-style cotton shirt over wide white cotton pants with tapering legs. Outer robes (*chapans*) were worn by both boys

and girls. A boy was usually presented with an expensive robe for the occasion of his circumcision (*sunnat*). A girl would be given a feminine robe upon reaching the age of twelve. As long as it was customary to wear the *paranja*, urban girls as young as nine wore them whenever they left the house. All females were expected to keep their heads covered with a scarf or cap.

The English ethnographer Annette Meakin was one of the first Western women to visit Central Asia (in 1896 and again in 1902). Being female, she was able to gain access to native women inside their homes—unthinkable for any men but their husbands. Her book *In Russian Turkestan* is particularly fascinating as it was written from a woman's perspective. Meakin took the photograph on page 118, in which one little girl is wearing a *paranja*; the smallest child, an ikat robe under her coat; and the boy and girl to the left wear printed cotton robes.

Children, especially boys, were highly valued in Central Asia's patriarchal society, and the more sons a woman had, the higher her position in her husband's family. From a very early age, daughters were expected to help their mothers with household chores, while their brothers played. As soon as an acceptable bride-price (*kalym*) could be arranged with the prospective husband's family, a daughter was betrothed. A young girl from a wealthy family could cost forty horses and a thousand sheep, while a poor servant girl, as little as one horse or cow. If the prospective husband was unable to pay the bride-price all at once, an agreement might be reached whereby he could pay in installments of a few animals each year. Although it could take as long as eight years for a poor man to pay off a *kalym* of sixteen sheep, the girl was promised at a very tender age. It was not uncommon for girls as young as twelve to marry, at which point they belonged to their husband's household. While the family of a son had to provide the hefty bride-price, he did not have to leave home. His wife (or wives) provided additional labor, and her children would increase the size and prestige of her husband's family. In the marriage trade-off, a son was considered the more valuable.

CHILDREN'S ROBES (*Bekasab*)

Children's robes were basically smaller versions of their parents' robes. However, since a child was considered especially vulnerable to sickness and the jealous Evil Eye, amulets were frequently attached to their clothing. Like adult robes, everyday children's robes were usually made from printed cotton or striped silk warp/cotton weft *bekasab*.

1, 2. ROBE. Uzbekistan, mid-20th c. *Bekasab*; handwoven trim; printed-cotton lining. 22" length; 35"cuff to cuff

3. SCHOOLCHILDREN. Uzbekistan, 1930s–40s. The barefoot boy in front is wearing a *bekasab* robe. Photograph by Max Penson.

4. ROBE. Uzbekistan, 3rd quarter, 20th c. *Bekasab*; printed-cotton lining. 21" length; 33" cuff to cuff

5. FAUX-*BEKASAB* ROBE. Uzbekistan, 3rd quarter, 20th c. Printed silk warp/cotton weft; printed-cotton lining. Like their faux-ikat cousins, a printed pattern cost less than a woven one. 24" length; 39" cuff to cuff

6, 7. ROBES. Uzbekistan, c. 1940s. *Bekasab*; printed-cotton linings. (fig. 6) 28" length; 37" cuff to cuff; (fig. 7) 36" length; 45" cuff to cuff

4.

5.

6.

7.

1.

2.

3.

4.

5.

CHILDREN'S ROBES

Once children were past the stage when protective garments such as *eleks*, *kirliks*, and patchwork (*caroq*) were necessary to ward of evil spirits, they were dressed in much the same way as their parents.

1. VELVET ROBE. Bukhara, Uzbekistan, 3rd quarter, 20th c. Silk velvet; metallic gold embroidery; Lurex; spangles; cotton lining. 22" length; 39" cuff to cuff

2. CHILD'S BOOTS. Uzbekistan, 4th quarter, 20th c. Velvet; metallic gold embroidery; spangles. 7 x 7"

3. IKAT ROBE. Uzbekistan, c. 1970s. *Bekasab* with ikat; printed-cotton lining. 32" length; 44" cuff to cuff

4. "A SART LADY AND CHILD." Uzbekistan, 1911. Photograph by Annette Meakin.

5. IKAT ROBE. Uzbekistan, mid-20th c. *Atlas* ikat; machine-embroidery; printed- and plain-cotton lining. 20" length; 28" cuff to cuff

6. TURKMEN ROBE. Tekke Turkmen, 3rd quarter, 20th c. Handwoven silk; silk lacing stitch; printed-cotton lining. 38" length; 46" cuff to cuff

7. TURKMEN ROBE. Tekke Turkmen, mid-20th c. Handwoven silk; silk hand-embroidery; loop-manipulation trim; printed lining. 19" length; 24" cuff to cuff

8. TURKMEN ROBE. Turkmen, mid-20th c. Silk velvet; hand-embroidery; loop-manipulation trim; printed-cotton lining. 20" length; 28" cuff to cuff

6.

8.

7.

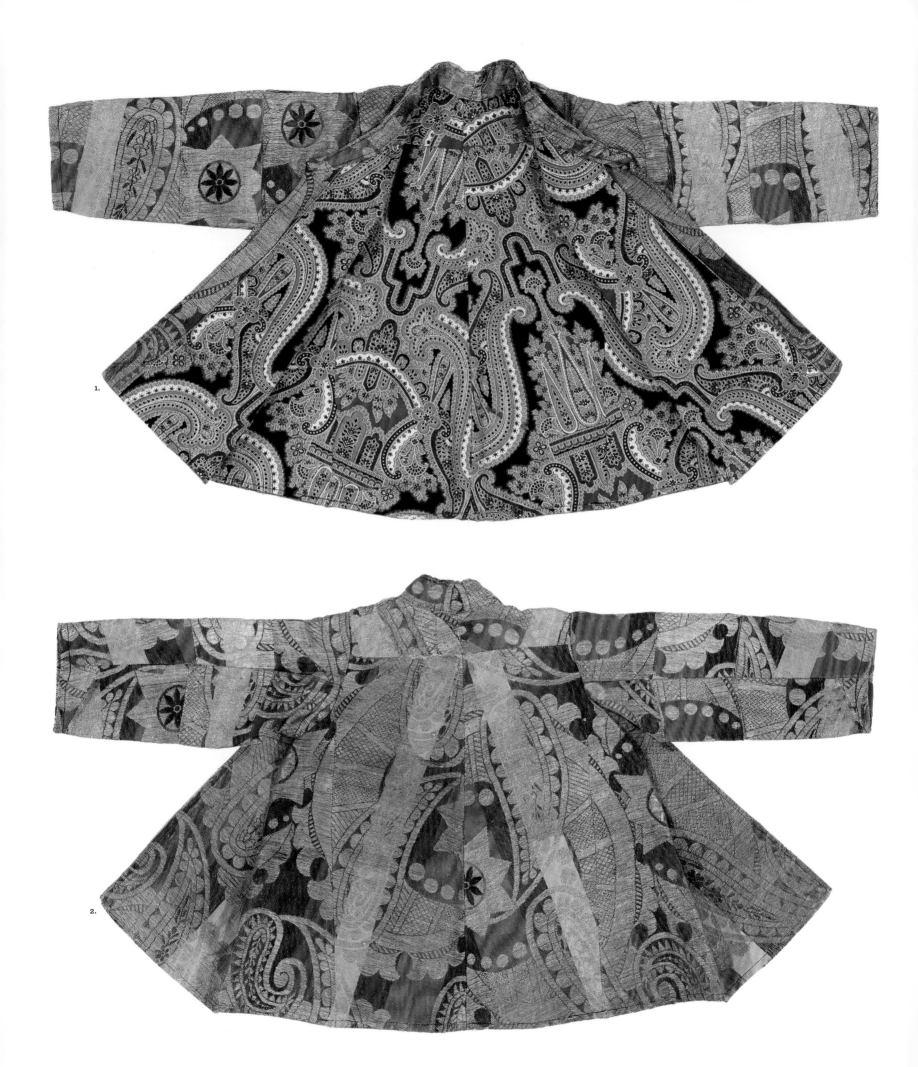

CHILDREN'S ROBES Brocade

Imported brocade was an expensive fabric—not the stuff of everyday wear. Most was imported from Russia, but Chinese and Indian brocades could also be found in the bazaars. The brocade pattern shown in fig. 1 is evocative of the so-called "bizarre" silks of the early eighteenth century—strange designs that probably originated in India and were widely copied in the West. The brocade pattern shown in fig. 3 has an Ottoman feeling to it, yet, like fig. 1, the cloth could well have been imported from Russia.

1, 2. ROBE (front and back). Uzbekistan, c. 1900. Imported silk and cotton brocade with silver-wrapped weft threads; probably Russian printed-cotton lining, which may have been inspired by a paisley shawl pattern. 18" length; 34" cuff to cuff

3. ROBE. Uzbekistan, c. 1900. Imported silk and cotton brocade with gold-wrapped weft threads; Russian printed-cotton lining. 33" length; 50" cuff to cuff

3.

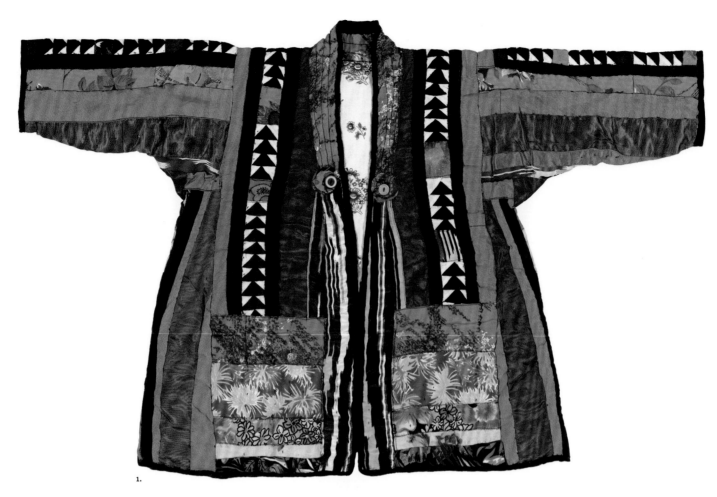

1.

2.

3.

4.

CHILDREN'S ROBES Patchwork (*Caroq*)

Caroq (*kurok*) is the general term for patchwork, whether a quilt of joined pieces, or clothes such as these, which were made from bits of recycled cloth. These little robes were probably made by a family member for a child to wear on special occasions. The many small pieces were thought to confuse evil spirits and drive them away. Triangles were considered talismanic, and they were often incorporated into patchwork.

1. ROBE. Urgut, Uzbekistan, late 20th c. Silk and cotton; cloth binding; printed-cotton lining. 21" length; 35" cuff to cuff

2. ROBE. Samarkand, Uzbekistan, 3rd quarter, 20th c. Silk velvet on cotton; sequins; cloth binding; cotton lining. 19" length; 24" cuff to cuff

3. ROBE. Urgut, 3rd quarter, 20th c. Silk and Lurex patches on cotton; silk binding; printed-cotton lining. Blue bead, rhinestone, and velvet amulet (*doga*) on back. 13" length; 26" cuff to cuff

4, 5. HAT and ROBE. Urgut, 3rd quarter, 20th c. Ikat, cotton, and silk triangles on printed cotton; printed-cotton lining. This robe and hat were made as a set. (fig. 4) 6" hat diameter; (fig. 5) 19" length; 34" cuff to cuff.

5.

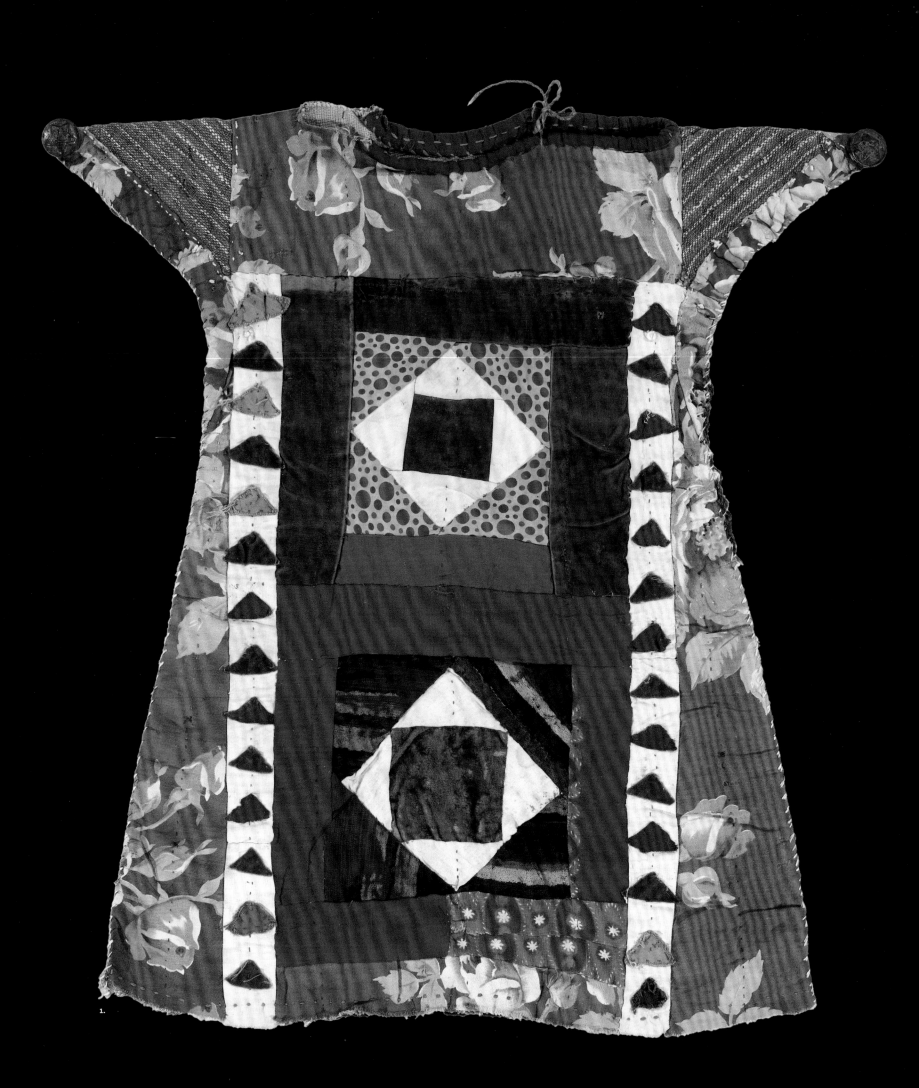

CHILDREN'S CLOTHES (*Kurte*)

Open-sided, poncholike *kurtes* were worn by Turkmen boys and girls from the time they could walk to about five years of age. Protective amulets were liberally added, and the *kurte* itself was considered a magical garment. Short, triangular cap sleeves were attached at the shoulders. The bottom hems were left unfinished to ensure that the child would thrive and continue to grow—and that the mother would bear more children.

1. *KURTE.* Turkmen, mid-20th c. Cotton, silk velvet, handwoven *alacha* stripes; handwoven cotton lining. A metal button embossed with the Soviet hammer and sickle within a five-pointed star is sewn to each sleeve. 20" length; 19" across top

2–4. *KURTE* **and BIB.** Turkmen, 2nd quarter, 20th c. Machine-made cotton; hand-embroidery; Russian printed and woven striped-cotton lining; cloth amulet; two metal buttons. A biblike *kirlik* (fig. 4) was often worn over the *kurte* (figs. 2, 3). It, too, had protective power. Most of the amulets are missing, but a blue glass bead and two small coral beads are still on guard. (figs. 2, 3) 15" length; 14" across top; (fig. 4) 15 x 16"

5. *KURTE.* Turkmen, 2nd quarter, 20th c. Silk handwoven *keteni*, printed cotton; printed-cotton lining. A short length of chain and seven Russian ten-kopek coins (1925–50) are still attached—it appears that many more were sewn across the front and back. 18" length; 17" across top

2.

3.

4.

5.

1.

2.

3.

4.

CHILDREN'S CLOTHES (*Kurte*)

There is nothing exceptional about these particular *kurtes*, and therein lies their appeal. They were made out of bits and pieces of recycled fabrics. The colors have faded; moths have nibbled holes in the wool; and amulets have disappeared. But the very fact that these little *kurtes* have survived so long is a testament to how cherished they and the children who wore them were.

1. ***KURTE.*** Probably Yomut Turkmen, 2nd quarter, 20th c. Handwoven and machine-made cotton and silk; imported wool-broadcloth triangles; cloth amulet (*doga*); black/white "snakes" trim; ladder and running stitches; printed-cotton lining; two Russian ten-kopek coins dated 1925. 12" length; 18" across top

2. ***KURTE.*** Turkmen, 2nd quarter, 20th c. Handwoven silk and machine-made gray cotton; local block-printed homespun cotton lining (*chit*); metal plaques and twenty-kopek coin dated 1949. 17" length; 17" across top

3. ***KURTE.*** Turkmen, 2nd quarter, 20th c. Plain and printed cotton, wool, Russian striped cotton, plain and printed cotton lining, protective cloth triangles (*doga*) down front and back. 18" length; 16" across top

4. ***KURTE.*** Turkmen, 3rd quarter, 20th c. Synthetic fabrics; machine- and hand-embroidery; cotton binding; silk cross-stitching on "buttons"; silk and cotton tassels; printed-cotton lining. 18" length; 16" across top

5. ***KURTE.*** Turkmen, 3rd quarter, 20th c. *Atlas* ikat and cotton; *doga* down front and back; blue buttons; cloth tassels; printed-cotton lining. 14" length; 14" across top

6. ***KURTE***[1] **and *KIRLIK*.** Tekke Turkmen, 2nd quarter, 20th c. Handwoven silk; imported red wool broadcloth; silk hand-embroidery; printed-cotton lining on bib (*kirlik*); black cotton lining on *kurte*; silk fringe; Russian kopek coins and small silver medallions inlaid with carnelian on *kurte*. *Kurte*: 19" length; 20" across top; *kirlik*: 21 x 21"

1 This *kurte* is shown in its entirety in Meller, *Russian Textiles*, 28.

5.

6.

CHILDREN'S BIBS (*Kirlik*)

The biblike *kirlik* (also called an *elek*) was worn over a young child's *kurte* to further deter evil spirits. The *kirliks* shown in figs. 1 and 2 are traditional Tekke Turkmen, while those shown in figs. 3, 4, 6, and 7 are more whimsical. Fig. 5 is Ersari Turkmen and unusually elaborate.

1, 2. KIRLIKS. Tekke Turkmen, 2nd quarter, 20th c. Handwoven silk; imported wool broadcloth; silk fringe; lacing stitch; loop-manipulation trim; printed-cotton linings. (fig. 1) 24 x 24"; (fig. 2) 18 x 19"

3. KIRLIK. Probably Yomut Turkmen, 2nd quarter, 20th c. Silk embroidery on cotton; ram's horn motifs; unlined. 16 x 14"

4. KIRLIK. Probably Yomut Turkmen, mid-20th c. Plain-weave cotton, red cotton jacquard; printed-cotton lining; black/white "snake" ties. 16 x 13"

5. KIRLIK. Ersari Turkmen, 1st quarter, 20th c. Silk lacing stitch on indigo *alacha*; loop-manipulation trim; metallic gold ribbon; unlined. 24 x 15"

6. KIRLIK. Probably Yomut Turkmen, 2nd quarter, 20th c. Wool and cotton patchwork on cotton twill; loop-manipulation trim; silk embroidery; unlined. 15 x 15"

7. KIRLIK. Probably Yomut Turkmen. 2nd quarter, 20th c. Imported silk and red wool broadcloth; silk; *keteni*; cotton; hand-embroidery; printed-cotton lining. 21 x 13"

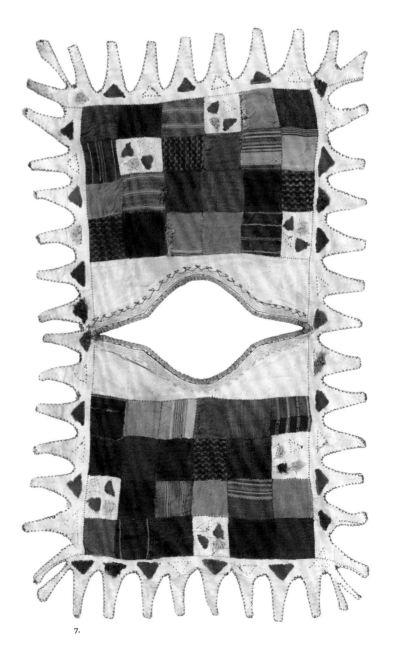

1.

2.

CHILDREN'S SHIRTS (*Kurta*)

While these shirts (*kurta*) may not have been considered as magical as the *elek*, they too were protective. Boys and girls wore them until about the age of five. Patchwork (*caroq*) confused the Evil Eye, as did shiny buttons and beads that reflected light and the Evil One's image. Pieces of cloth belonging to people blessed with many children, longevity, or prosperity were used whenever possible; and certain colors, particularly red and blue, were believed to have magical properties. An owl feather was an especially powerful amulet—but a chicken feather would do (fig. 1)—as was the ram's horn motif seen around the neckline shown in fig. 4.

1. KURTA. Probably Turkmen, mid-20th c. Machine-made cotton and silk; cotton lining; chicken feather amulet. The *caroq* panel evokes the American patchwork quilt patterns "Pinwheel" and "Pineapple." 13" length; 19" cuff to cuff

2. KURTA. Turkmen, mid-20th c. Silk handwoven *keteni*; machine-made cotton and silk; printed-cotton lining. 21" length; 24" cuff to cuff

3. TURKMEN CHILDREN. Afghanistan, late 20th–early 21st c. The baby in this photograph is wearing a *caroq* shirt.

4. KURTA. Turkmen, mid-20th c. Plain-weave cotton; silk hand-embroidery; unlined. 19" length; 40" cuff to cuff

5. KURTA. Turkmen, 1st quarter, 20th c. Plain cotton and cotton jacquard; several hundred glass buttons across the front; Russian printed-cotton lining. Only three beads remain, but probably more continued down the front. 13 x 14"

3.

4.

5.

1.

2.

3.

4.

5.

6.

7.

AMULETS (*Doga*)

Even today, amulets wield their protective powers. In Central Asia the triangular-shaped cloth *doga* or *tumar* can be found in yurts and apartments, over shop doors and taxi mirrors, and on donkeys and horses. Shiny buttons and beads (especially blue beads), clinking coins, dangling tassels, lots of little triangles, twisted black and white threads (simulating snakes), and the color red all enhance the *doga*'s ability to ward off malevolent spirits (*jinns*).

A *doga* can be a simple cloth triangle stitched to a child's garment, or a triangular pouch worn around the neck that holds a little salt, coal, other amuletic bits, or a verse from the Koran.

1, 2. AMULETS. Probably Yomut Turkmen, 2nd quarter, 20th c. Silk lacing stitch; wool broadcloth triangles; cotton tassels; human-hair braids; cotton backings. (fig. 1) 20 x 6"; (fig. 2) 17 x 9"

3, 4. AMULETS. Yomut Turkmen, 1st quarter, 20th c. Part of a camel trapping. (fig. 3) silk lacing stitch and chain stitch on silk; cotton backing; 4 x 8"; (fig. 4) wool broadcloth on cotton; black/white cotton "snake" tassels; 5 x 4.25" as shown

5, 6. AMULETS. Ersari Turkmen. 1st quarter, 20th c. Silk lacing stitch; silk tassels. (fig. 5) same on reverse; gold-wrapped trim; bone beads; 7 x 7" as shown; (fig. 6) printed cotton backing; loop-manipulation trim; glass beads; 9.5 x 6.5" as shown

7. BAMIYAN GIRL. Bamiyan, Afghanistan, 2001. This Afghan girl is wearing many amulets—blue and red beads, dangling triangular-shaped earrings, and an amulet in her hair. Photograph © Luke Powell.

8. AMULET. Uzbekistan, mid-20th c. Silk cross-stitch embroidery (same on reverse); glass beads; Russian kopek coins dated 1933–56. 5 x 7" as shown

9. BOY WITH TEARS. Roghani refugee camp, Charman, Balochistan, Pakistan, 2001. Simple cloth *doga* are sewn to this Afghan boy's vest and a group of amulets hang from his neck. Photograph © Luke Powell.

8.

9.

3

HEADWEAR

"Everybody wears little skull caps . . . and they are embroidered with gold and silver braid or silks of brilliant colours. The cap shops are among the most numerous and attractive in the bazaars."
—William Eleroy Curtis, *Turkestan: The Heart of Asia*, 1911

Central Asian headwear is a world unto itself. In nineteenth-century Central Asia it was said that you could tell a man by his skullcap. His specific ethnic group, tribe, region, or even the town he came from could be identified from the patterns and style of his hat. Women also wore distinctive headdresses. Even at a distance, one knew where a Kyrgyz woman was from based on how she arranged her massive white turban: *Ileki* was the southern style and *elechek* the northern. During the Soviet period, brightly colored embroidered skullcaps continued to remain popular with girls and young women as well as with boys and men. In 1936 sociologist Fannina W. Halle wrote, "There are crowds and hubbub and gay colours in old Bukhara . . . where you may see quite different colours and patterns among the crowd from those of Tashkent and Samarqand . . . There are new colours in the *tyubeteikas* [skullcaps], which always show great variety."[1] Together with ikat chemises, colorful embroidered skullcaps became an integral part of Uzbek women's national costume. Although men continued to wear them as well, by far the most common ones were black Chust-style hats with white capsicum pepper motifs (see pages 140–41), which are still widely worn today, particularly on special occasions.[2]

Except for caps sewn by nomadic women or by mothers for their young children, most skullcaps were made by individual craftswomen and sold in the bazaars. However, during the 1920s and '30s, the Soviets began organizing these women into cooperatives (artels), with names such as *Mehnat Guli* (Flower of Labor).[3] At this time, the variety of traditionally based patterns expanded and modern ones were introduced. Regional styles, designs, and stitching were retained, although there was more overlap, and three basic shapes prevailed—square, round, and conical. From the 1950s onward, colored glass beads, metal spangles, and metallic threads were added.

Skullcaps go by many names: *tyubeteika, duppi*, or *do'ppi* (Uzbek); *takhya* (Turkmen); *takiya* or *tobetai* (Kazakh); *topu* or *takiya* (Kyrgyz); *takiya* (Karakalpak); and *toki* (Tajik). Traditionally, each style of hat and each embroidery pattern had its own regional name. Women tended to use embroidery stitches specific to their area, such as small cross-stitches (*iroki*) in Tashkent and the Ferghana region; even finer cross-stitches (*tirma*) in Shakhrisabz; ribbed (*piltado-zi*) stitching in south Uzbekistan; and lacing stitch (*kesdi*) in Turkmenistan. An embroidered band or woven braid (called *jiyak, sheroza, tizma*, or *zeh*) usually encircled the edge of the hat. This decorative border also served as protection from evil spirits, since the head was considered an especially vulnerable part of the body.

Customarily, most adult Muslim men shaved their heads and covered them with various types of skullcaps. When a turban was worn, it was wrapped around the cap. The quality of a man's skullcap and turban was an indication of his wealth and social standing. The turbans (*salla*) themselves differed in both the way they were worn and the material from which they were made. One end was often arranged so as to fall over the left shoulder. Muslin, plain and fancy, was the most commonly used cloth, much of it imported from India, Russia, and England. The length of a man's turban could measure thirty feet, and often served as his funeral pall. Nomadic men tended to wear hats made from fur or felt over their skullcaps. The tall, distinctive Turkmen hats (*telpek*) were made of black, brown, or white sheepskin and worn year-round. Kyrgyz and Kazakh men wore white felt hats with upturned brims (*kalpak*), or in winter, fur hats with long earflaps (*malakay*). Jewish men were required to wear a small black cap trimmed with fur when in public.

Women always covered their heads, either with scarves or shawls (*rumol, doka*), skullcaps, or their traditional tribal headdresses. Married Kungrat women in the Boysun region of southern Uzbekistan wore a tall cylindrical headdress (*bosh*) constructed from many scarves intricately wound over a soft cap (*kulta*). A long, embroidered extension to the *kulta* hung down their backs in order to conceal their braids. Kyrgyz women wore their towering white turbans over a similar cap (*chach kep*) with exquisitely embroidered patterns and silver amulets decorating the plait-cover. Turkmen women wore tall headdresses of tightly wound silk scarves with the addition of a wide, engraved and carnelian-encrusted silver headpiece on special occasions. For their weddings, wealthy Kazakh, Kyrgyz, and Karakalpak brides wore very high conical hats (*saukele*) that were adorned with coral, precious stones, and embroidery. Some Jewish, Kazakh, Kyrgyz, Uzbek, and Tajik women wore a wimple-like white headdress called a *kimeshek* (Kazakh, Kyrgyz) or *lachak* (Uzbek, Tajik).

1 Fannina W. Halle, *Women in the Soviet East* (London: Martin Secker & Warburg, 1938), 326.

2 For more in-depth information about Uzbek skullcaps, see Irina Bogoslovskaya and Larisa Levteeva, *Skullcaps of Uzbekistan: 19th–20th Centuries* (Tashkent, 2006).

3 In 1932–33 Swiss traveler Ella Maillart visited an embroidery artel in Samarkand, where she saw stacks of skullcaps "among piles of brocade, cut into sections, waiting to be sewn. 'I am having brought from Moscow two wagon-loads of priests' chasubles and surplices that I have to pay cash for,' said the Armenian directress. 'Nowadays it is just these skullcaps that are most in demand in the mountains of the Pamirs [Moscow's way of recycling confiscated ecclesiastical garments].'" Ella K. Maillart, *Turkestan Solo: One Woman's Expedition from the Tien Shan to the Kizil Kum* (New York: G. P. Putnam's Sons, 1935), 201.

1.

4.

Самаркандъ. Типы сартовскихъ дѣтей.

t'assure que nous nous sommes partagés de bonnes parts
je t'embrasse ainsi que M__ __ et M__ __ Chérie

2.

5.

3.

6.

7.

HATS Children's

Skullcaps were an integral part of Central Asian national dress. With the exception of elderly women, most everyone wore them—even babies. Protective amulets such as beads (especially blue), owl feathers, tassels, twisted black and white strings (representing snakes), and cloth triangles (*doga*) were added to children's hats. Patchwork also helped to ward off evil spirits.

1. FIRST LESSONS. Samarkand, Uzbekistan 1871–72. Jewish man and boy. (The boy's hat is similar to fig. 3, page 152). Photograph from the Turkestan Album.

2. "SART NATIVE CHILDREN." Samarkand, c. 1910. Russian period postcard.

3. ON A HOLIDAY. Uzbekistan, May 1, 1936. Some of the children's hats were made in Tashkent, Bukhara, and Samarkand. Photograph by Max Penson.

4. GIRL WITH VIOLETS. Uzbakistan, 2nd quarter, 20th c. Photograph by Max Penson.

5. HAT. Afghanistan, mid-20th c. Cotton, wool, and silk patchwork and embroidery; small bone amulet; twisted black/white "snakes"; loop-manipulation trim; printed-cotton lining. 5 H. x 7" D.

6. CHILD. Afghanistan, 2001. The little girl is wearing a homemade hat of printed cotton with an amulet that appears to be an amber-colored stone surrounded by white beads strung on blue thread. A border of small protective triangles frames her face. Photograph © Luke Powell.

7. HAT. South Uzbekistan, mid-20th c. Silk embroidery on cotton with almond (*bodum*) motifs. Silk tassels with small glass beads; embroidered trim; printed-cotton lining. 4.5 H. x 5.5" D.

8. HAT. Probably Chodor Turkmen, mid-20th c. Silk embroidery on cotton; ram's horn motifs; velvet *doga*; glass beads and buttons; printed-cotton lining. 4 H. x 5.5" D.

9. HAT. Turkmen, 3rd quarter, 20th c. Silk, corduroy, and velvet patches on cotton; plain-cotton lining. 3 H. x 4.5" D.

10, 13. BABY HATS. Tekke Turkmen, 2nd half, 20th c. Silk embroidery on silk (fig. 10), on cotton (fig. 13); small bone amulet (fig. 10); loop-manipulation trim; plain-cotton lining. (fig. 10) 2.5 H. x 5" D.; (fig. 13) 4 H. x 4" D.

11. HAT. Turkmen, mid-20th c. Cotton patchwork; silk and cotton tassels; twisted black/white "snakes"; seed pods; printed-cotton lining. 5 H. x 4.5" D.

12. HAT. Yomut Turkmen, mid-20th c. Silk embroidery on silk; plain-cotton lining. 3 H. x 5" D.

8.

9.

11.

12.

10.

13.

HATS Turkmen

Turkmen women used a type of lacing or ladder stitch embroidery called *kesdi* on their clothing and hats. All of the skullcaps (*takhya*) shown here feature it. Children and unmarried girls wore skullcaps. Married women wore a tall headdress composed of many wrapped scarves (see fig. 8, page 49). Men wore their skullcaps under tall sheepskin hats (*telpek*).

1–3. HATS. Yomut Turkmen, mid-20th c. Silk lacing stitch on cotton; plain-cotton lining. (fig. 1) 3.5 H. x 5.5" D.; (figs. 2, 3) 3 H. x 6.5" D.

4. HAT. Tekke Turkmen, mid-20th c. Silk lacing stitch on cotton; loop-manipulation trim; printed-cotton lining. 3.5 H. x 7" D.

5. HAT. Probably Ersari Turkmen, mid-20th c. Silk lacing stitch on cotton; loop-manipulation trim; printed-cotton lining. 4 H. x 6.5" D.

6–9. HATS. Turkmen, mid-20th c. Silk lacing stitch on cotton; plain-cotton lining. (figs. 6–9) 2.5 H. x 6.5" D.

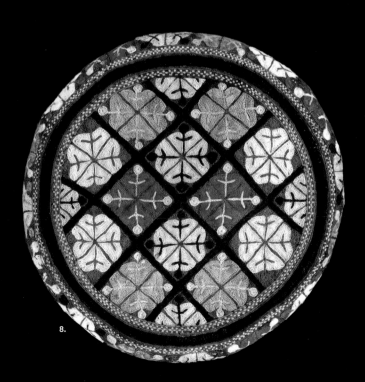

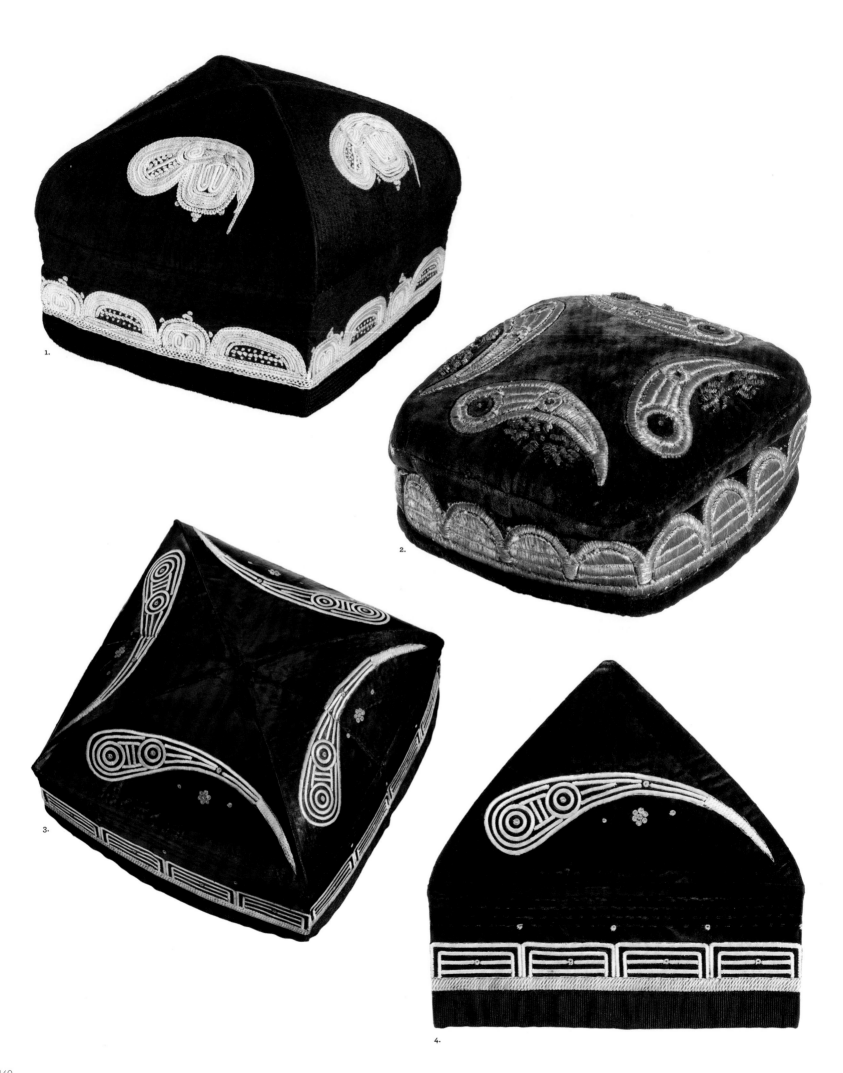

HATS Chust-style

The ubiquitous square black skullcap worn mainly by men and boys throughout Uzbekistan originated in the city of Chust, located in the Ferghana Valley. Called *tus do'ppi*, it is characterized by four highly stylized *kalampir* (capsicum peppers). The intense heat of the peppers was thought to protect the wearer from evil spirits. The crown of the hat is encircled by a border of arches, which some say symbolize gates through which no enemy can enter. The pattern varies by region, yet it has remained basically the same since it first gained popularity in the 1920s. Chust-style hats are considered necessary men's apparel for attending mosques, weddings, and funerals.

1. MAN'S HAT. Chust, Uzbekistan, late 20th c. Silk embroidery on cotton; silk trim; plain- and printed-cotton lining. 5.5 H. x 6" D.

2. MAN'S HAT. Bukhara, Uzbekistan, c. 1960s. Gold-wrapped threads embroidered on silk velvet; printed-cotton lining; black velvet trim. 2.5 H. x 6" D.

3, 4. MAN'S HAT. Kokand, Uzbekistan, late 20th c. Silk embroidery on cotton with a hard, polished finish; silk trim; printed-cotton lining. Chust-style hats can be folded into a flat triangle. (fig. 3) 4 H. x 6" D.; (fig. 4) 5 x 4" folded

5. BOY'S HAT. Kokand, 1990s. Silk embroidery on silk; cotton trim; red cotton lining. 4 H. x 5" D.

6. HOLIDAY. Uzbekistan, c. 1930s–40s. The men and most of the boys are wearing Chust-style hats. The dancer and musicians wear *bekasab* robes. Photograph by Max Penson.

5.

6.

1.

2.

3.

4.

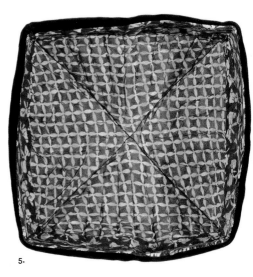

5.

6.

7.

8.

HATS Ferghana Region

Hats from the Ferghana Valley cities of Ferghana and Marghilan were typically square and made in such a way that the sides could be folded inward, creating a flat triangle for ease of carrying. The surface was entirely covered with tiny cross-stitches called *iroki*, which were often sewn on a base cloth of starched gauze (*bo'ronboy*). The hat shown in fig. 1 is probably from Tashkent, where square caps sewn with *iroki* were also very popular. All of the hats on this spread were worn by women and girls.

1–3. HAT. Probably Tashkent, Uzbekistan, c. 1970. Silk cross-stitch on starched gauze; velvet trim; small bluebirds (symbols of good luck and happiness) and pansies; plain- and printed-cotton lining. Fig. 3 shows a hat in progress. (fig. 1) 3 H. x 6" D.; (fig. 2) 4.5 x 5" folded; (fig. 3) 9 x 9"

4–6. HAT. Marghilan, Uzbekistan, 3rd quarter, 20th c. Silk cross-stitch; velvet trim; printed-cotton lining. (fig. 4) 4.5 x 5" folded; (figs. 5, 6) 3 H. x 6" D.

7. HAT. Ferghana region, Uzbekistan, early 1970s. Silk cross-stitch with small birds and the girl's name *GULNOZ* ("Blooming"); velvet trim; printed-cotton lining. 3 H. x 6" D.

8. HAT. Ferghana region, early 1970s. Silk cross-stitch; velvet trim, red cotton lining. 4.5 x 5.5" folded

9. HAT. Ferghana region, early 1970s. Silk cross-stitch; velvet trim; printed-cotton lining. The Cyrillic letters translate as "Let the flowers flourish in the world." 3 H. x 6" D.

10. HAT. Ferghana region, 3rd quarter, 20th c. Silk cross-stitch; velvet trim; printed-cotton lining. 3 H. x 6" D.

10.

9.

4.

HATS Ferghana Valley Region

The hats shown in figs. 1–5 were acquired in Leninabad (currently Khujand), Tajikistan, and were probably made by Tajik women. The one shown in figs. 6 and 7 came from Andijan and was said to be of the style worn by Uyghur men in the Ferghana Valley region during the 1930s and '40s. The small white stitches that form irregular cellular patterns on figs. 4–7 are referred to as *chakmatur*. These hats were constructed in such a way that they could be folded into flat triangles.

1–3. MAN'S HAT. Leninabad, Tajikistan, 2nd quarter, 20th c. Silk embroidery on cotton; cotton trim; plain- and printed-cotton lining. (figs. 1, 2) 4 H. x 5.75" D.; (fig. 3) 5.25 x 5" folded

4, 5. MEN'S HATS. Leninabad, 2nd quarter, 20th c. Silk embroidery on green silk; velvet trim; printed- and plain-cotton linings; (fig. 4) 4.5 x 6.5" D.; (fig. 5) 4.5 x 5.5" folded

6, 7. MAN'S HAT. Andijan, Uzbekistan, c. 1930s. Silk embroidery on blue silk; velvet trim; green cotton lining. (fig. 6) 5 x 5.25" folded; (fig. 7) 4 H. x 5.5" D.

5.

6.

7.

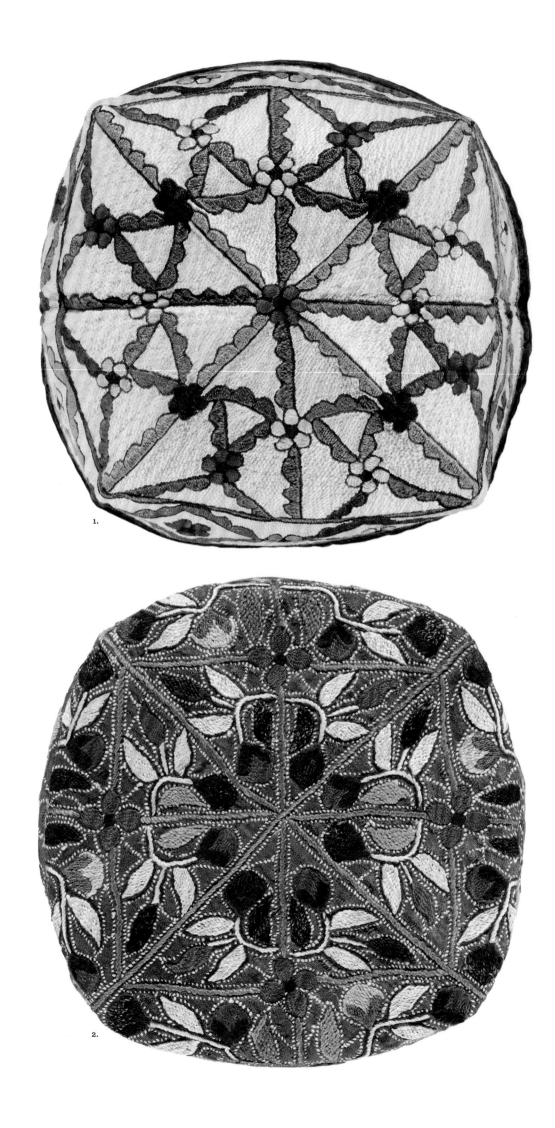

1.

2.

3.

HATS Tashkent

Hats from Tashkent often feature satin and couching stitches, as well as cross-stitch *iroki* and *chakmatur*. The latter forms an allover pattern of small white stitches (figs. 2, 3, 5). All of these hats can be folded into flat triangles.

1. HAT. Tashkent, Uzbekistan, 2nd quarter, 20th c. Silk embroidery on cotton; velvet trim; silk and printed-cotton lining. The entire surface of the hat is covered with embroidery. 3.5 H. x 6" D.

2. HAT. Tashkent, 2nd quarter, 20th c. Silk embroidery on green silk; silk trim; plain-cotton and gauze lining. 2.5 H. x 6" D.

3. HAT. Tashkent, 2nd quarter, 20th c. Silk embroidery on faded purple silk; missing trim; brown cotton and ikat lining. 3.5 H. x 6" D.

4. A MOTHER AND CHILD. Tashkent, c. 1935. This photograph is a variation of Max Penson's "Uzbek Madonna," which won a gold metal at the Paris World Exposition in 1937. The young mother's cap is sewn with the *chakmatur* technique. Photograph by Max Penson.

5. HAT. Tashkent, 2nd quarter, 20th c. Silk embroidery on faded black silk; cotton trim; printed-cotton lining. 4 H. x 6" D.

4.

5.

HATS Tashkent

Hat patterns were given names such as *chamanda gul* (flowers on the lawn), *qizil gul* (red flower), and *oq par* (white feather). Both women and men wore hats embroidered with flowers and birds. Beaded hats were worn primarily in Tashkent and only by girls. Figs. 1–3 can be folded into flat triangles.

1. HAT. Tashkent, Uzbekistan, 2nd quarter, 20th c. Silk embroidery on violet silk; *chakmatur* technique; cotton trim; plain-cotton lining. 4 H. x 7" D.

2. GIRL'S HAT. Tashkent, c. 1960s. *Chamanda gul* pattern. Silk embroidery on silk brocade; velvet trim; red cotton lining. 4 H. x 5.5" D.

3. HAT. Tashkent, c. 1930s. *Qizil gul* pattern. Silk embroidery on cotton; velvet trim; printed-cotton lining. 4 H. x 6" D.

4. GIRL'S HAT. Tashkent, mid-20th c. White glass beads and metal spangles on silk velvet; velvet trim; plain-cotton lining. 2.5 H. x 6" D.

5. GIRL'S HAT. Tashkent(?), mid-20th c. Clear glass beads on velvet; black silk velvet and red cotton jacquard; applied embroidered trim; woven plaid and printed-cotton lining. The shape of this hat says Khorezm, yet beads are almost exclusively Tashkent. 2.5 H. x 7" D.

6. HAT. Tashkent, c. 1940s. Glass beads and metal spangles on silk velvet; silk velvet trim; plain-cotton lining. 4 H. x 7" D.

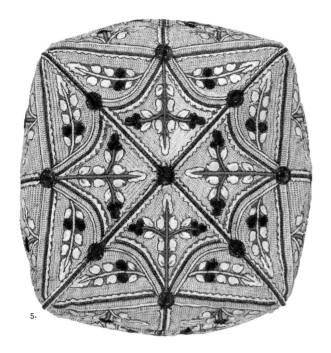

5.

6.

7.

HATS Tashkent/Ferghana Region

Some hats were made with narrow ribbing, a technique called *piltado'zi* (figs. 1, 3, 8). After the crown of the hat had been secured to the lining, rolled wadding (*pilta*) of cotton or paper was inserted inside rows of quilting with a special iron needle. The band was treated in the same way, and then the two were joined together. The hat shown in fig. 8 is made from imported gold brocade. Since most men wore a turban (*salla*) wrapped around their skullcap, only the crown would have been visible. Figs. 2, 7, and 8 can be folded into flat triangles.

1, 3, 4. GIRLS' HATS. Ferghana region, Uzbekistan, 1930s. Silk embroidery on silk velvet; *piltado'zi* technique with paper *pilta*; velvet trim; plain- and printed-cotton linings. (fig. 1) 3 H. x 6.5" D.; (fig. 3, unfinished) 7.5 x 8" as shown; (fig. 4, band) 22 x 1.5" as shown

2. GIRL'S HAT. Tashkent, Uzbekistan, 3rd quarter, 20th c. Silk embroidery on silk velvet; velvet trim; printed-cotton lining; *chamanda gul* pattern. 3 H. x 6" D.

5. MAN'S HAT. Andijan, Uzbekistan, last quarter, 20th c. Silk embroidery on cotton; velvet trim; red cotton lining. This style hat was worn by Uyghur men in the region. 3.5 H. x 7.5" D.

6, 7. HATS. Tashkent, c. 1930s. Silk embroidery on cotton; *chakmatur* technique (fig. 6); embroidery covers the entire surface of fig. 7; velvet trim; plain- and printed-cotton linings. (fig. 6) 2.5 H. x 6" D.; (fig. 7) 4 H. x 6" D.

8. MAN'S HAT. Probably Tashkent, c. 1900. Russian silk brocade with gold-wrapped threads; wide silk band with gold threads; silk trim; Russian printed-cotton lining. This style of tall, conical hat was called a *kulokh* or *kulox*. 8 H. x 7" D.

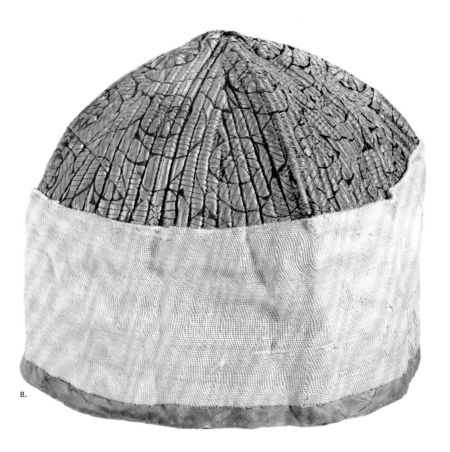

8.

HATS Shakhrisabz/Samarkand

Located fifty miles south of Samarkand, Shakhrisabz is perhaps best known historically as the birthplace of Timur (Tamerlane). But in the textile world, the city is renowned for its fine embroidery, especially *suzanis* and hats. The hats are embroidered in small cross-stitches (*iroki*) that cover the entire surface. Even smaller *iroki* are called *tirma*. Sometimes the stitches are so fine that a magnifying glass is needed to see them clearly.

1, 2. MAN'S HAT. Shakhrisabz, Uzbekistan, c. 1930s. Silk cross-stitch embroidery; silk plaid- and cotton-gauze lining. 6.5 H. x 6.5" D.

3, 6. MEN'S HATS. Shakhrisabz or Samarkand, c. 1930s. Silk cross-stitch embroidery on cotton; hand-embroidered silk trim; printed- and plain-cotton lining. (fig. 3) 4 H. x 7" D.; (fig. 6) 6.5 H. x 6.5" D.

4, 5. MAN'S HAT. Samarkand, c. 1920s–30s. Silk embroidery on purple silk; chain-stitch (*yurma*) outlines; *piltado'zi* technique; hand-embroidered silk trim; plain cotton lining. 5.5 H. x 7" D.

4.

5.

6.

4.

HATS Shakhrisabz/Urgut

Shakhrisabz hats are embroidered with particularly intricate patterns. Fig. 2 appears (inadvertently) to be a strange face, while fig. 3 is a commonly seen pattern based on a stylized lotus flower. It is named *chinni* for the Chinese porcelain that inspired it.

Urgut, situated about twenty-five miles from Samarkand, is known for its large weekend market, where a wide variety of traditional handicrafts are sold.

1, 3, 4. MEN'S HATS. Shakhrisabz, Uzbekistan, mid-20th c. Silk cross-stitch embroidery on cotton; cross-stitch borders; black cotton linings. (fig. 1) 3.5 H. x 6" D.; (fig. 3) 3.5 H. x 7" D.; (fig. 4) 3.5 H. x 6" D.

2. MAN'S HAT. Shakhrisabz, mid-20th c. Silk cross-stitch embroidery on cotton; applied handwoven silk trim; printed-cotton lining. 3.5 H. x 6.5" D.

5, 6. GIRL'S HAT. Urgut, Uzbekistan, 1960s. Silk chain and couching stitches on orange silk; applied hand-embroidered silk trim; clear glass beads; printed-cotton lining; pom-pom. 3.5 H. x 6.5" D.

7. A WOMAN'S PORTRAIT. Uzbekistan, 1930s. Photograph by Max Penson.

5.

6.

7.

HATS Bukhara/Khiva

Hats from Bukhara were prized for their intricate gold embroidery (*zarduzi*). Traditionally, the master embroiderers were only men, as it was thought that a woman's breath and hands would tarnish the gold. In the 1930s the Soviets set up gold-embroidery artels, and in a short time most of the masters were women. Today, gold-embroidered hats are an important part of wedding attire.

During the early twentieth century, women's and girls' hats made from imported brocade with gold-wrapped threads became popular in the Khorezm region of Uzbekistan, where Khiva, the capital of the former khanate of Khiva, is located.

1, 2. GIRL'S HAT. Bukhara, Uzbekistan, c. 1950. *Tovus Nusqa* (peacock) pattern.[1] Silver- and gold-wrapped threads on velvet; hand-embroidered silk trim; silk pom-pom (*popuk*); printed-cotton lining. 2.5 H. x 6" D.

1 The peacock-pattern hat is shown in *Applied Art of Uzbekistan*, 185.

3. HAT. Bukhara, 2nd quarter, 20th c. Silk and metallic-gold embroidery on silk velvet; applied hand-embroidered trim; silk pom-pom; plain-cotton lining. 3 H. x 7" D.

4, 5. WOMEN'S HATS. Bukhara, c. 1970s–80s. Gold-wrapped threads on velvet; glass beads; metal spangles; velvet trim; plain- and printed-cotton linings. 2.5 H. x 6" D.

6. HAT. Bukhara, early 20th c. Gold-wrapped threads on silk velvet; applied woven gold trimming band; *adras* ikat lining. 4.5 H. x 6" D.

7. MAN'S HAT. Bukhara, late 20th c. Metallic threads and Lurex on velvet; spangles; printed-cotton lining. 4 H. x 7" D.

8. HAT. Bukhara, mid-20th c. Russian velvet brocade with silk and gold-wrapped threads; hand-embroidered silk trim; silk pom-pom; printed-cotton lining. 3 H. x 6.5" D.

9. GIRL'S HAT (*taxiya*). Khiva, c. 1900. Russian silk brocade with gold-wrapped threads; wide, woven red silk trim; silk pom-pom; Russian printed-cotton lining.[2] 2.5 H x 6" D.

2 The same printed-cotton fabric is shown in Meller, *Russian Textiles*, 13.

1.

2.

3.

4.

5.

HATS South Uzbekistan

Kashkadarya and Surkhandarya are the two southernmost provinces of Uzbekistan. Bright colors and ribbed *piltado'zi* technique are typical hallmarks of hats from this region. The embroidery stitches follow the pattern of the ribbing, completely covering the surface of the hat.

1, 2. MEN'S HATS. Boysun, Surkhandarya, Uzbekistan, c. 1970s. Silk embroidery on cotton; *piltado'zi* technique; hand-embroidered and braided trims; plain- and printed-cotton linings. (fig. 1) 5 H. x 7" D.; (fig. 2) 5 H. x 6.5" D.

3, 6. HATS. Boysun, Surkhandarya, last quarter, 20th c. Silk embroidery on cotton; *piltado'zi* technique; hand-embroidered trim; silk tassels; plain- and printed-cotton linings. (figs. 3, 6) 2.5 H. x 6.5" D.

4, 5. MEN'S HATS. Uzbek-Lakai, South Uzbekistan, mid-20th c. Wool and silk embroidery on ikat; *piltado'zi* technique; cross-stitch trim; silk tassels; glass beads; printed-cotton linings. (figs. 4, 5) 4 H. x 7" D.

7, 8 HAT. South Uzbekistan, early 20th c. Silk embroidery on cotton; *piltado'zi* technique; four narrow bands of gold-wrapped threads; loop-manipulation trim; plain- and printed-cotton lining. (figs. 7, 8) 5.5 H. x 6" D.

6.

8.

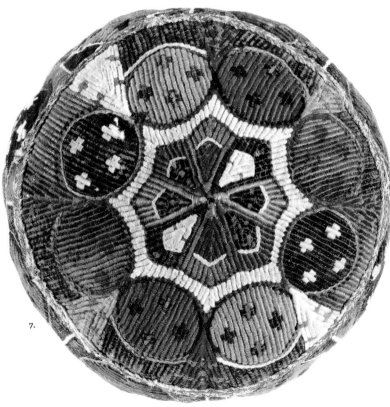

7.

HATS Uzbek-Lakai

These hats were probably made in southern Uzbekistan by women from the Uzbek-Lakai tribe. Except for fig. 6, all are embroidered with variations of the ram's horn (*qo'chqor muguz*) motif, which was used throughout Central Asia. The ram was considered a magical, protective animal, and people would attach its skull and horns outside their homes to ward off evil spirits.

1, 2. UZBEK-LAKAI HATS. 3rd quarter, 20th c. Silk embroidery on cotton; cross-stitch trim; silk tassels with glass beads; printed-cotton linings. (figs. 1, 2) 4.5 H. x 6.5" D.

3. MAN'S UZBEK-LAKAI HAT. c. 1950s. Silk cross-stitch on cotton; cross-stitch trim; silk tassel with glass beads; printed-cotton lining; thickly padded. 5 H. x 7" D.

4. CHILD'S UZBEK-LAKAI HAT. 3rd quarter, 20th c. Silk embroidery on cotton; cross-stitch trim; printed-cotton lining. 4.5 H. x 6.5" D.

5. WILD RAMS. Engraving, 1884. *Ovis poli* (foreground), also known as the Marco Polo sheep, is an endangered species that lives in the mountainous regions of Central Asia.

6. GIRL'S UZBEK-LAKAI HAT. 3rd quarter, 20th c. Silk embroidery on cotton; tulip (*lola*) motifs; hand-embroidered trim; silk tassels with glass beads; red cotton lining. 4 H. x 6.5" D.

5.

6.

CAPS (*Kulta* and *Chach Kep*)

Uzbek and Tajik women also wore soft, rounded caps with an embroidered plait-cover called a *kulta*, *kultapush*, or *kiygich* that extended down the back. Kungrat women from the Boysun region wore an elaborate headdress of multiple scarves called a *bosh* that was wrapped around the top of the *kulta*. The plait-cover served to hide a young woman's long braids, which might attract the Evil Eye.

The *chach kep* was a similar cap worn by Kyrgyz women in southern Kyrgyzstan. Made from undyed cotton, it had a loosely gathered top, elaborately embroidered earflaps, and a plait-cover with an assortment of amulets dangling from it. A long white turban (*ileki*) was wrapped around the top.

1. *KULTA*. South Uzbekistan, mid-20th c. Silk embroidery on purple silk; handwoven trim; printed-cotton lining. (cap) 6" D., (tail) 16 x 8"

2. *KULTA*. Probably Samarkand area, Uzbekistan, 2nd quarter, 20th c. Silk embroidery on cotton; hand-embroidered trim; printed-cotton lining. (cap) 7" D., (tail) 17 x 7"

3. *KULTA*. South Uzbekistan, 3rd quarter, 20th c. Silk embroidery on cotton; hand-embroidered trim; pearl buttons; glass beads; faux-ikat cotton lining. (cap) 7" D., (tail) 23 x 7.5"

4. KYRGYZ WOMAN. Pamir Region, Central Asia, c. 1932. This young woman's headdress is decorated with pearl buttons, small silver bells, and triangular amulets. Photograph by Maynard Owen Williams.

5. *CHACH KEP*. Southern Kyrgyzstan, c. 1900. Silk lacing stitch on plain-weave cotton; handwoven trim; seed pods; pearl buttons; silver ornaments; Russian printed-cotton lining. (cap) 6" D., (tail) 29 x 4"

6, 7. *KULTA*. Uzbekistan, c. 1900. Russian silk brocade with gold-wrapped threads; hand-embroidered trim; Russian printed-cotton lining. (cap) 7" D., (tail) 18 x 4.25"

4.

5.

6.

7.

4

SUZANI

"Naturally, any conclusions as to date and attribution which are based upon such a collage of unsubstantiated premises are best circumspect, and the interpretation of the multitude of variations observed is a potential minefield, but it seems unlikely that any more detailed information will come to light." —Michael Franses, Suzani: The Textile Art of Uzbekistan, 1750–1850[1]

These words, from a respected and prominent textile scholar, still hold true. We in the West would like to be able to provide precise attributions, especially for such magnificent and costly pieces as these early *suzanis*. But they were almost never signed or dated, nor were they specifically mentioned in the writings of eighteenth- and nineteenth-century travelers. Many remain beautiful enigmas.

The term "*suzani*" derives from the Farsi word for needle, "*suzan*," and it has come to refer to the large embroideries that a young girl and her female family members made for her dowry. These pieces were usually embroidered with silk floss on narrow lengths of handwoven, undyed cotton cloth (*karbos*). Hanks of silk threads were obtained in the bazaars, where most had been dyed by professional dyers. Beginning in the 1880s, silk was used as a ground cloth in addition to cotton, but it was more expensive and generally did not hold up as well. A master draftswoman called a *kalamkash* was often engaged to draw a traditional pattern onto the loosely joined panels (between three and seven in number). After the panels were separated, the embroidery was usually stitched by several women in the girl's family, including the bride-to-be, who learned to sew as a young child. As a result, when the completed panels were finally joined together, the pattern did not always match up perfectly.

The basic embroidery stitches used were couching (*basma*), chain stitch (*yurma*), and open chain stitch or ladder stitch (*ilmok* or *ilmoq*), with regional variations. Chain stitching was done with either a needle (*nina*) or a handheld tambour hook (*bigiz*, *daravsh*), which made very fine, even stitches.

*Suzani*s were made by settled people, mostly Uzbek and Tajik, and allowed the new bride (*kelin*) to show off her sewing skills and bring something very personal and beautiful with her to the household of her husband. Traditionally, after the marriage ceremony, the *suzani* was laid over the top of the marriage bed and later might be used to decorate the marriage chamber.

With Russian control over cities such as Bukhara and Samarkand solidified in the 1870s, commercialization of embroideries became more common. Men could be seen in the bazaars embroidering tablecloths, hats, and other textiles. These pieces were sold in the local markets or made on commission for well-to-do families and, it seems, traders.[2] It is likely that *suzanis* too were made for resale as they could be found in nineteenth-century Western homes and collections. As the twentieth century progressed, *suzanis* began to be displayed in places other than the newlyweds' room: in homes both modest and sumptuous, in synagogues, and, during Soviet times, in public buildings and even voting booths (see fig. 2, page 185).

Pre-Soviet-era *suzanis* were almost never signed or dated, and their origins were seldom documented. However, each region developed its own style (albeit with considerable overlap), which helps somewhat when trying to establish the provenance of a particular piece. The emirate of Bukhara was the trendsetting center of nineteenth-century *suzani* production, and the emir maintained his own embroidery workshops. Probably because of this, *suzanis* from Bukhara and other towns within the emirate (such as Shakhrisabz, Kermina, and Kitab) tend to share many characteristics and are, therefore, more difficult to precisely identify. Nurata and Ura-Tube *suzanis* have a distinctive appearance, as do those from Jizzak, Tashkent, and Pskent. During the Soviet era, certain Samarkand *suzanis* developed a very recognizable look: large-scale, boldly graphic, red medallions surrounded by dense black scrollwork. They were most likely commercial items made by women in Soviet-organized artels (see pages 178–81).

Throughout much of the twentieth century, girls continued to make *suzanis* for their weddings, although seldom with the very fine and intricate embroidery characteristic of those from the nineteenth century. Factory-woven cloth in wider widths and bright colors was readily available and often used instead of the traditional undyed cotton. However the embroidery thread continued to be silk floss. In the south of Uzbekistan, the province of Surkhandarya carried on a lively *suzani* tradition. Some of these bright, folksy embroideries with bold flowers, outsized medallions, and fanciful birds on predominately red backgrounds were signed, dated, and bore words of well wishes. Many *suzanis* from the southern provinces of Uzbekistan can be bought in the market today, with most dating from the 1950s through the 1980s. These are the embroideries that are finding their way into Western homes as bedspreads, furniture coverings, throw pillows, and wall hangings.

Like American patchwork quilts, one small area was often left unfinished. American women did so in deference to God as "only He is perfect," while Central Asian women were loathe to arouse the jealousy of the Evil Eye. Auspicious symbols, each bearing various meanings—such as pomegranates (fertility), birds (happiness), water vessels (purity), teapots (hospitality), and *tumars* (protective amulets)—were often integrated into the patterns. The borders themselves served as protective devices to keep out *jinns* (bad spirits). A *suzani* was not only an object of beauty; it held much of a young woman's past and would accompany her on the rest of her life's journey.

---

1 An Internet exhibit arranged by the Textile Gallery, London, 1998. (Michael Franses has confirmed that this statement is still valid.)

2 An interesting paragraph in *Turkestan: The Heart of Asia*, written by William Eleroy Curtis in 1911, rings true even today: "Very few pieces of embroidery are offered for sale there, however. You can buy to much better advantage in Constantinople or even the United States. A well-known Chicago gentleman, who has visited Turkestan twice and is a recognized authority on matters pertaining to that part of the world, carried home with him from his last trip a very handsome specimen of Bokhara embroidery. A few weeks after his return he was astonished to find an exact duplicate hanging upon the wall of a friend in Evanston, who had purchased it at a department store in Chicago. My friend went to that store the next day and found fifty pieces precisely like his own, offered for sale at a less price than he had paid in Bokhara." William Eleroy Curtis, *Turkestan: The Heart of Asia* (New York: Hodder & Stoughton, 1911), 172.

1.

SUZANI Bukhara Region

As the seat of the ruling emir of the khanate, nineteenth-century Bukhara was the Paris of Central Asia. The emir's embroidery workshops influenced *suzani* styles of the surrounding regions, including Kermina, Shakhrisabz, and Samarkand, which makes attribution far from exact. Bukharan *suzanis* often have a wide outer border with large floral medallions in two shades of red (an orange-red and a rose-red) that are intertwined with graceful, meandering vines. The embroidery is usually a type of couching stitch (*basma* or *kanda khayol*). *Nim suzanis* are literally "half-size" *suzanis*.

2.

1. *SUZANI*.[1] Bukhara region, Uzbekistan, mid-19th c. Silk chain stitch (*yurma*) on four joined panels of handwoven cotton (*karbos*); small water vessels (*oftoba*), symbols of purity and hospitality, in the borders; unlined. It appears that this *suzani* was made without secondary borders. 5'11" x 3'11"

2, 3. *NIM SUZANI* (and detail). Bukhara region, early 19th c. Silk couching stitch (*basma*) and open chain stitch, also called ladder stitch (*ilmok*), on four joined panels of *karbos*; relined. This is a rare *suzani*, thought to be a variant of the "large medallion" *suzani*. (fig. 2) 6.5 x 7"; (fig. 3) 3'10" x 4'9"

1 For a similar *suzani*, see Christina Sumner and Guy Petherbridge, *Bright Flowers: Textiles and Ceramics of Central Asia* (Sydney: Powerhouse Publishing, 2004), 38; and Ignazio Vok and Jakob Taube, *Vok Collection: Suzani: A Textile Art from Central Asia* (Munich: HeroldVerlagsauslieferung, 1994), no. 8

3.

2.

SUZANI

This *suzani* is more of an enigma than most because it has characteristics of several regions. The "parasol" flowers in the field are similar in form to a *suzani* attributed to the Samarkand region[2]; the pale aubergine is likely made from logwood, which is almost only found in *suzanis* from Kermina; the attention to detail in the large border flowers, especially the checkered chain stitch around the outer petals and flower centers, and the many different colors suggest Shakhrisabz (although chain stitch was more commonly used in Kermina and Samarkand); and the narrow red/white/blue outside border is a typical finish of the Lakai tribe. (By the time this *suzani* was made, the Lakai had settled in all three regions.)

2 Franz Bausback, *SUSANI: Stickereien aus Mittelasien* (auction catalog, Mannheim, Germany: April 1981), 40.

1. SUZANI. Uzbekistan, 3rd quarter, 19th c. Silk and wool chain stitch on three joined panels of factory-made tan cotton; lined with Russian printed cotton. 8'9" x 6'2"

2. DETAIL. Central panel motifs. Note how the filling stitches follow the shapes of the motifs, creating a pleasing pattern themselves. 31 x 20" as shown

3. LINING DETAIL. Russian roller-printed cotton; handwoven silk warp/cotton weft stripe border. 7 x 6" as shown

4, 5. DETAILS. Bottom right corner. The two-color patterned chain stitching used in the border flowers is called checkered chain stitch and is achieved using two different colored threads in one needle. (fig. 4) 26 x 20" as shown; (fig. 5) detail of fig. 4

3.

4.

5.

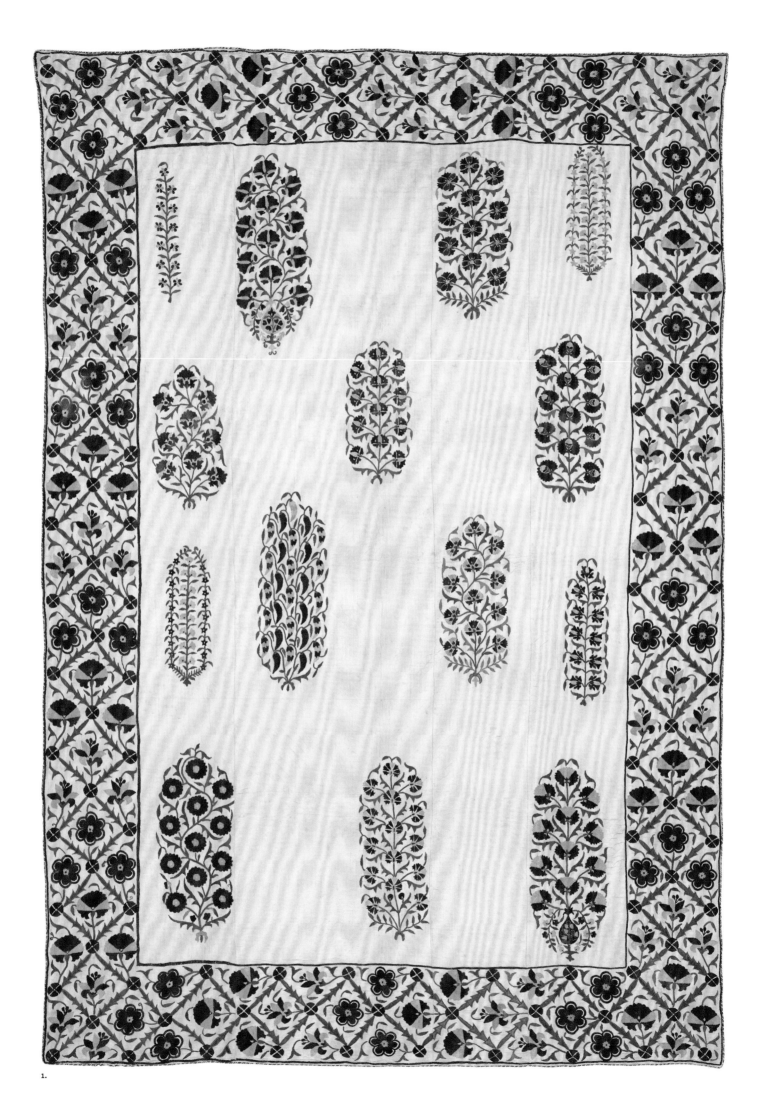

1.

2.

SUZANI Nurata Region

Nurata is a small historic town situated approximately 220 miles northeast of Bukhara. Said to have been founded by Alexander the Great in the fourth century BCE, it was a provincial center for trade between Kazakhstan and the emirate of Bukhara. One characteristic of Nurata *suzanis* is the use of naturalistic flowers that often evoke Mughal floral motifs. They frequently appear as spaced flowering plants on a field of undyed handwoven cotton cloth (*karbos*).[3]

3 For a similar *suzani*, see Sumner and Petherbridge, *Bright Flowers*, 54.

1. SUZANI. Nurata, Uzbekistan, mid-19th c. Silk couching stitch (*basma*) and double chain stitch (*ilmok*) on four joined panels of *karbos*; finely quilted and lined with undyed *karbos*. 7'5" x 5'3"

2. DETAIL. Irises. 13 x 4" as shown

3. DETAIL. Carnations. 15 x 7" as shown

4. DETAIL. Capsicum peppers. The intense heat of capsicum peppers (*kalampir*), was believed to ward off malevolent spirits. 17.5 x 6.5" as shown

5. DETAIL. Carnations. This stylized five-petaled carnation flower is found in Mughal, Persian, and Ottoman textiles, as there was much cross-pollination among the design forms of these cultures. 15 x 6" as shown

3.

4.

5.

1.

SUZANI Nurata Region

This *suzani* has been attributed to the Nurata region by several authorities on the subject, although the allover pattern is not typical of most Nurata *suzanis*. The formal layout is enlivened by a profusion of delicately embroidered flowers—carnations, irises, poppies, pomegranate, and *bodum* (almond)—all rendered in exquisitely fine detail. At least thirteen shades of natural dyes have been used.

1. SUZANI. Nurata region, Uzbekistan, early to mid-19th c. Silk couching and double chain stitch on four joined panels of *karbos*; relined. 8' x 5'8"

2. DETAIL. Top left corner; 10 x 10" as shown

3. DETAIL. Bottom third left border. 8.5 x 15" as shown

2.

3.

SUZANI Ura-Tube and Nurata

While the nineteenth-century *suzani* shown in fig. 1 is laid out in Nurata fashion, with a central starlike motif surrounded by spaced flowering plants or shrubs, experts in the field attribute it to Ura-Tube, a town formerly in the khanate of Kokand. The profusion of curling tendrils and multitude of colorful, freely drawn flowers give this piece a joyful, folk-art quality. The poppy flowers (upper right) and the curling tips and subtle roots of the two plants on either side of the central star are evocative of early Mughal flower forms. The elongated green seedpods and black-and-yellow striped buds are Ura-Tube *suzani* motifs.

The floral forms in the twentieth-century *suzani* shown in fig. 2 have been simplified with greatly stylized capsicum peppers being the only recognizable plants. *Basma* (couching) and *yurma* (chain stitch) are still employed, but in a far less refined way than in nineteenth-century examples.

1. URA-TUBE *SUZANI*. Tajikistan, early to mid-19th c. Silk couching and chain stitch on five joined panels of *karbos*; eighteen shades of natural dyes; relined. 6' x 5'5"

2. NURATA *SUZANI*. Uzbekistan, mid-20th c. Silk couching and chain stitch on factory-made cotton; central panel and border framed by narrow chain-stitched borders; machine-embroidered black trim; unlined. 4'7" x 7'4"

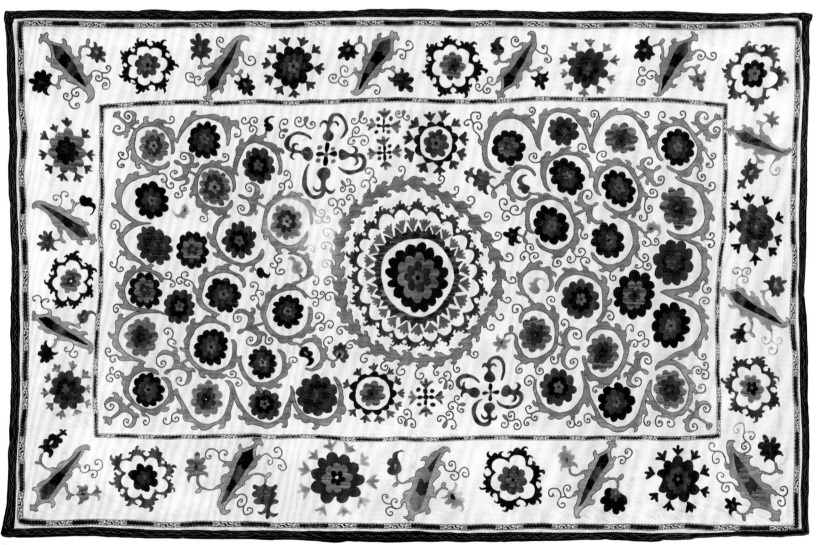

2.

SUZANI Samarkand

Two features that distinguish this *suzani* from its Bukharan relatives are the very narrow borders and the placement of the large medallions. While the eight-pointed star-within-a-rosette motif is found in both types, they usually appear within the wide borders of Bukharan *suzanis*, rather than as repetitive main elements in the central field. The layout of this particular *suzani* appears to be a forerunner of the two twentieth-century Samarkand examples on pages 178–81.

1. *SUZANI*. Samarkand, Uzbekistan, third quarter, 19th c. Very fine silk chain stitch (made with a handheld tool called a *bigiz*) on four joined panels of *karbos*; lined with Russian printed-cotton and *adras* ikat borders. Small blue irises peek out from the garlands of green lotuslike vines, and small water vessels (*oftoba*), symbols of purity, hospitality, and life, are worked into the pattern. 5'2" x 8'5"

2. DETAIL. Lining of *suzani* shown in fig. 1. Russian printed-cotton lining; *adras* ikat borders. 7.5 x 7" as shown

2.

As the twentieth century progressed, Samarkand *suzanis* took on their own distinctive look. They became commercial products, and the embroiderers followed what the customer, or the artel to which they belonged, wanted: huge *suzanis* (around 12' x 8') that were almost entirely covered with embroidery. Co[lors] were reduced to a few shades of red, ochre, and black; and the delicate green lo[ng] vines of nineteenth-century *suzanis* were stylized into heavy black scrollwork, referred to as "melon vines." At times different dye lots of embroidery thread resulted in a variegated effect, as seen in the dark-red medallions. When this occurs in traditional handwoven carpets it is called *abrash*.

1. SUZANI. Samarkand, Uzbekistan, c. 1950.
Silk couching outlined with chain stitch on
four joined panels of factory-made plain-
weave cotton; black cotton trim; unlined.
9' x 12'6"

1.

SUZANI Samarkand

These commercial *suzanis* are far removed from the nineteenth-century pieces that a young girl made for her dowry—in fact they probably were sewn in Soviet-established artels. However, from a purely design point of view, examples such as this one succeeded in abstracting traditional motifs into a dynamic new look. The mismatched bottom row of medallions was not an uncommon occurrence, since *suzanis* were worked as separate panels, at times by different women, and later joined together.

1. *SUZANI.* Samarkand, Uzbekistan, mid-20th c. Silk couching outlined with chain stitch on four joined panels of factory-made plain-weave cotton; machine-embroidered cotton trim; unlined. 7' x 9'

1.

SUZANI Samarkand

Another distinct group of Samarkand *suzanis* are the so-called "flowering bushes." Composed of rows of highly stylized plant forms, usually in a limited palette, their bold, graphic quality is reminiscent of the paper cutouts that Henri Matisse made during the period from 1940 until he died in 1954.

2.

1. *SUZANI*. Samarkand, Uzbekistan, 2nd quarter, 20th c. Silk and cotton couching and chain stitch on three joined panels of factory-made cotton; black cloth trim; unlined. It appears that different dye lots of dark blue thread were used, resulting in some areas fading to shades of gray. 8'5" x 6'8"

2. EMBROIDERING *SUZANIS*. Samarkand, 1997. Women would often gather together in an informal setting to sew quilts and *suzanis*. Referred to as *kashkar*, it was like an American quilting bee. Photograph by Anatoly Rahimbaev.

3. *SUZANI*. Samarkand, mid-20th c. Cotton couching and chain stitch on two joined panels of factory-made cotton; capsicum pepper or *bodum* (almond) motifs in border and around niches; machine chain-stitched black cloth trim; unlined. 5'5" x 4'7"

3.

1.

SUZANI Tashkent Region

Certain types of *suzanis* from Tashkent and the neighboring town of Pskent to the southeast have a distinctive look. Called *palyak* or *paliak*, perhaps derived from the Arabic word "*falak*" (firmament), they are easily recognized by large circular disks known as *oy* or *oi* (moon) that are worked in shades of red. These circles may be solid red, or filled with ornate renderings of stars (fig. 1). The ground cloth is usually entirely covered in silk couching (*basma*) with ladder stitch (*ilmok*) or chain stitch (*yurma*) outlines. During the nineteenth century, red-orange wool embroidery was used for accent color. The *suzani* shown in fig. 3 is a typical twentieth-century square Tashkent *oy palyak*.

1. *PALYAK SUZANI*. Pskent, Uzbekistan, late 19th c. Silk and wool *basma* and *ilmok* on seven joined panels of *karbos*; unlined. 8'6" x 6'5"

2. ELECTIONS TO THE SUPREME SOVIET. Tashkent, Uzbekistan, 1937. Several *suzanis* hang on the wall, including an *oy palyak* similar to the one shown in fig. 3. Photograph by Max Penson.

3. *OY PALYAK SUZANI*. Tashkent, mid-20th c. Silk *basma* outlined in *yurma* entirely covers three joined panels of factory-made cotton; stylized striped-snake motifs (protective symbols) in center; unlined. 8' x 7'7"

2.

3.

1.

SUZANI Southern Uzbekistan

Kashkadarya and Surkhandarya are the two southernmost provinces of Uzbekistan. Cultural traditions have remained strong here, and many brightly colored, cheerful wedding *suzanis* like these can still be found. Fanciful birds and large floral medallions, often on red cotton, are a recurring theme, but sometimes a woman puts her own spin on things—such as fig. 3 on this page and figs. 1 and 3 on pages 188–89.

2.

1. SUZANI. Boysun region, Surkhandayra, c. 1970s. Silk couching stitch on red cotton; scattered spangles; machine-embroidered black cotton trim; silk fringe; unlined. 6'5" x 5'5"

2. SUZANI. Kosan, Kashkadarya, mid-20th c. Silk and cotton couching on cotton; machine-embroidered cotton trim; unlined. 5'9" x 3'5"

3. SUZANI. Surkhandarya, dated 1976. Silk couching stitch on cotton; unlined. The words translate as: "A memory left from my youth—a fragrance from the flower of love." "Hursana" [woman's name] and "Mengboy" [man's name]. 3'6" x 5'2"

3.

SUZANI Southern Uzbekistan

The *suzani* shown in fig. 1 is a true piece of folk art, replete with auspicious motifs. Snakes (*ilon*) were considered protective, especially of women, children, family, and home; the pomegranate (*anor*) symbolizes abundance and fertility; the teapot (*chainik*) offers welcoming hospitality; and the bird (*qush*) brings happiness. Ram's horns (*quo'chqoroq*) stand guard along the borders.

1. *SUZANI*. Probably southern Uzbekistan, signed and dated 1965. Silk couching, stem, and buttonhole stitches on cotton; black commercial ribbon; machine-embroidered red cloth trim; unlined. This *suzani* was said to be Lakai, and though this attribution is often too readily given, the ogive-shaped motifs with ram's horns and the circular medallions that appear in the borders are similar to those found in Lakai embroideries.[4] 4'3" x 3'

4 See Kate Fitz Gibbon and Andrew Hale, *Uzbek Embroidery in the Nomadic Tradition: The Jack A. and Aviva Robinson Collection* (Minneapolis: Minneapolis Institute of Arts, 2007), 25.

2. *SUZANI* WORKSHOP. Tashkent, Uzbekistan, 2004. In this photograph, the cotton base cloth with a pattern either stenciled or drawn on it has been fastened to a wooden frame. The women are needle-embroidering the *suzani* in chain stitch.

3. *SUZANI*. Southern Uzbekistan, dated 1971. Silk couching stitch on cotton; machine-embroidered black cotton trim; unlined. This is an unusual design for a *suzani* and is evocative of Kyrgyz motifs (see pages 208–9). 4'8" x 6'5"

2.

3.

1.

2.

3.

4.

5.

SUZANI Machine Embroidery

The sewing machine (*popuk mashina*) was introduced into Central Asia during the late 1800s. Some machines produced only chain stitch and others, such as the old treadle Singer machines, only lock-stitch straight seams. Urban Uzbek robes and *paranjas* from the late 1800s onward were often machine-stitched by professional tailors called *mashinachi*. During the Soviet era, large workshops were set up where *suzanis* were embroidered with modern machines that created a variety of stitches.

1. TRADE CARD. Singer Manufacturing Co., USA, dated 1894. Kazakh women in ikat robes and traditional headdresses at a treadle-operated Singer sewing machine.

2, 3. *SUZANI* TRIM. Tajikistan, mid-20th c. Cotton thread on black cotton cloth. Edging trim in general was considered protective—the complex patterns on these machine-stitched borders, an art in itself, served to further deter harmful spirits. (fig. 2) 4.5 x 9"; (fig. 3) 3.5 x 10" as shown

4. *KIRPECH*. Tashkent, Uzbekistan, dated 1949. Silk machine-made chain stitch on black velvet; peacocks; unlined. (Note the cotton boll tucked in by the date.) 79 x 24" as shown

5. *KIRPECH*. Tashkent, dated 1973. Silk, machine-made chain stitch on black cotton velvet; unlined. A *kirpech* is a long, narrow embroidery traditionally used as a niche cover. This example would have hung in a guest room (*mehmonkhana*) and says: "Welcome Dear Guests." 82 x 28"

6. *SUZANI* FACTORY. Tashkent, c. 1980. In this photograph, women are machine-embroidering chain-stitched *suzanis* similar to the one shown in fig. 5.

6.

5

HOUSEHOLD

"... The most potent forms of cultural continuity exist within the woman's sphere—as domestic ritual and, especially, in the creation of handmade textiles." —Kate Fitz Gibbon and Andrew Hale, *Uzbek Embroidery*, 2007

Textiles were steeped in tradition and integral to Central Asian life. Every piece a woman made had its specific function and place in the home, whether yurt or mud-brick house. The nomad's tent itself was made from textiles: On the exterior, heavy wool felt kept out the fiercest winds, cold, and heat. Inside, knotted-pile and flat-weave carpets or felt rugs (*shyrdak*) covered the earthen floor. Patterned wool tent bands (*terme*), woven on a narrow ground loom, helped secure the wooden frame. Along the back wall, painted wood and leather-covered chests (*sanduk*) were piled high with the family's bedding—quilts often made of patchwork and padded with cotton. Storage bags of all sizes and shapes hung from the interior trellis framework. The largest bags (*chuval* and *torba*) were rectangular and often intricately woven, like knotted wool carpets. They hung hammocklike and usually held clothing and headdresses. Other large storage bags were placed on low wooden platforms against the back wall. Smaller bags were used to hold items such as scissors (*kaichi kap, kaichidon*), spoons (*kashik kap, tchemthcedon*), salt (*tuz kap, tuz khalta*), tea (*chai kap, chai khalta*), and personal items. These bags were both functional and objects of considerable beauty. Other fabric hangings were purely decorative, such as Kungrat and Lakai *ilgich*, which displayed the woman's sewing skills. It appears that very few textile items went unadorned; embroidery, tassels, and fringe were all lavishly employed. The tassels themselves were works of art (see page 104). In addition to the nomadic family's household textiles, colorful, ornate animal trappings were hung on the yurt's walls. To be surrounded by wide-open spaces yet snug inside the family yurt with beautiful textiles of one's own creation and a plentiful source of meat, milk, wool, and transportation just outside the door, gave rise to the appreciation many Westerners felt for the pastoral nomadic life.

Sedentary women did not have as much freedom in movement and dress as nomadic women. They had to veil whenever they went outside, and most seldom left their own *mahalla* (neighborhood). Some were totally secluded by their husbands and never allowed to leave the women's quarters (*ichkari*) of their own houses. Even within the home, the sexes were strictly segregated (except in Jewish homes). Women in well-off households usually had servants and, aside from their children, little to occupy themselves. They did, however, spend time embroidering various textiles for the home or dowry. Besides the requisite *suzanis*, there were wedding bedsheets (*ruijo, ruydjo*); prayer mats (*joinomoz, joinamaz*); curtains to cover niches (*kirpech, tokchapush*); narrow, decorative, friezelike embroideries (*zardevor, dorpech*) that hung just below the ceiling and were often long enough to wrap around an entire room; brazier covers (*sandalpush*) that the family would sit under to keep warm; and small bags, such as mirror bags (*aina khalta*) and comb bags (*shona khalta*). Both nomadic and sedentary peoples used very little furniture—a few storage chests and, in the urban homes, perhaps a low table for serving food. Cushions and thick quilts (*kurpa*) took the place of chairs and beds. A cloth (*dastarkhan*) was spread on the floor and families ate their meals sitting around it. Textiles were the furnishings of a Central Asian home.

1.

2.

3.

4.

CRADLE COVERS (*Beshikpush*)

A traditional baby cradle, called a *beshik* (Uzbek) or a *gavara* (Tajik), was crafted of wood, with a horizontal turned handle and a round hole in the bottom board (fig. 6). A mattress, also with a hole (fig. 7), was laid on top of the board, with the holes aligned. A clay pot (*beshik tuvak*, fig. 8) was placed under the cradle. The baby was laid in the cradle with its bare bottom over the mattress hole, and a clay or wooden pipe (*sumak*), designed specifically for the job, directed the urine into the pot. After the baby was swaddled and strapped in, a cover (*beshikpush*) was draped over the top rail to keep out drafts, light, insects, and any jealous evil spirits. The pattern on the cover was designed to conform to the cradle structure.

1, 3, 4. CRADLE COVERS. Samarkand (figs. 1, 4), Uzbekistan, 3rd quarter, 20th c. Silk and cotton couching and chain stitch on cotton; black cotton trim; unlined. (fig. 1) 57 x 64"; (fig. 3) dated 1974; 56 x 74"; (fig. 4) 50 x 55"

2. CRADLE WITH BESHIKPUSH. Samarkand area, c. 2004.

5. THE BROTHERS. Bukhara, Uzbekistan, c. 1960s. Baby in an Uzbek cradle with a *beshikpush* draped over one end. Photograph by Fitzroy Maclean.

6. CRADLE MAKER. Samarkand bazaar, 1871–72. Photograph from the Turkestan Album.

7, 8. MATTRESS and CLAY POT. Uzbekistan. (fig.7) Mattress: 1st quarter, 20th c. Silk *atlas* ikat; black cotton trim; Russian printed-cotton lining. A silk ikat mattress was believed to ensure a rich future for the baby. 15 x 38". (fig.8) Handmade pot: Tashkent bazaar, 2009. 5.5 x 5"

5.

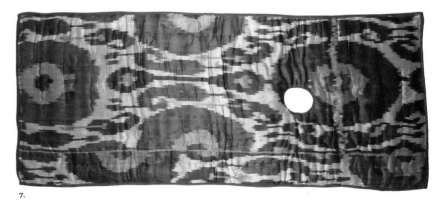
7.

8.

6.

1.

2.

3.

PRAYER MATS (*Joinomoz*)

According to Islamic law a Muslim must pray five times a day; the place he prays must be clean, and he must be facing Mecca. An embroidered prayer mat, called a *joinomoz*, was often part of a woman's dowry. Far lighter to transport than a carpet, these mats allowed a man to have a clean, defined area available for prayer wherever he might be. The arch represents the *mirhab* in a mosque, which points the way to Mecca.

1. PRAYER MAT. Kashkadarya region, Uzbekistan, mid-20th c. Silk chain stitch on cotton; unlined. 63 x 40"

2. PRAYER MAT. Nurata region, Uzbekistan, 3rd quarter, 20th c. Silk couching and chain stitch on cotton; factory-made trim; unlined. 58 x 45"

3. PRAYER MAT. Kashkadarya region, mid-20th c. Silk chain stitch on cotton; machine-embroidered cotton trim; printed-cotton lining. 54 x 43"

4. THE CALL TO PRAYER. Samarkand, Uzbekistan, c. 1929. A *muezzin* summoning the faithful to prayer from high above the rooftops of the city.

5. PRAYING IN THE REGISTAN. Samarkand, 1920s. "There in the bright sun of the market-place, forming a color picture that only an Eastern sun could harmonize, hundreds of men bow and kneel and rise in unison."[1] The Registan was the central public square and main marketplace of Samarkand. It was surrounded on three sides by imposing *madrassahs*: Tilia-Kari, Shir-Dor, and Ulugh Beg.

1. Maynard Owen Williams, "Russia's Orphan Races," *National Geographic*, October 1918, 269.

4.

5.

1.

2.

3.

4.

5.

WEDDING *SUZANI* (*Bolinpush* and *Ruijo*)

During an Uzbek wedding ceremony, an embroidered square cloth called a *bolinpush* (in Samarkand and Bukhara) was held like a canopy over the bride to shield her from malevolent spirits (fig. 2 is a typical Samarkand *bolinpush* pattern). After the wedding, it was laid over the pillows on the couple's bed.

Another dowry item was an embroidered bedsheet that would be used on the newlyweds' bed. Called a *ruijo* (in the Bukhara region) or *choishab* (in Tashkent), it was patterned on three sides. The center panel was traditionally left unadorned (in order to display proof of the bride's virginity). While similar in style to the prayer mat (*joinomoz*), the *ruijo* was larger and the niche was not pointed.

1, 2. *BOLINPUSH.* Samarkand, Uzbekistan, mid-20th c. Silk and cotton couching on cotton; cotton trim; plain cotton lining; melon-vine scrollwork. (fig. 1) 59 x 95"; (fig. 2) 60 x 62"

3. FAMILY BY SAMOVAR. Uzbekistan, c. 1930s–40s. A *ruijo* hangs on the wall and a photo of Stalin watches over the family. Photograph by Max Penson.

4. UZBEK WEDDING. Uzbekistan, 2005. A *bolinpush* is held over the bride.

5–7. *RUIJOS.* Samarkand, mid-20th c. Silk couching and chain stitch on cotton; cotton trim; unlined. (fig. 5) 85 x 60"; (fig. 6) 79 x 63"; (fig. 7) 80 x 61"

6.

7.

1. 2.

NICHE COVERS (*Kirpech* and *Tokchapush*)

Niches inset into thick walls served as storage spaces. In well-to-do urban homes, they were elaborately carved from plaster and left uncovered in order to display prized possessions such as fine porcelain. Other niches held folded bedding or clothing, and these were covered with embroidered cloths (*tokchapush* and *kirpech*). *Tokchapush* were generally square (and also used as pillow covers); *kirpech* were long and narrow.

1, 2. *KIRPECH.* Tashkent, Uzbekistan, 2nd quarter, 20th c. Silk couching and chain stitch on cotton; silk fringe; unlined. The embroidery covers the entire surface. The central medallion and border pattern of fig. 2 are similar to the Tashkent *suzani* on page 185. (fig. 1) 84 x 26"; (fig. 2) 93 x 25"

3–5. *TOKCHAPUSH.* Samarkand, Uzbekistan, mid-20th c. Silk and cotton embroidery on cotton; cotton trim; spangles and small glass beads. (fig. 3) printed cotton lining; 36 x 35"; (figs. 4, 5) unlined; 38 x 38"

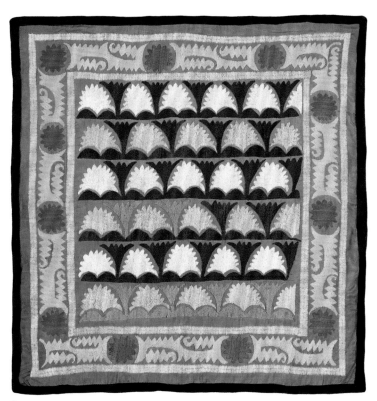

5.

3.

4.

201

1.

2.

ДЎСТЛИГИМИЗ   АБАДИЙ   ГУЛНОРА   КАРОМАТ   1981   ЙИЛ   ИСТАРДИМКИ   КАЛБЛАРА

3.

WALL HANGINGS (*Zardevor*)

Many different types of embroideries were, and still are, used as wall hangings, whether in urban homes or nomadic tents. A *zardevor* (also called a *dorpech*) was a very long, narrow embroidery that hung just below the ceiling of an important room and served as a sort of frieze along one or more walls. Often it was embroidered with words of good wishes.

1. ZARDEVOR. Kattakurgan (forty miles northwest of Samarkand), Uzbekistan, 2nd quarter, 20th c. Silk couching and chain stitch on cotton; machine-embroidered cotton trim; silk netting and tassels; unlined. 25 x 121"

2. ZARDEVOR. South Uzbekistan, dated 1981. Silk couching stitch on cotton; machine-embroidered cotton trim; unlined. The Uzbek words loosely translate as "Friendship is eternal—*Gulnora Karomat*—1981—May the friendship in our hearts stay as pure as a spring." 26 x 185"

3. ZARDEVOR. Surkhandarya region, Uzbekistan, 3rd quarter, 20th c. Silk couching stitch on cotton; machine-embroidered cotton trim; cotton fringe; unlined. Birds (in this piece, peacocks) often appear on Central Asian embroideries. They are thought to bring happiness—especially into the home of a newlywed couple. 26 x 176"

УСТЛИК, ЧАШМАДЕК ПОК ТУГАНМАС БУЛСА!

1.

WALL HANGINGS Tajik

Leninabad (formerly Khodjent and now called Khujand) is a city in northern Tajikistan, a short distance from the Ferghana Valley of Uzbekistan. Figs. 1, 2, and 4 have a look typical of mid-twentieth-century Tajik embroideries from this area—bold, flat patterns in a limited palette on black. They are usually bordered by intricately machine-embroidered black cotton trim. The distinctive white border pattern is said to symbolize snakes, which were thought to protect against evil spirits, as were capsicum peppers.

1, 2, 4. TAJIK HANGINGS. Leninabad, Tajikistan, mid-20th c. Silk couching on cotton; capsicum pepper motifs; stylized snake borders; machine-embroidered cotton trims; unlined. (fig. 1) 47 x 34"; (fig. 2) 57 x 52"; (fig. 4) 50 x 50"

3. TAJIK HANGING. Late 20th c. Silk couching on cotton; block-printed cotton (*chit*) lining. This piece may well have been made in Samarkand, although dealers in the Istanbul bazaar (where it was obtained) call this type of *suzani* "Tajik." The heavy black scrollwork is very similar to that in the Samarkand *suzani* shown on pages 178–79. 31 x 31"

2.

3.

4.

1.

2.

3.

TENT HANGINGS Lakai and Kungrat

The Lakai and Kungrat were seminomadic Uzbek tribes—the former noted for their horse breeding, fierce independence, and plundering raids upon their neighbors.

Historically they lived in what is now southern Uzbekistan and Tajikistan. Lakai and Kungrat embroideries reflect their shamanistic roots. The symbolic motifs of swirling disks, spirals, and stylized scorpions and spiders have a primal quality about them. They exude a magical energy.

1. *AT TORBA ILGICH* (**square** *ilgich* **without a triangular flap).** Lakai, late 19th c. Silk slanted buttonhole and chain-stitch embroidery on imported wool broadcloth (*banot*); applied cross-stitch border; striped silk warp/cotton weft *bekasab* (see fig. 7, page 265) and Russian printed-cotton lining; silk fringe. 29 x 31" as shown

2. *ILGICH.* Probably Kungrat, late 19th–early 20th c. Silk chain- and double chain–stitch embroidery on imported wool broadcloth; striped cotton lining; black cotton binding. 22 x 14"

3. *TABALAU ILGICH* (**square** *ilgich* **with triangular flap).** Lakai, late 19th–early 20th c. Silk slanted buttonhole and chain-stitch embroidery on imported wool broadcloth; block-printed cotton lining (*chit*); silk fringe. 24 x 24" as shown

4. *UUK KAP ILGICH* (**shield-shaped Lakai** *ilgich*). Late 19th–early 20th c. Silk slanted buttonhole and chain-stitch embroidery on imported wool broadcloth; red wool broadcloth lining; applied silk cross-stitch trim; silk tassels with eternal knots. 35 x 16" as shown

5. *ILGICH.* Kungrat, late 19th–early 20th c. Silk chain-stitch embroidery on imported wool broadcloth; block-printed cotton lining (*chit*). 26 x 16"

1.

2.

3.

4.

TENT HANGINGS Kyrgyz

Traditionally, the type of hanging illustrated here, called a *bashtyk*, was backed with fabric to form a pouch that held small personal items. *Bashtyks* were also hung hammocklike from the lattice framework of a yurt wall and might hold hats or other small articles of clothing. Later, they were simply used as decorative hangings. The patterns of Kyrgyz embroideries were often laid out within four sections.

1. TENT HANGING. Kyrgyz, early 20th c. Silk chain and lacing stitch on imported wool broadcloth; silk tassels with Turk's head knots and gold-wrapped thread, Russian printed-cotton lining. 28 x 26" as shown

2. TENT HANGING. Kyrgyz, early 20th c. Silk chain and lacing stitch on cotton; cotton fringe; wool braided-net with gold-wrapped wool tassels; Russian printed-cotton border and lining. 29 x 29" as shown

3. TENT HANGING. Kyrgyz, 2nd quarter, 20th c. Silk chain and lacing stitch on cotton; cotton fringe; Russian printed-cotton lining. 27 x 19" as shown

4. TENT HANGING. Kyrgyz, late 19th–early 20th c. Silk and wool chain and lacing stitch on handwoven, dark indigo wool; tan cotton border; wool gold-wrapped tassels; remnants of Russian printed-cotton lining. 33 x 28" as shown

5. A NOMAD HOSTESS. Tekes Valley, c. 1935. The Kyrgyz woman in this photograph is serving tea to her husband's guests. An embroidered hanging is on the wall. Photograph by Edward Murray.

6. KYRGYZ YURT FRAMEWORK. Tekes Valley, c. 1935. Photograph by Edward Murray.

7. TENT HANGING. Kyrgyz, c. 1930s. Imported wool broadcloth; silk cording; printed cotton trim; cotton lining; cotton fringe. The same "mosaic" technique was used to make this piece as was used on a felt bag (see fig. 4, page 227). 24 x 21" as shown

8. TENT HANGING. Kyrgyz, late 19th–early 20th c. Silk chain and lacing stitch on imported wool broadcloth; scorpion motifs on right border; remnants of Russian printed-cotton lining. 16 x 27"

5.

6.

7.

8.

1.

2.

TENT HANGINGS (Kazakh *Tus Kiiz*)

Tus kiiz (Kazakh) and *tush kiyiz* (Kyrgyz) were often made by a grandmother for a newly married couple, or handed down from mother to daughter. They were left unfinished at the bottom to ensure that the marriage would continue to bring unbounded happiness. As part of the wedding ceremony, the bride sat in a curtained-off area in front of the *tus kiiz*. Later, it was either hung over the newlyweds' bed or in the place of honor (*tor*)—along the back wall of the yurt, facing the entrance.

The motifs of many *tus kiiz* made by Kazakhs living in the Altai Mountain region of westernmost Mongolia, where the borders of Kazakhstan, China, and Russia meet, show a distinct Mongolian/Chinese influence (figs. 1, 2), while others, such as the one shown in fig. 5, are evocative of Russian folk embroidery.[2] Kazakh and Kyrgyz versions are similar, although in Kyrgyz *tush kiyiz*, the small center panel (as seen in figs. 1 and 2) is usually left unadorned, or not included at all.

3.

2 *Tus kiiz* such as the ones illustrated here are often attributed to the Kyrgyz. However, an exhibit in 2009 at the Brunei Gallery, London, focused on textiles made by Kazakh women living in the Altai Mountain province of Bayan-Oigii in western Mongolia. Figs. 1 and 2 are almost identical to the *tus kiiz* shown in the exhibition.

1, 2, 5. *TUS KIIZ.* Kazakh, 1960s–80s. Fig. 2 is dated 1967. Cotton chain stitch on cotton; machine-stitched red velvet borders; unlined. (fig. 1) 48 x 76"; (fig. 2) 55 x 82"; (fig. 5) 51 x 80"

3. STITCH BY STITCH A KAZAKH MAID HELPS WITH HER MISTRESS'S DOWRY. Tekes Valley, Central Asia, c. 1935. The caption under this photograph reads, "The little servant girl . . .

is embroidering a wall decoration of Russian design . . . Now many nomad warlords have tamed down, adopting Russian arts and culture." Photograph by Edward Murray.

4. KAZAKH/KYRGYZ COUPLE. Tekes Valley, Central Asia, c. 1935. Ahmed, a Kazakh man, and his Kyrgyz wife are sitting in their yurt; a *tus kiiz* hangs on the wall behind them. Photograph by Edward Murray.

4.

5.

1.

2.

IKAT PANELS

The ikat panels on this spread were woven on extra-wide looms that enabled the creation of large-scale, one-piece ikats used as hangings or quilt (*kurpa*) tops. This type of ikat was produced as early as 1918 (figs. 1, 2) and as late as the 1960s (figs. 3, 4).

The photograph of French portrait photographer Georgette Chadourne (1897–1983) was taken at her home in 1918. The ikat hanging behind her is very similar to fig. 2, which also belonged to Chadourne and now hangs in the California home of her daughter.

1. GEORGETTE CHADOURNE. Paris, 1918. At this time, it was the fashion to pose with exotic textiles. Like Matisse (whom Chadourne photographed), she collected beautiful textiles, including those shown in figs. 1 and 2. Chadourne's work also includes portraits of Picasso and Colette.

2. IKAT PANEL. Uzbekistan, early 20th c. Silk *shohi* ikat with white weft; unlined. This ikat is made with finer silk than those shown in figs. 3 and 4 and has a much softer hand. The overall feeling is subtler and more refined. 84 x 61"

3, 4. IKAT PANELS. Uzbekistan, 1960s. Silk *atlas* ikat with red weft (fig. 3) and light blue weft (fig. 4); unlined. These ikats were produced in the Samarkand silk factory 26 Bakinskih Komissarov, which is no longer in operation. They were probably used as quilt covers. 84 x 56"

3.

4.

1.

2.

3.

4.

5.

6.

7.

8.

MIRROR BAGS (*Aina Khalta*)

Small embroideries called *aina khalta* and *ainak push* traditionally had a cloth backing; open at the top, they served as pouches to store mirrors and other household items. Most twentieth-century examples such as these were used only as decorative hangings.

1, 3, 4, 6. *AINA KHALTAS.* Uzbekistan, 3rd quarter, 20th c. Silk and cotton chain stitch and couching on cotton; machine- and hand-embroidered trims; silk fringe with spangles and small glass beads; printed-cotton lining. (figs. 1, 4) 18 x 16"; (fig. 3) 22 x 22"; (fig. 6) 26 x 26"; all as shown

2. *AINA KHALTA.* Uzbekistan, 2nd quarter, 20th c. Silk couching, buttonhole, and chain stitch on cotton; Russian printed-cotton lining. 18 x 19"

5. *AINA KHALTA.* Uzbekistan, mid-20th c. Silk and cotton couching and chain stitch on cotton; silk tassels; printed-cotton lining; machine-embroidered border. 17 x 15" as shown

7, 8. *AINA KHALTA* (back and front). Uzbekistan, 2nd quarter, 20th c. Silk chain stitch on cotton; cotton fringe; three ewers; Russian printed-cotton lining. 27 x 27" as shown

9. DOMESTIC METALWARE. Uzbekistan, 1870–71. The vessel on the left is a chased and engraved teapot. The other two are ewers (*oftuba*). All three are most likely brass. Photograph from the Turkestan Album.

9.

1.

2.

3.

4.

SMALL BAGS (*Khalta*)

Among the most utilitarian (and beautiful) textiles found in Central Asian homes were bags. Every one of them—from large, woven transport bags (*chuval*) to small, finely embroidered bags such as these—had a purpose. Figs. 1, 2, 3, and 5 (*chai khalta*) often held loose tea. Bags with a drawstring top (fig. 4) or a long neck that folded closed (see fig. 2, page 219) were used for coins. A man could either hang the bag from his belt, or tuck it into his sash when he went to the bazaar (see fig. 1, page 218).

1, 2, 5, 6. KHALTAS (and detail). Uzbek-Lakai, 1st quarter, 20th c. Silk cross-stitch (*iroki*) on cotton; ram's horn motifs; silk tassel with glass beads; Russian printed-cotton linings. (figs. 1, 2, front and back) 8.5 x 7"; (fig. 5) 6.5 x 6"; (fig. 6) .75 x .75"

3. KHALTA. Probably Uzbek-Lakai, 1st quarter, 20th c. Silk cross-stitch on cotton; Russian printed-cotton lining. The patterns of the three primary bands are almost identical to figs. 4 and 5 on page 113. 7.25 x 4.75"

4. KHALTA. Uzbekistan, 2nd quarter, 20th c. Silk chain stitch on worn purple silk velvet; silk tassels with glass beads and metal spangles; Russian printed-cotton lining. The central motif is probably a stylized scorpion—a talismanic symbol. 6.75 x 5.75"

5.

6.

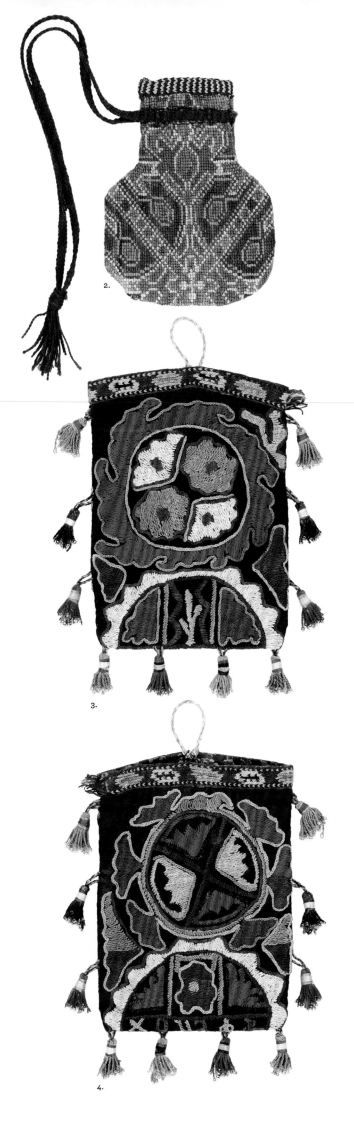

SMALL BAGS (*Khalta*)

The official in fig. 1 has three small, embroidered bags attached to his belt. His striking ikat robe mirrors the painted stripes on the column behind him. Fig. 2 was likely used for carrying coins, as the neck could be folded over and secured with the long cord. Figs. 3 and 4 show an odd little bag, possibly made up from a larger embroidery. The letters spell out a proper name. Fig. 5 was found in an Israeli bazaar. When Jews from Soviet Central Asia were allowed to emigrate in the 1970s, many came to Israel, bringing *suzanis* and other textiles with them.

1. BUKHARAN OFFICIAL. Bukhara, 1911. This building was one of the emir of Bukhara's country palaces, Shirbudin (see fig. 6, page. 323). The emir preferred to stay here rather than at his official residence, the Ark (see fig. 6, page 277) in the city of Bukhara. Photograph by Prokudin-Gorskii.

2. *KHALTA*. Uzbekistan, mid-20th c. Silk cross-stitch on cotton; loop-manipulation trim; printed-cotton lining. 5 x 4"

3, 4. *KHALTA* (front and back). Southern Uzbekistan, mid-20th c. Silk couching and chain stitch on cotton; silk tassels with glass beads; printed-cotton lining. 7 x 5"

5. *KHALTA*. Probably Uzbek, early 20th c. Silk chain stitch on cotton; chain-stitch border embroidered directly onto piece; woven red band at top; Russian printed-cotton backing; open at top. 9.5 x 8.5"

5.

1.

2.

3.

4.

5.

SMALL BAGS Turkmen

Turkmen women often used a type of fine lacing or ladder stitch called *kesdi* when embroidering clothing and bags such as these. *Chai khalta* (figs. 1, 4, 5, 7) were embroidered by women for their husbands to carry loose tea and small personal possessions. They might also be given away as special gifts and served to show off the sewing skills of the women. All of the bags shown here have the same pattern on both sides.

1, 4, 5, 7 CHAI KHALTAS. Ersari Turkmen, 1st quarter, 20th c. Silk lacing stitch on cotton; loop-manipulation trim; silk tassels with glass beads and metal caps; Russian cotton linings. (figs. 1, 4) 7 x 5.5"; (figs. 5, 7) 6.5 x 5"

2. *KHALTA*. Yomut Turkmen, 2nd quarter, 20th c. Silk lacing stitch on cotton; plain cotton lining; drawstring. 7.5 x 4.5"

3. *KHALTA*. Yomut; 1st quarter, 20th c. Silk lacing stitch on cotton; local block-printed cotton lining. 4.25 x 3.5"

6. *KHALTA*. Yomut, dated 1954. Silk lacing stitch on cotton; loop-manipulation trim; plain cotton lining. 8 x 5"

6.

7.

1.

2.

3.

4.

5.

SMALL BAGS Turkmen

Russian teapots (*chainik*) such as the one shown in fig. 2 were specifically made for export to Central Asia. The pattern on this teapot was very popular, and archival photographs show it being used in both teahouses and private homes (see fig. 1, page 31 and fig. 1, page 278). Small hollow gourds (fig. 3) of various shapes were used to hold a mixture of finely ground fresh tobacco leaves, slaked lime, and wood ash called *naswar*. Men would visit the teahouses with their tobacco gourds and small bags of tea (*chai khalta*) and spend hours socializing with friends.

1, 4, 5, 8. *CHAI KHALTAS.* Ersari Turkmen, 1st quarter, 20th c. Silk lacing stitch on cotton; loop-manipulation trim; cotton linings. (figs. 1, 4) 6 x 5"; (fig. 5) 7 x 6"; (fig. 8) 7.5 x 5.5"

2. TEAPOT. Gardner Manufacturer, Moscow, Russia, early 20th c. Porcelain with hand-painted design; Gardner stamp on bottom; metal spout repair (see fig. 5, page 278). 4 x 6.5"

3. *NASWAR* GOURD. Turkmen or Uzbek, mid-20th c. Gourd with painted design; stopper with silk tassel. 4 x 1.5" (without tassels)

6, 7. MINIATURE DOUBLE-BAGS. Turkmen, date unknown. (fig. 6) wool and cotton appliqué on cotton; 10.5 x 3.5"; (fig. 7) wool and silk lacing stitch on cotton; plain cotton lining; 6.5 x 2.25"

6.

7.

8.

5.

TURKMEN BAGS (*Bokche*)

Embroidered envelope-shaped bags such as these were used by the Turkmen to hold personal possessions and, at times, flatbread. They varied in size from very small ones to large felt storage bags (see figs. 4 and 5, page 227).

1, 2. *BOKCHE* (front and back). Yomut Turkmen, c. 1920s–30s. Silk and cotton lacing and chain stitch on silk and cotton; loop-manipulation trim; cotton and silk tassels; printed-cotton lining. 16 x 10" as shown

3, 4, 6. *BOKCHES*. Turkmen, mid-20th c. Silk embroidery on cotton; silk velvet; loop-manipulation trim; cotton linings. (fig. 3) 11 x 12"; (fig. 4) 11 x 11"; (fig. 6) 7 x 5"

5. *BOKCHE* (back). Turkmen, early 20th c. Silk lacing stitch on imported wool broadcloth; cotton lining. 12 x 12"

7. *BOKCHE*. Turkmen, early 20th c. Silk embroidery on imported wool broadcloth, cotton, and silk; loop-manipulation trim; cotton lining. 17.5 x 11.5"

6.

7.

1.

2.

3.

KYRGYZ BAGS

Archival photographs show teardrop-shaped bags such as those shown in figs. 1 and 2 hanging from the lattice framework inside Kyrgyz tents. Fig. 4 (and 5) was made from pieces of felt that were cut into the desired shapes then stitched together (often referred to as a "felt mosaic"). The same technique was used to make Kyrgyz felt carpets (*shyrdak*) such as the one shown in fig. 3.

1. BAG. Kyrgyz, early 20th c. Silk and wool lacing and chain stitch on imported wool broadcloth; cotton backing with pouch; cotton fringe. 17 x 15"

2. BAG. Kyrgyz, early 20th c. Silk lacing and chain stitch on velvet; red cotton trim (probably not original); coarse natural felt backing; fringe missing. 14 x 11.5"

3. KYRGYZ FAMILY. Tekes Valley, c. 1935. Sayjan Beg, a Kyrgyz chieftain (center), with his family. Seated to his right is a Kazakh woman, the family "nanny," wearing a traditional headdress (*kimeshek*). The *beg*'s mother is in the checkered dress. A felt rug (*shyrdak*) covers the floor, a woven-pile carpet and striped *dastarkhan* lie on top of it, a Russian samovar is in the foreground, and bedding quilts (*kurpa*) are stacked against the wall. Photograph by Edward Murray.

4, 5. *BOKCHE* (back and front). Kyrgyz, mid-20th c. Red, yellow, and undyed brown wool felt with wool embroidery over the seams. (fig. 4) 34 x 22" as shown; (fig. 5) 22 x 22" as shown

6. KYRGYZ MEN. Central Asia, 1931. An embroidered felt hanging covers the yurt entrance. Photograph by Walter Bosshard.

4.

5.

6.

STORAGE BAGS (*Napramach*)

Traditionally, long storage bags such as these (*napramach, mapramach, mafrash*) were made of woven wool pile. More recently, the bag faces and ends were embroidered on sturdy cotton and the back and bottom made from coarse, flat-weave striped cotton. The classic octagon *gol* motifs (figs. 1–3) remained basically the same. In figs. 4 and 5 the *gols* have been replaced by swirling sun disks, often seen on Lakai embroideries (see fig. 3, page 206).

Napramaches were placed along the back wall of a yurt or house and formed a base for the family's bedding quilts, which were stacked on top in a pile called a *chuk* (see fig. 5, page 209 and fig. 3, page 226).

1–3. ***NAPRAMACH.*** Probably Uzbek-Lakai, 3rd quarter, 20th c. Silk and wool chain stitch and cross-stitch on cotton; woven striped-cotton back; unlined. (fig. 1) 14 x 43 x 10"; (fig. 2) 16 x 43 x 10"; (fig. 3) 16 x 38 x 11"

4, 5 ***NAPRAMACH* FACES.** Probably Uzbek Lakai, 3rd quarter, 20th c. Silk couching, chain stitch, and cross-stitch on cotton; woven and embroidered trims; cotton fringe; cotton backing. (fig. 4) 22 x 39"; (fig. 5) 18 x 39"

4.

5.

1.

PATCHWORK (Caroq)

Patchwork (caroq, kurok) not only recycled pieces of material into something functional and aesthetically pleasing, it also possessed powerful protective and auspicious properties. Cloth used on a special occasion, from a respected person, or from a woman with many children was often incorporated. The intricate patterns of multicolored fabrics, usually composed with many small talismanic triangles, were thought to confuse evil spirits and drive them away. A family sleeping under caroq quilts and wall hangings could feel quite secure from the Evil Eye.

1. **QUILT.** Uzbekistan, 3rd quarter, 20th c. Printed and plain cotton (most of the fabrics appear to have been printed in Uzbek textile combines); embroidered fragments; machine-embroidered trim; printed-cotton lining. 74 x 64"

2. **HANGING.** Probably Afghanistan, 1st quarter, 20th c. Cotton, silk, and imported wool broadcloth; silk cross-stitch; printed-cotton lining. 22 x 25"

3. **HANGING.** Uzbekistan, mid-20th c. Printed and plain cotton, adras ikat; silk fringe; printed-cotton lining. 32 x 32"

4. **HANGING.** Uzbekistan, mid-20th c. Printed and plain cotton, silk ikat, silk velvet, artificial silk jacquard border; silk fringe; printed-cotton lining. 36 x 32"

5. **SEWING QUILTS.** Uzbekistan, c. 1930s. These women are probably working in a Soviet-organized workshop or cooperative making patchwork (caroq) bedding quilts (kurpa). Photograph by Max Penson.

6. **HANGING.** Uzbekistan, 2nd quarter, 20th c. Plain cotton, adras ikat; silk chain stitch embroidery on wool; unlined. 24 x 24"

2.

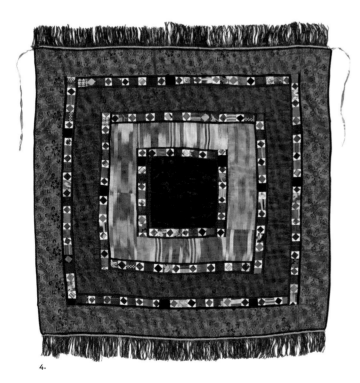

3.

5.

4.

6.

1.

2.

PATCHWORK (*Caroq*)

The quilt top shown in fig. 1 is composed of 148 different late nineteenth-century Russian roller-printed cotton fabrics, many of which appear to have been unused. (Only the ikat central square is not original to the piece.) This is highly unusual. Perhaps the woman who made it had access to fabrics left over from a robe-making workshop or samples from an importer of Russian cloth—or she may have had many friends and relatives who contributed.

1. QUILT TOP. Uzbekistan, late 19th c. Russian roller-printed and plain cotton; hand-stitched; unlined. Rows of triangles are a typical Central Asian quilt pattern device and are used as a talisman (like the cloth triangle amulet, *doga*). It is also a favorite pattern among American quilters, who call it "flying geese." 80 x 80"

2. HANGING. Uzbekistan, 3rd quarter, 20th c. Printed and plain cotton, silk jacquard; cotton fringe with glass beads; printed-cotton lining; machine-embroidered trim. 31 x 29"

3. UZBEK FAMILY. Uzbekistan, c. 1930s–40s. *Caroq* and printed whole-cloth quilts (including a faux-ikat and the same floral print as fig. 4, page 262) are in the stacks of bedding shown here. Quilts (*kurpa*) were neatly folded and stored in a pile along a wall of a house or tent. The stack of bedding, called a *chuk*, was a status symbol of sorts—the higher the pile, the more prosperous the family. This was obviously a well-off family with a radio, phonograph, and Russian samovar. Photograph by Max Penson.

3.

1.

2.

3.

BEDDING QUILTS (*Kurpa*)

A typical Central Asian home, whether tent or house, had little furniture besides a few storage chests and perhaps a low table. Pillows served as seating. Family and guests slept on thickly padded reversible quilts (*kurpa*) laid out on the floor. Long, narrow ones (fig. 3) served as both bottom and top quilt when folded in half. When not in use, bedding quilts were carefully folded and stacked against a wall. The stack (*chuk*) might be decorated with embroideries such as the ones shown on pages 236–37.

Today *kurpas* are still very much a part of everyday life. The bazaars are well stocked with satin and plush quilts (fig. 4).

1. A MOTHER AND A CHILD. Uzbekistan, late 1940s. A faux-ikat *kurpa*. Photograph by Max Penson.

2. KURPAS. Uzbekistan, 3rd quarter, 20th c. A stack of printed *kurpas*. Factory-made cotton fabric, probably produced in Uzbekistan. Faux-ikat prints were popular for whole-cloth quilts (see page 272).

3. *CAROQ KURPA*. Uzbekistan, mid-20th c. Printed and plain cotton; printed-cotton lining. 140 x 42"

4. KURPA BAZAAR. Tashkent, Uzbekistan, 2010. Stacks of plush and satin quilts, probably made from imported fabric.

4.

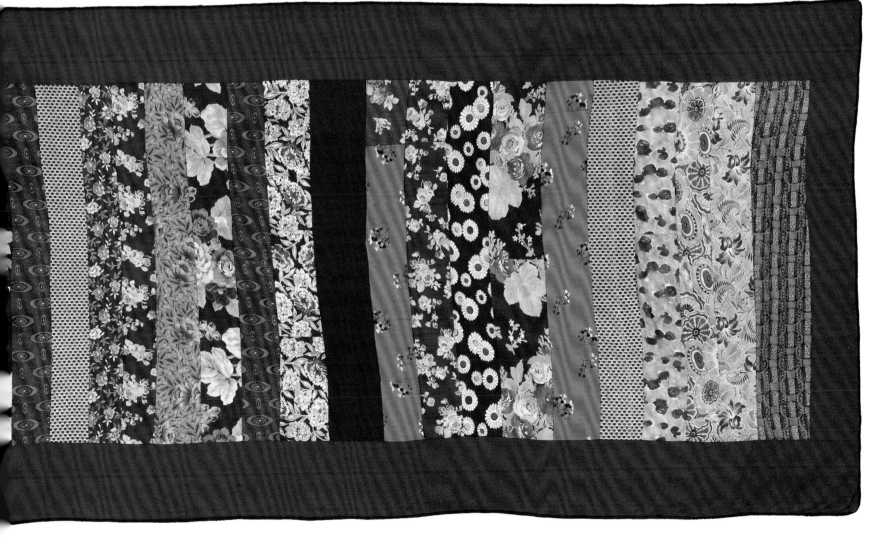

SEGUSHA AND BUGJAMA

Segusha, or *saye gosha* (figs. 1–5), are V-shaped embroideries used to embellish the *chuk* (bedding stack). They were usually part of a larger piece of cloth (fig. 4) that was laid between the quilts with the decorative embroidery hanging down in front. With time, the plain red cotton or wool cloth (red was the usual color) was often discarded and only the embroidery retained.

A *bugjama*, or *bugzhoma*, was used to wrap clothing and bedding (figs. 6 and 7 show a complete *bugjama*). These days far more *segusha* and *bugjama* corners survive than complete pieces.

1. **SEGUSHA.** Uzbek, 2nd quarter, 20th c. Silk couching on cotton; silk fringe with glass beads; printed-cotton lining. 14 x 43" as shown

2. **SEGUSHA.** Uzbek, mid-20th c. Silk embroidery on cotton; glass beads; silk cross-stitch trim; braided netting with metal spangles; unlined. 12 x 36" as shown

3. **SEGUSHA.** Uzbek, 2nd quarter, 20th c. Silk chain stitch; silk braided netting; silk tassels with glass beads; plain-cotton lining. 9 x 36" as shown

4. **SEGUSHA.** Uzbekistan, 3rd quarter, 20th c. Silk couching and chain stitch on cotton; chain-stitch trim; silk fringe with glass beads and metal spangles; printed-cotton lining. 47 x 47"

5. **SEGUSHA.** Uzbekistan, dated 1984. Silk cross-stitch and Lurex on cotton; silk braided netting; tassels with glass beads; red cotton lining. The words translate as "Unforgettable Youth." 30 x 38"

6, 7. **BUGJAMA.** Uzbekistan, 3rd quarter, 20th c. Silk couching on cotton; silk embroidered trim; silk braided netting, tassels with glass beads; faux-ikat cotton lining. (fig. 6) as it would appear when in use; (fig. 7) open; 78 x 78"

4.

5.

6.

7.

Старая Бухара.
Угощеніе пловомъ во дворцѣ
Эмира бухарскаго въ Керминѣ.

1.

2.

3.

SPREADS (*Dastarkhan*)

The term "*dastarkhan*" is used in much the same way as the English noun "spread." It can refer to the cloth on which a meal is laid, or the meal itself. The cloth might be woven, embroidered, or perhaps block-printed (see fig. 9, page 255). It could be long enough for a banquet, or small enough for a merchant in his stall to serve some tea and refreshments. Western travelers often recount the many (at times, too many) *dastarkhans* that were so hospitably offered them by *begs* and villagers alike. British politician Henry Norman, M.P., wrote this description of his reception at the Ark in Bukhara: ". . . a most picturesque *dastarkhan*, or spread, of sweetmeats of every kind was on the table, too obviously the prelude to a corresponding feast."[3]

3 Henry Norman, *All the Russias* (New York: Charles Scribner's Sons, 1902), 305.

1. "OLD BUKHARA." Kermine, Uzbekistan, c. 1910. Russian period postcard. The words read: "Old Bukhara. Refreshments pilaf in [the] palace [of the] emir of Bukhara at Kermine." This was one of the emir's country palaces. Kermine (also called Kermina and now known as Navoi) is about seventy miles northeast of Bukhara. The dignitaries are seated inside a huge tent with brightly colored cloth appliqué hangings, a *dastarkhan* laid out before them.[4]

4 A color photograph of a very similar Bukharan tent is shown in Johannes Kalter and Margareta Pavaloi, *Uzbekistan: Heirs to the Silk Road* (London: Thames & Hudson, 1997), 196.

2. "TYPES OF CENTRAL ASIA." c. 1910. Russian period postcard. An imported porcelain teapot and bowl, water ewer, melons, flatbread, and hookah are laid out on the *dastarkhan*.

3. *DASTARKHAN*. Uzbekistan, 3rd quarter, 20th c. Wool flat-weave; three joined strips with multicolored wool embroidery and tassels. 74 x 34"

4. *DASTARKHAN*. Central Asia, mid 20th c. Weft-patterned cotton. It appears that this was made up from factory-woven cloth. At some point, this piece was also used as a hanging. 67 x 105"

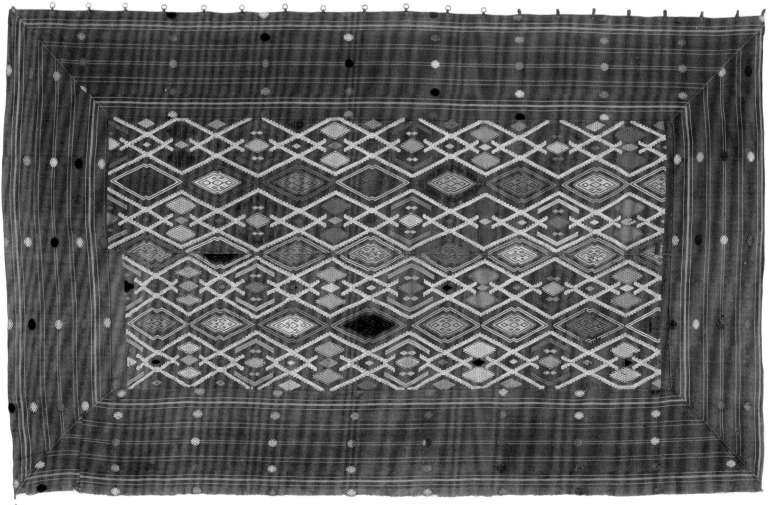

4.

6

ANIMAL TRAPPINGS

"For coloring, the saddlery bazaar ranked high. The wooden saddles, with their pommel in front, painted in a species of lacquer, whose glorious reds shone amid the various inlaid designs . . . The horse trappings, sufficient to deck a horse from head to tail, were of leather, covered with metal ornaments . . . coloured bosses, beads, feathers; nothing omitted that could make a pony as gay as a macaw."
—Ella Christie, *Through Khiva to Golden Samarkand, 1925*[1]

The horse enabled the Mongol hordes to conquer most of Eurasia, giving rise to a horse culture among nomadic peoples that continues to this day. The Turkmen, Kyrgyz, and Kazakhs bred horses well-suited for their needs and environments: Turkmen horses for their speed and stamina (necessary for long-distance raiding parties, called *alamans*) and for their refined beauty; the considerably smaller Kyrgyz horses for their toughness, endurance, and sure-footedness (traits needed for rugged mountain terrains); and the hardy, swift, muscular Kazakh horse for life on the steppes. A fine horse was the pride and joy of every man, whether nomad or settled, and no man would walk even a short distance if he could ride.[2] Most families, except for the very poorest, owned at least one horse. The khans had stables full—for their own use and for presenting as gifts.

The basic trappings for a horse consisted of a saddle blanket, saddle pad, saddle, girth, bridle, and various neck ornaments. The blanket had a trapezoidal shape with a straight front and flaring sides. It could be as plain as tan wool flannel with an underlay of felt, or as costly as crimson silk velvet, elaborately embroidered with gold and silver, and backed with silk ikat. The latter were made in the khan's workshops for his own stable of horses and for use as gifts to officials and visiting dignitaries—at times with the horse as well. The Turkmen generally made their saddle blankets out of knotted wool pile with traditional patterns, while Kyrgyz blankets were embroidered felt or made from coarsely woven, felt-backed cotton or wool. The saddle was cushioned by a saddle pad that rested on top of the blanket. A fanlike embroidery with tassels that extended from the back of the saddle pad added even more embellishment. The saddle itself was usually made of painted wood, sometimes with ornate designs, and a small decorative saddle cover might be placed over it. The girth could be a simple leather strap or a richly embroidered cloth belt. Bridles, neck collars, and breastplates might be so encrusted with gilt ornaments, turquoise, and carnelians that they would cost as much as the horse.

Camels (the two-humped Bactrian was the most prevalent Central Asian camel) were also decked out with sets of trappings during migrations and for wedding ceremonies. In a Turkmen wedding procession, the camels' flanks might be decorated with pentagonal wool-pile weavings (*asmalyk*), or colorful patchwork hangings (*kuroma*). Smaller versions called *duye dizlyk* were tied around their knees. A long trapping (*duye bashlyk*), often made of patchwork, rested on the camel's head and draped down both sides of its neck. The bride would be ensconced in a specially constructed tentlike litter (*kejebe*, see fig. 2, page 245) atop the camel's back. Female relatives and friends would also ride on camels, while the men were on horseback. Lots of little bells attached to the camels announced the approaching procession.

The spring migration of the Kyrgyz to their high summer pastures (*jailo'o*) was a cause for great celebration. Symbolically it marked a time of rebirth, of life's eternal cycle. Traditionally, everyone dressed in their best clothes, and a newly married young woman, resplendent in her wedding garb, would ride the lead camel or horse. The animals too would wear their finest trappings. It was said to be quite a spectacular sight.

---

1 Traveler, gardener, and fellow of the Royal Scottish Geographical Society, Ella Christie made two trips to Central Asia, one in 1910 and another in 1912.

2 In 1935 Edward Murray, an American teacher at Roberts College in Istanbul, spent the summer with Kyrgyz nomads in the Tekes Valley. At one point his Kyrgyz guide pointed to a yurt a hundred yards away and summoned a servant to bring their horses. Murray spoke up, "But we can easily walk." The guide replied in amazement, "And why? Have we not horses? Are we servants?" Murray was careful after that never to jeopardize his reputation by being seen on foot.

1.

2.

HORSE TRAPPINGS

A man's horse was often his most prized possession, especially if it was an Akhal Tekke, the renowned Turkmen purebred. For special occasions, men decked their horses with large ornamental horse covers, saddle bolsters, headdresses, and bridles—trappings that also imparted prestige to the owner. In 1924 the Austrian adventurer Gustav Krist was befriended by a chief of the Yomut Turkmen and lived with his tribe for a time. He wrote, "Second only to his love of hospitality is the Turkoman's love of his horse. He may live in rags himself; his horse will be covered in costly saddlecloths, while its harness and saddle gleam bright with silver platings. The favorite horse is also housed in the family yurt."[1]

1 Gustav Krist, *Alone through the Forbidden Land: Journeys in Disguise through Soviet Central Asia* (London: Faber and Faber, 1938), 44. During World War I, Krist was a private in the Austro-Hungarian army. He was wounded and captured by the Russians on the eastern front and interned in various prisoner-of-war camps in Turkestan, where he was eventually freed by the Bolsheviks. He engaged in numerous escapades while there, before settling in Vienna in 1926.

1. HORSE COVER. Kyrgyz, early 20th c. Wool lacing and chain stitch on handwoven cotton; woven wool trim and fringe; Russian printed- and striped-cotton lining. 50 x 71" as shown

2. HORSE COVER. Uzbek, 2nd half, 19th c. Silk chain stitch and gold metallic stitches on imported red wool broadcloth; silk tassels, fringe, netting; narrow chain-stitched border embroidered directly on the piece. 54 x 59" as shown

3. SADDLE GEAR. Samarkand, Uzbekistan, 1871–72. This elaborate cover was probably embellished with gold embroidery. Photograph from the Turkestan Album.

4. SADDLE PAD SKIRT. Uzbek, 2nd quarter, 20th c. Silk couching and chain stitch on cotton; silk fringe; unlined. This piece would have been attached to the back edge of the saddle pad.[2] 12 x 44"

2 Color photographs of two saddle bolsters with skirts are shown in Kalter and Pavaloi, *Uzbekistan*, 173.

5. SELLING SADDLE CLOTHS. Samarkand bazaar, 1871–72. Saddle cloths; bolsters; saddle pad with skirt; wooden saddles; girths; stirrups, etc. Photograph from the Turkestan Album.

6. HORSE COVER (*dauri*). Uzbek, border dated 1970. Five joined wool flat-weave strips woven in the *gajeri* technique; narrow woven wool border; braided-wool fringe and tassels; machine-embroidered partial *suzani* lining. 54 x 64"

3.

5.

6.

4.

1.

CAMEL TRAPPINGS

These trappings were made to adorn the camels in a Turkmen bridal procession. The piece shown in fig. 1, called a *duye bashlyk*, rested on the camel's head, with the patchwork panels hanging down on either side of its neck. Fig. 3, a *kuroma*, is one of a pair of trappings that hung along each flank. Trappings were usually backed with a variety of different fabrics, such as Russian printed cotton; handwoven striped *alacha*; or local block-printed *chit* (see figs. 6 and 7, page 247).

1. CAMEL TRAPPING (*duye bashlyk*). Probably Yomut Turkmen, early 20th c. Russian printed and plain cotton; imported wool broadcloth; silk; Russian printed-cotton lining. The feathers, buttons, triangles, and patchwork are all talismanic. The Turkey-red rectangular fabric at the base of the trapping is part of a Russian scarf. 87 x 73"

2. TURKMEN WEDDING. Central Asia, 1924. The bride sits inside a tentlike structure (*kejebe*). Woven pile carpets are wrapped around its base and a pair of wool *asmaylks* hang on each side of the camel. A *duye bashlyk* is draped across its neck. The men wear traditional sheepskin hats (*telpek*) Photograph by Hudaibergen Divonov.

"... the men were grouped, mostly wearing their white fur caps in honour of the festival ... many of them were taking trouble to curb their horses—Akhal-Tekke— whilst dozens of camels, festively adorned, yawned appallingly loud and shrill. All around stood a whole host of women from the neighborhood ... their long robes, scarlet and wine red ... their tall crowns shimmering with silver and precious stones ... Everyone was waiting eagerly for ... the new arrivals who came from the bridegroom's aul ... Some approached with rhythmic majesty on their high, four-legged ships of the deserts ... some came galloping on their swift thoroughbred horses, and some like a whirlwind on their bicycles.

"... But inside, in the unsightly clay hut that belonged to all this, crouched a little trembling girl, hardly more than a child ... the bride was carried out into the courtyard, now wrapped like a parcel in the blanket and carpet ... was placed on a camel ... and the young thing rode at the head of the newly formed cavalcade, which started to move forwards slowly and solemnly, on to a totally new, unknown life in an absolutely strange aul."
—Fannina W. Halle, *Women in the Soviet East*, 1938

3. CAMEL TRAPPING (*kuroma*). Yomut, early 20th c. Wool embroidery on imported wool broadcloth; Russian printed-cotton lining. 33 x 42"

2.

3.

1.

2.

3.

4.

CAMEL TRAPPINGS

The photograph is of a Tekke Turkmen family sitting inside their tent dressed in their best clothes. Sunlight streams in through the spoked wooden roof wheel at the top of the tent (see fig. 6, page 209), making a pattern on the woven wool carpet. The latticework walls are hung with patchwork camel trappings (fig. 8) and a wool-pile trapping (center).

1. CAMEL TRAPPING (*asmalyk*). Turkmen, 1st half, 20th c. Factory-made cotton; handwoven wool trim; wool fringe; Russian printed-cotton lining. This is a very plain example of the traditional trapezoid-shaped flank decoration called an *asmalyk*. Always made in pairs, these trappings were woven, embroidered, or appliquéd. 41 x 54"

2, 3. TALISMANIC TRAPPING PATCHES. Yomut Turkmen, early 20th c. Imported wool broadcloth on cotton; glass beads; silk embroidery; printed- and checked-cotton linings. (fig. 2) 3.5 x 4"; (fig.3) 5 x 5"

4. TURKMEN FAMILY. Tekke Turkmen, 1911. Photograph by Prokudin-Gorskii.

5–7. BACKING FABRICS. Tekke Turkmen, early 20th c. Block-printed cottons (*chit*); handwoven cotton check; natural dyes. Backing fabrics from fig. 8. (figs. 5, 6) 3.5 x 3.5"; (fig. 7) 10 x 8"

8. CAMEL TRAPPING (*kuroma*). Tekke Turkmen, early 20th c. Handwoven silk stripes and checks, imported wool broadcloth; silk embroidery and fringe; block-printed cotton lining (fig. 7). One from a pair of flank trappings. 42 x 56"

6.

5.

7.

8.

1.

2.

3.

4.

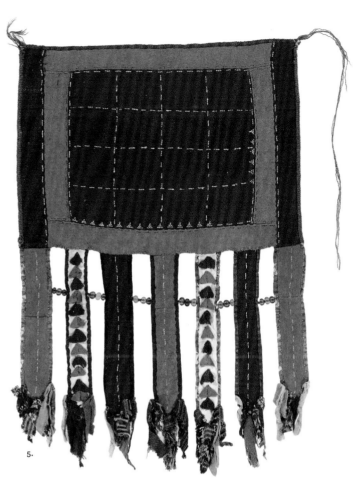

5.

CAMEL KNEE TRAPPINGS

The camels in a wedding procession had their forelegs decorated with small trappings called *duye dizlyk*, which looked like miniature flank covers. They could be woven from wool pile or sewn from cloth such as these. Strips of various pieces of cloth made up the fringe. Always made in pairs, they were tied just above the knees and often hung with little bells that jingled as the camels walked.

1. **KNEE TRAPPING.** Probably Yomut Turkmen, early 20th c. Silk lacing stitch on imported wool broadcloth; cotton trim; glass beads; Russian printed-cotton lining; ram's horn motif. 16 x 12"

2. **KNEE TRAPPING.** Turkmen, early 20th c. Russian printed-cotton, imported wool broadcloth, handwoven silk-plaid center; Russian printed- and plain-cotton lining. 16 x 12"

3, 5. **KNEE TRAPPINGS.** Probably Yomut, early 20th c. Russian plain and printed cotton, imported wool broadcloth, silk; glass beads; Russian printed- and plain-cotton linings. (fig. 3) 18 x 17"; (fig. 5) 18 x 13"

4. **KNEE TRAPPING.** Turkmen, mid-20th c. Silk and cotton; machine-embroidery; costume jewelry; printed-cotton lining. 23 x 16"

6, 7. **PAIR OF KNEE TRAPPINGS.** Turkmen, early 20th c. Russian plain and printed cotton, imported wool broadcloth; Russian printed-cotton lining. 17 x 14"

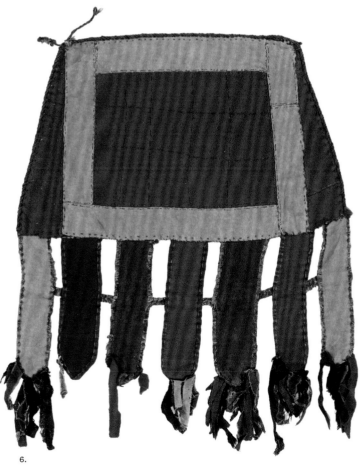

6.

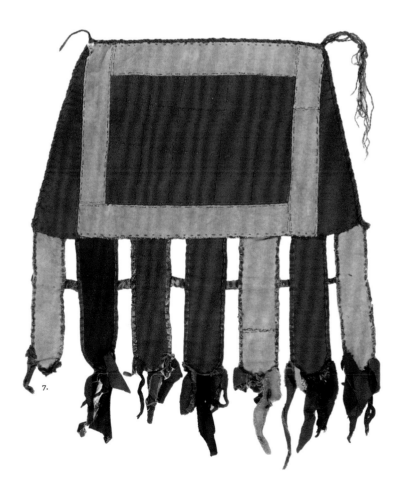

7.

7

CLOTH

The Great Game between Russia and Britain was also played out in the textile bazaars of Central Asia. Russian cloth was obtained by merchants from the huge fair at Nizhny Novgorod (250 miles northeast of Moscow) and transported by camel caravans to Central Asia, while English material entered the region by way of Afghanistan and Persia. Until the mid-nineteenth century, Russian fabrics were cheaper, but the English goods were often of higher quality. However, as Russia gained more and more control, it enacted high tariffs; and by the late nineteenth century, it had a virtual monopoly on all cloth imported into Central Asia.

Nomadic women traditionally wove their own cloth on narrow horizontal ground looms. Wool came from their sheep, camels, and goats, while raw cotton was usually acquired in the market. The fibers were carded, spun, wound, and woven into cloth. Vegetable dyes were used until the introduction of imported synthetic dyes in the late nineteenth century began to replace them. At the same time, inexpensive factory-made cloth from Russia, and to a lesser extent England, was readily available in the bazaars and from peddlers, who traveled to the nomad camps with goods to trade. These imported fabrics—cotton calico and chintz, velvet, felted-wool broadcloth (*banot*), and silk brocades (*parcha*)—began to be preferred over handwoven cloth. As ready-made robes of imported and locally made material (such as striped *alacha,* silk *shohi,* and ikat) could also be bought in the marketplace, nomadic people began dressing more like their settled neighbors. The Turkmen, however, continued to wear their traditional handwoven fabrics—silk *keteni* for women's dresses (see fig. 2, page 48) and striped red *gyrmyzy donlyk* for men's robes (see fig. 4, page 51).

Long-established traditions of fabric-weaving existed in the oasis cities. Small workshops, historically organized like guilds, specialized in the weaving and dying of particular types of cloth, including ikat; rustling plain-weave silk *shohi;* glossy satin-weave silk *atlas* and *khanatlas;* silk warp/cotton weft *adras;* luxurious silk-velvet *baghmal;* multicolored striped *alacha* and *bekasab;* pinstriped silk warp/cotton weft *banoras* (commonly used for *paranjas*); and the staple hand-loomed cotton cloth called *buz, boz, karbos,* or *mata* (widely used for men's shirts and trousers, block-printed *chit,* and the ground cloth of *suzanis*).

By the middle of the nineteenth century, imported fabrics, primarily from Russia, had begun to flood the local markets. In 1860 textiles accounted for 53 percent of Russia's total exports to Central Asia.[1] Block-printers had a difficult time competing with the huge selection of cheap, brightly patterned, roller-printed cotton cloth, called *sitetz* in Russian. They were constrained by a limited selection of natural dyes and the relative crudeness of carved wooden blocks. (In a futile and self-defeating action, the emirate of Bukhara passed a law forbidding the use and sale of aniline dyes.[2]) Archival photographs show people of all social stations wearing factory-printed cotton robes. The designs were not gender-specific—men were just as fond of bold floral prints as women. Even robes made from costly silk were usually lined with Russian printed cloth. (Strict Islamic law forbade men to wear pure silk cloth next to their bodies. This was circumvented by weaving cloth with a silk warp and cotton weft, and it also contributed to the extensive use of inexpensive imported cotton cloth as lining material.) Weavers of *alacha/bekasab* fared better. No imported cloth was equivalent to this striped fabric, with its highly glazed and moiré surface. It remained a favorite material for robes well into the twentieth century, although the number of workshops that produced it decreased dramatically under the Soviets.

During the Soviet era, artisans were collectivized into cooperatives (artels). Production of more labor-intensive and costly fabrics such as *adras* and *baghmal* ikat came to a halt. Large vertical textile combines were built by the Soviets as early as the late 1920s–30s. They produced many of the same types of fabrics that were being imported from Russia, as well as machine-made ikat, faux-ikat, and *bekasab.* Most traditionally made cloth ceased being produced. After the Central Asian republics gained their independence, artisans revived some of the old textile techniques and today, handwoven ikats, including silk-velvet *baghmal,* are once again available.

1 Seymour Becker, *Russia's Protectorates in Central Asia: Bukhara and Khiva, 1865–1924* (Cambridge: Harvard University Press, 1968), 21.

2 Curtis, *Turkestan: The Heart of Asia,* 170.

1.

2.

3.

4.

CHIT PRODUCTION

Before the introduction of machine-printed cloth, the only printed fabrics available were locally produced woodblock prints called *chit*. Homespun, handwoven, plain-weave cotton (*karbos, karbas, karbaz, bos, boz, buz, mata*) was the fabric most frequently used to print on. Vegetable dyes were made from native wild and cultivated plants: shades of red, orange, purple, and brown from madder root (*ruyan*); yellow from larkspur (*isparak*) or the buds of the Japanese pagoda tree (*tukhmak*); black from pomegranate peels (*anor pusti*) or pistachio galls (*buzgunch*). Blocks of indigo (*nil*) were imported from India and Afghanistan. *Kirmiz* (also called cochineal), made from tiny dried scale insects, was imported from Russia and imparted a rich red, but it was used for dyeing silk, not cotton.

1. CLEANING COTTON FROM THE SEEDS. Samarkand, Uzbekistan, 1871–72. Wooden cotton gin (*chirik*) with rollers. Photograph from the Turkestan Album.

2. WOMEN SPINNING COTTON. Marghilan, Uzbekistan, c. 1900. Most raw cotton preparation and spinning was done by women in their homes. The spinning wheel was called a *charkh*. Photograph by Annette Meakin.

3. WORKSHOP FOR PRINTING *CHIT*. Samarkand, 1871–72. The printing workshop was called a *chitkarkhana*. Photograph from the Turkestan Album.

4, 5. *CHIT*. Uzbekistan, early 20th c. Natural dyes (madder red) on *karbos*. (fig. 4) 10.5 x 9"; (fig. 5) backing of camel trapping (see fig. 8, page 247); 3.5 x 3.5"

6. WOODBLOCKS. Uzbekistan, 20th c. Carved hardwood stamps (*kolyb, kolib*). 4.5 x 4.5"; 6 x 1.25"

7. FABRIC PRINTING PRODUCTION. Samarkand, 1871–72. The men who printed the cloth were called *chitkar* or *chitagar*. Photograph from the Turkestan Album.

5.

6.

7.

1.

2.

4.

5.

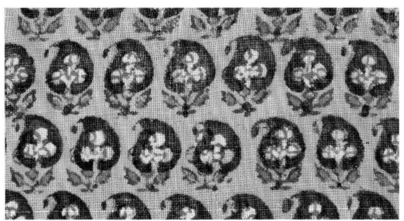

3.

6.

7.

BLOCK-PRINTED COTTON (*Chit*)

Chit was used for household items such as quilts and spreads, and as lining material. Turkmen clothing, particularly *chyrpys*, were often lined with it—as were robes, including costly silk ikats, although these tended to be earlier than ones lined with Russian printed cotton.[1] One seldom comes across garments made entirely from *chit*. Perhaps they were simply worn till no longer serviceable and then the cloth recycled. *Karbos* ranged in quality from the soft, tightly woven cloth used for spreads (fig. 9) and *suzanis* to the coarse *chit* used to back camel trappings (fig. 4). The dervishes in Vereshchagin's painting (see fig. 5, page 31) are wearing robes made from patches of *chit*.

1 Ikat robes lined with *chit* are shown in Sumru Belger Krody, *Colors of the Oasis: Central Asian Ikats* (Washington, DC: The Textile Museum, 2010).

1. *CHIT* SPREAD (detail). Uzbekistan, early 20th c. Center of a large bedspread (*kurpachit*), or cloth on which to serve food (*dastarkhan*). 40 x 43" as shown

2. *CHIT* LINING (detail). Uzbekistan, late 19th c. Madder flowers on resist-printed indigo ground; lining from the sleeve of a late nineteenth-century silk brocade robe. 10 x 8"

3. *CHIT* (detail). Uzbekistan, 1st quarter, 20th c. Five joined panels in a popular pattern; from the front or back of a quilt. 30 x 24" (selvedge to selvedge) as shown

4–6. *CHIT* (details). Uzbekistan, late 19th–early 20th c. (fig. 4) backing of a Turkmen camel trapping, 3.25 x 1.75"; (fig. 5) length of cloth; 14 x 11.5"; (fig. 6) lining of an ikat robe; 3 x 5"; all as shown

7–9. *CHIT* SPREAD (and details). Uzbekistan, early 20th c. This piece could have been used as a *kurpachit* or *dastarkhan*. (fig. 7) 27 x 27"; (fig. 8) 18 x 4.5"; (fig. 9) 81 x 101"

8.

9.

1.

2.

3.

4.

5.

6.

7.

8.

COTTON PRODUCTION Collective Farms (*Kolkhoz*)

By the mid-1880s Russia controlled all of Central Asia and was actively developing wide-scale cotton cultivation. During the late 1920s the Soviets started to collectivize cotton production. Cotton (*pakhta*, or "white gold," as it came to be called) rapidly became a monoculture with disastrous human and environmental consequences.

1. COTTON BOLL PANEL. Uzbekistan, 3rd quarter, 20th c. Silk cross-stitch on cotton; silk fringe with glass beads; printed-cotton lining. 11 x 42" as shown

2. SOWING. Uzbekistan, c. 1920s–30s. Collective farmers sowing the field with horse-drawn seeder. Photograph by Max Penson.

3. WATER DISTRIBUTOR IN COTTON FIELD. Uzbekistan, c. 1920s–30s. The man responsible for controlling the flow of the irrigation channels (*arik*) was called a *mirab*—his was one of the most important positions in the community. Photograph by Max Penson.

4. COTTON-PICKERS. Uzbekistan, c. 1930s. An iconic image of a woman holding a bundle of cotton on her head. By this time, cropped vests such as these had become part of women's national dress. Photograph by Max Penson.

5. IN THE COTTON FIELD. Uzbekistan, c. 1930s. Passing the banner on to the brigade that picked the most cotton. Photograph by Max Penson.

6. TRANSPORTATION OF COTTON. Uzbekistan, 1949. Kaganovich collective farm. The notorious Lazar Kaganovich was one of Stalin's right-hand men and instrumental in implementing and overseeing collectivization. Photograph by Max Penson.

7. COTTON COLLECTION POINT. Uzbekistan, c. 1930s. Photograph by Max Penson.

8. SORTING THE SEED COTTON. Uzbekistan, c. 1930s. Photograph by Max Penson.

9. RED SQUARE. Tashkent, Uzbekistan, c. 1930s. Women in ikat dresses holding cotton bolls (and a picture of Stalin) during a rally in Tashkent's Red Square. Photograph by Max Penson.

9.

1.

2.

3.

4.

5.

6.

7.

COTTON PRODUCTION Collective Farms (*Kolkhoz*)

In 1939 the Great Ferghana Canal was constructed to carry water to the cotton-growing regions of the Ferghana Valley. An estimated 160,000 Uzbeks and 20,000 Tajiks built the 168-mile canal in 45 days, mostly with picks and shovels. In Central Asia, extensive irrigation, heavy use of chemical fertilizers and pesticides, collectivized labor, railways, construction of cotton-processing plants, and to some extent farm machinery all enabled the Soviet Union to reach its goal of becoming cotton self-sufficient.

1. NIGHT TRACTOR. Uzbekistan, c. 1930s. By day or by night, the fields must get plowed. Photograph by Max Penson.

2. TRACTOR. Russia, c. 1930. Designed by S. Burylin. Printed cotton. By the early 1930s, it became apparent that agitprop textiles celebrating industry with motifs such as tractors and gears were not well received by the workers for whom they were designed. These fabrics were satirized in an article published in *Pravda*, September 1933, titled "Tractor in Front, Grain Harvester Behind."[2]

2 G. Ryklin, "Speredi traktorszadi kombain," *Pravda*, September 6, 1933, quoted in Tatiana Strizhenova, *Soviet Costume and Textiles 1917–1945* (Paris: Flammarion, 1991), 199.

3. ON COTTON FIELD. Uzbekistan, c. 1930s. Two men wearing traditional Kyrgyz felt hats ride a cotton-seeding machine. Photograph by Max Penson.

4. COTTON COMBINE. Russia, 1958. Cover of the Soviet magazine *Science and Life*. The Soviet-built factory Tashselmash in Tashkent, was the largest producer of cotton harvesters in the USSR.

5. TRACTOR PLOWING COTTON FIELD. Uzbekistan, c. 1930s. Photograph by Max Penson.

6. COLLECTIVE FARM (*kolkhoz*). Kazakhstan, 1931. Period Russian postcard. Machine for cotton harvesting with long hoses used to suck up the cotton bolls.

7. GATHERING COTTON. Russia, early 1930s. Designed by M. Nazarevskaya. Printed cotton sateen; agitprop pattern with cotton-harvesting machine (fig. 6).

8. TRUCKS WITH COTTON. Uzbekistan, 1950. A cotton convoy with banners celebrating the thirty-third anniversary of the "Great October Socialist Revolution" and "Cotton delivery ahead of schedule." Photograph by Max Penson.

9. ON A STORAGE CENTER. Uzbekistan, c. 1930s. Mountain of cotton. Photograph by Max Penson.

8.

9.

1.

2.

3.

4.

5.

6.

7.

8.

TEXTILE COMBINES Printed Cloth

As early as the 1920s and '30s, the Soviets built large vertical textile factories (combines) in Uzbekistan, Tajikistan, and Kyrgyzstan. Printed cotton was produced in the Uzbek cities of Tashkent, Ferghana, Bukhara, and in Dushanbe, Tajikistan. Combines in Marghilan, Uzbekistan; Leninabad (Khujand), Tajikistan; and Osh, Kyrgyzstan, all printed silk. The fabrics on this spread most likely came from these factories.

1. SOVIET EMBLEM. Moscow, 1926. From a booklet of Soviet "clip art" titled "POLYGRAF," issued by VSNKH, the "Supreme Council on the National Economy."

2, 4, 5, 7, 8. COTTON FABRICS (details). Probably Uzbekistan, 3rd quarter, 20th c. (fig. 2) cotton bolls, printed robe; 19 x 15"; (fig. 4) patchwork quilt; 10 x 8"; (fig. 5) prayer mat lining; 8 x 14"; (fig. 7) quilt; 27 x 12"; (fig. 8) *suzani* lining; 25 x 23"

3. SILK FABRIC. Osh, Kyrgyzstan, 3rd quarter, 20th c. Length of fabric with attached label from "VLKSM" silk combine built in 1926 in Osh. 19 x 11"

6. A TEXTILE COMBINE. Tashkent, Uzbekistan, 1938. The Tashkent Textile Combine, originally called the J. V. Stalin Textile Combine, began operating in 1934. It was the largest cotton-textile enterprise in Central Asia and one of the largest in the entire USSR. Photograph by Max Penson.

9. A TEXTILE COMBINE. Tashkent, 1938. Probably the Tashkent Textile Combine. Photograph by Max Penson.

9.

1.

2.

3.

4.

TEXTILE COMBINES Faux-Ikat

The Soviets equipped the Central Asian textile combines with machinery similar to that used in Russian plants. At first, cloth was printed with engraved copper rollers. In the late 1950s flatbed screen-printing was probably introduced. (A Soviet photo from 1965 of the "im. Kirova" combine in Marghilan shows a modern flatbed operation.) Mills from Ivanovo and Moscow sent specialists to train local workers. For the most part, the patterns continued to look similar to their Russian counterparts, except for the large number of faux-ikat designs, which were very popular in Central Asia.

1. A TEXTILE MILL. Probably Tashkent Textile Combine, Uzbekistan, c. 1938. The Russian man is operating a large roller-printing machine. The cloth being printed is the same pattern as fig. 4 (see also fig. 3, page 233). Photograph by Max Penson.

2. COTTON FABRIC. Tashkent, c. 1983. This faux-ikat cloth bears the Tashkent Textile Combine stamp. Probably screen-printed, it is the same pattern as the women are holding in fig. 5.

3, 4. *KURPA.* c. 1960s–70s. The faux-ikat printed cotton was probably produced in either the Tashkent or Dushanbe Textile Combine. The faux-ikat cloth dates from the 1960s–70s, while the floral print was probably first produced in the late 1930s. (fig. 3) 98 x 74"; (fig. 4) roller-printed cotton; Tashkent Textile Combine; detail; 25 x 16"

5. TASHKENT TEXTILE COMBINE. Tashkent, c. 1983. Two women workers examining a length of faux-ikat cloth with the same pattern as fig. 2.

6. IN STORE. Uzbekistan, late 1940s–early '50s. Uzbek men in *bekasab* robes looking at printed home-furnishing fabrics. Photograph by Max Penson.

5.

6.

1.

2.

3.

4.

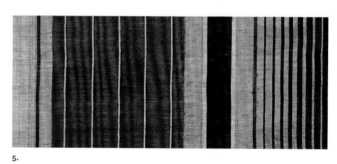

5.

6.

7.

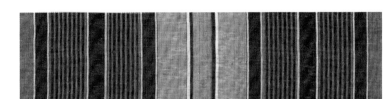

8.

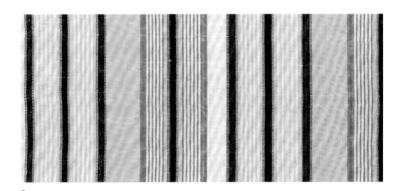

9.

HANDWOVEN CLOTH (*Bekasab/Alacha*)

The words "*bekasab (bekasam)*" and "*alacha*" can be confusing. "*Bekasab*" is a late nineteenth- and twentieth-century term, while "*alacha*" has been in use for at least four hundred years. They basically refer to the same type of cloth—a glazed silk warp/cotton weft striped fabric. It was handwoven in what is now Uzbekistan and a part of Tajikistan. The terms are regional: "*Bekasab*" was used in the eastern silk-weaving centers of Ferghana, Marghilan, Kokand, Namangan, and Khodjent (Khujand). The cloth was called *alacha* in the south-central textile-weaving areas of Bukhara, Karshi, and Shakhrisabz, and in regions further west, such as Khiva. However, Khivan *alacha* was usually made with a cotton warp and cotton weft.[3] Probably more robes were made from this material than any other. Worn by men, women, and children, the variations in patterns and colors were seemingly endless.

3 For a detailed description of the polishing and weaving process of *alacha* in Khiva, see Richardson, *Qaraqalpaqs of the Aral Delta*.

1. UNWINDING SILK. Samarkand, Uzbekistan, 1871–72. Cocoons are being boiled and the filaments wound on a reel (*charkh*, see fig. 2, page 252). Photograph from the Turkestan Album.

2. LOOM FOR *ALACHA*. Samarkand, 1871–72. Photograph from the Turkestan Album.

3. SELLING SILK. Samarkand, 1871–72. Silk was spun and dyed locally in specialized workshops. Photograph from the Turkestan Album.

4–9. *BEKASAB/ALACHA*. Uzbekistan, c. 1890s-1930s. Lining details from robes shown on pages 39 (fig. 2), 40 (fig. 3), 42 (fig. 1), and 47 (fig. 6). (fig. 4) 3" wide; (figs. 5–7) 8.25" wide; (figs. 8, 9) 12" wide

10. *KUDUNGIARI*. Samarkand, 1871–72. *Kudungiari* were the men who specialized in polishing cloth, usually *bekasab*, *alacha*, and *adras* ikat. The fabric was coated with egg whites or a mixture containing animal sinew, and then either pounded with heavy hardwood hammers (*kudung*) or polished with half-spheres of heavy glass. The result was a crisp, highly glazed finish. A moiré effect was achieved by laying the cloth on a wooden table with rounded hardwood protuberances and pounding it with the hammer.[4] Photograph from the Turkestan Album.

4 This process is described in Henry Lansdell, *Russian Central Asia, Including Kuldja, Bokhara, Khiva and Merv*, vol. 1 (London: Low, Marston, Searle, and Rivington, 1885), 316.

10.

1.

SILK PRODUCTION

Although Central Asia produced silk textiles with imported Chinese thread from about 1000 BCE, it wasn't until the fourth century CE, with the introduction of Chinese silkworms, that sericulture was thought to have begun. Even today the process of making silk remains basically the same. Most silkworms are raised in private homes. The eggs ("grains") are placed inside trays in warm rooms where they hatch. The newborn caterpillars grow quickly on a diet of fresh mulberry leaves and, in four to six weeks, spin their cocoons These are promptly removed, cleaned (fig. 2), sorted, and steamed (or dropped in boiling water) to kill the pupae before they hatch and damage the cocoons. The filaments are then wound into threads (fig. 1). After several more steps, the silk is ready to weave into cloth or to be made into silk floss for embroidery.

1. BOILING COCOONS. Yodgorlik Silk Factory, Marghilan, Uzbekistan, c. 2005. The cocoons float in a cauldron of simmering water as the woman pulls the filaments of several dozen cocoons at a time up and into a wire loop, from which they are wound on a reel by another woman sitting nearby. The boiling water removes the sticky sericin that binds the filaments together.

2. AT WORK. Ferghana, Uzbekistan, c. 1930s. Women cleaning bits of debris from the cocoons. Photograph by Max Penson.

3. COCOONS. Small ceramic Uzbek bowl with cocoons.

4. DYEING SILK THREAD. Ferghana Valley, Uzbekistan, c. 2005. This man is dyeing silk warp threads in a small area adjacent to his home.

5. DRYING OF COCOONS. Uzbekistan, c. 1930s–40s. Soviet collective farm. Photograph by Max Penson.

2.

3.

4.

5.

1.

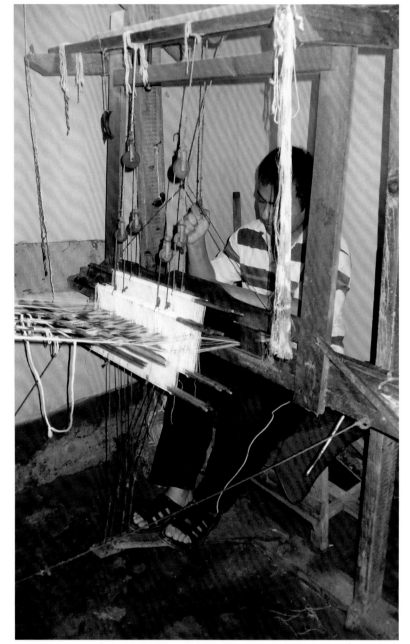

2.

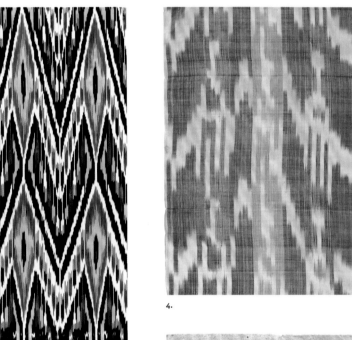

3.

4.

5.

6.

IKAT PRODUCTION

The ikat-weaving process begins with the warping master, who winds the de-gummed silk threads on a huge reel. Once this stage is complete, the warp is removed from the reel and stretched onto a long frame, where a master designer (*abrbandchi*) marks the outlines of the pattern onto the threads. Binders (fig. 6), following the designer's markings, wrap the sections of the warp that will resist the first dye bath. The warp is then taken off the frame, wound onto a pole, and immersed in the first dye bath. When removed from the bath, it is rewound onto the patterning frame and the process is repeated. Once all the colors have been dyed, the wrappings are removed and the resist-dyed warp is carefully unwound from the frame and ready to be set up on a loom (fig. 7). Handlooms are often in private homes (fig. 2) and the warps are installed by loom masters who travel from household to household.

1. **SPRAYING THE WARP.** Yodgorlik Silk Factory, Marghilan, Uzbekistan, 2004. The young woman is using her mouth to spray a fine mixture of flour and water onto the section of warp that is about to be woven. Acting as a spray starch, it helps keep the threads from tangling and breaking.

2. **IKAT WEAVING.** Ferghana Valley, Uzbekistan, 2005. Silk *atlas* ikat being woven on a handloom in a private home.

3–5. **IKAT FABRICS AND LABEL.** Marghilan. Silk ikat fabrics that were produced at the former Atlas combine, a division of which exists today as Yodgorlik. (figs. 3, 5) *Khanatlas* with label dated 1994; 92 x 25" selvedge to selvedge; (fig. 4) *shohi* ikat, Baynalminal division, c. 1960s; 33 x 21" selvedge to selvedge as shown

6. **BINDING THE WARP.** Yodgorlik Silk Factory, 2004. The orange sections have already been dyed. The binders (*abr-bands*) are now removing the wrapping from the next areas to be dyed and rewrapping the orange sections to protect them from the next dye bath.

7. **WEAVING THE WARP.** Yodgorlik Silk Factory, 2004. The dyed warp is strung on the loom and ready to be woven with the plain weft.

8. **IKAT PRODUCTION.** Namangan, Uzbekistan, c. 2008. Silk *khanatlas* ikat is still being produced by Soviet-era machines in small enterprises.

9. *KHANATLAS* **IKAT.** Marghilan, c. 1960s. This all-silk ikat was produced in what was once the huge Atlas Textile Combine. 93 x 32" selvedge to selvedge as shown

7.

8.

9.

1.

IKAT PANELS

Traditionally, ikat cloth was woven by hand in prescribed lengths and narrow widths of approximately eight to twenty-two inches, depending on the size of the loom. In the early 1960s Soviet textile combines began producing ikat fabric on machines that enabled wider widths to be woven. Far less expensive and more readily available, it became popular throughout Central Asia for girls' and women's dresses as well as bedding quilts (*kurpa*).

1. *KURPA.* Probably Bukhara, Uzbekistan, 1st quarter, 20th c. Five joined panels of silk warp/cotton weft satin-weave ikat; printed-cotton lining. Pairs of red *bodum* (almond), green *tumar* (triangular amulets), and pomegranates. 84 x 77"

2. PANEL. Marghilan, Uzbekistan, late 19th–early 20th c. Two joined panels of silk warp/cotton weft satin-weave ikat. 104 x 26"

3. PANEL. Ferghana region, Uzbekistan, late 19th–early 20th c. Silk warp/cotton weft *adras* ikat. 71 x 16" selvedge to selvedge

4. PANEL. Bukhara, 1st quarter, 20th c. Silk warp/cotton weft satin-weave ikat. 93 x 17" selvedge to selvedge

5. PANEL. Marghilan, c. 1960s. Silk warp/silk weft *atlas* ikat. Made in the Baynalminal factory. 96 x 15" selvedge to selvedge

2.

3.

4.

5.

1.

2.

3.

4.

5.

6.

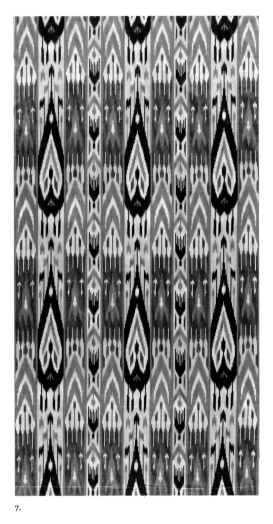

7.

FAUX-IKATS

During the second half of the nineteenth century, when Russian printed cottons were flooding the Central Asian markets, faux-ikats (printed imitations) could be bought in the bazaars for a fraction of the price of the real thing. But it was not until the 1960s, when the Soviet-built textile combines in Uzbekistan and Tajikistan began turning out faux-ikat cotton and silk fabrics, that they really caught on. For the next thirty years, until the combines closed in the early 1990s, faux-ikats (cheaper still than machine-woven *atlas* ikat) were everywhere—as *kurpas* (quilts) in the home and on women's dresses. All widths below are selvedge to selvedge.

1, 9. FAUX-IKAT CLOTH. Tashkent Textile Combine, Uzbekistan, c. 1980s. Details of cotton *kurpas*. (figs. 1, 9) 50 x 30"

2, 8. FAUX-IKAT CLOTH. Dushanbe Textile Combine, Tajikistan, c. 1960s–70s. Details of cotton *kurpas*. (figs. 2, 8) 56 x 28"

3, 6. FAUX-IKAT CLOTH. Uzbekistan or Dushanbe, 1960s–80s. Details of cotton *kurpas*. (figs. 3, 6) 50 x 29"

4, 5. FAUX-IKAT CLOTH. "im. Kirova" silk combine, Marghilan, Uzbekistan, c. 1990. Lengths of silk cloth. The writing on fig. 5 reads: "Uzbekistan 6 Years." (figs. 4, 5) 70 x 37"

7. FAUX-IKAT CLOTH. Marghilan textile combine, c. 1970s. Length of silk cloth. 68 x 38"

10. FAUX-IKAT CLOTH. Leninabad textile combine, Tajikistan c. 1980s. Length of silk cloth. 68 x 36"

8.

9.

10.

8

THE BAZAAR

The old bazaars of Central Asia are best described by travelers who were there:

"The chief articles imported to us are cotton, dry fruit, rice, raw and dyed silks, indigo, dyed and white *baz*, silk *khalats*, half of silk and half of cotton, small caps, known as *tubeti*, silk sashes, turquoises, shawls and furs. But of all the above imported articles, raw cotton occupies the chief place . . . In exchange for the articles we have enumerated, our merchants furnish Central Asia, chiefly through the medium of Bokharians themselves, with chintz, calicoes, muslins, some silk stuffs, broad cloth, brocades, etc. The raw materials are hides, and some metallic productions, such as iron and cast iron." —Nikolai Khanikoff (Russian diplomat), *Bokhara: Its Amir and Its People*, 1845

"Bukhara is the chief point of Central Asiatic trade, and is very important to us, because the state and direction of this trade must govern our further movements in Central Asia . . . Who can guarantee that with our carelessness . . . all the trade with Central Asia will not pass into the hands of the English or the Afghans; and there are signs of that already. In that case we should of course have nothing left to do in Central Asia . . . Even the bare enumeration of countries and goods is enough to confirm my opinion of the commercial importance of the Bukharan market, the yearly transactions of which are estimated at not less than forty million of rubles [about $25,000,000]." —Petrofsky, agent of the Russian Minister of Finance, upon his return from a mission to Bukhara in 1872, as quoted by Eugene Schuyler, *Turkestan*, vol. 2, 1876

"When a Sart wants amusement he turns his steps instinctively to the bazaar; when he wants news of what is going on in the world he is off to the bazaar, and when in fact there is no urgent reason why he should be there, you will find him in the bazaar." —Annette M. B. Meakin, *In Russian Turkestan: A Garden of Asia and Its People*, 1903

"The bustle of life is greatest in the bazaars where all shades of the population of Central and Mid Asia afford an exceedingly picturesque sight in a literal sense of the word. Tadjiks and Usbegs [sic] with their many coloured silk and cotton *khalats* and white-, blue-, or red-striped turbans are in the majority; then there are Kirghiz in fur-dresses with black fur-caps or felt-caps set with coloured ribbons or braids or in camel brown *khalats*. Afghans in snow-white woolen caftans, Jews in *khalats* of one colour with a string around their waists and a small fur-cap, tall Turkomans with the gigantic fur-cap (*chugerma*), Hindoos [sic] with black silk calottes, a motley swarm of riders, pedestrians, *arbas*, caravans of horses, dromedaries, camels and donkeys among which at long intervals a European is seen making his way, or a small procession of calandars, a single dervish, an Arabian lay preacher." —Ole Olufsen, *The Emir of Bokhara and His Country*, 1911

"Each bazaar (*tim*) has its own *Aksakal* [whitebeard] who maintains order among its merchants and artisans. A few of these bazaars have their special articles, thus in Tim-I-Abdullah-Khan they deal in velvet, muslin, brocade, and satin; in another, Tim-I-Tanninga, in silk; in a third, Tim-I-Gilam, in carpets . . . In another street they deal in nothing but Russian manufactured goods of the bright colours known from the annual markets in Central Russia . . . In a very long covered bazaar street ready-made men's dresses are disposed of from the simple grayish brown over-dress of camel's wool (*chapan*) and the thin many coloured cotton *khalat* or *don* to the caftan embroidered with gold, which is worn by those of high rank, and here we also see a splendid display of long boots embroidered with gold and large saddle-cloths for the horses of the well-to-do . . . Here is a sight to tempt the foreigner, namely the most magnificent articles of silk velvet of many, but beautifully arranged colours. As in the case of silk the pieces are always narrow strips not exceeding one foot . . . All the merchants themselves seem very well-to-do . . . It is practically a favor to procure anything even at an absurd price, but their wares are indeed of the best industry of Bokhara." —Ole Olufsen, *The Emir of Bokhara and His Country*, 1911

"The Jews are a very large and important element in the population of Bokhara . . . They are the leading merchants; they control the silk market; they own most of the camel caravans; and are so skillful in dyeing wools and silk that they practically monopolize that business . . . half the Jews you see in the bazaars . . . and elsewhere, are stained up to the knuckles with the dyes they use." —William Eleroy Curtis, *Turkestan: The Heart of Asia*, 1911

"Merchants [in Bukhara] sit cross-legged on the rugs which decorate the floors of their little booths, and their customers either stand in the street or squat down on the threshold . . . Every possible article that a human being can need or desire may be found, from a cake of soap to a sewing machine or a phonograph. The latter articles, with revolvers,

are about the only goods that come from the United States. Nearly everything else is from Russia." —William Eleroy Curtis, *Turkestan: The Heart of Asia*, 1911

"It is not considered the thing for a respectable Sart woman to go to the bazaar. Anything she wants must be bought by her husband or brother." —Paul Nazaroff, *Hunted Through Central Asia*, 1932

"Now I am in all the bustle of the crowd [in Tashkent]: the vendors of sherbert, of mineral water, and the barbers operating at each house corner . . . Outside the bakery an impressive queue waits for the door to open . . . The men are wearing '*khalats*'—wide, quilted robes with vertical stripes of green, mauve, black, and white . . . The large piece of cloth that serves as a belt forms a triangle over the loins . . . A weeping willow bends over the rapid waters of a main *arik*, in which a water-carrier is filling his two buckets suspended from a thick staff: then the water disappears under the platform of a cool *chai-kana*, where skewers of mutton sputter over a brazier." —Ella Maillart, *Turkestan Solo*, 1934

"Behind the Shir-Dar [in Samarkand] we come to a bazaar—a series of arcades under a high domed roof. There is a dense crowd here, Oriental motley; veiled women in the flowing robes of the *paranjas* . . . a few unveiled women wearing coloured velvet skullcaps on their dark hair. But mostly the crowd is male, a dense throng of padded coats, flowered robes, turbans, velvet caps, huge round fur busbies, shaggy sheepskins . . . young Uzbeks, clean-shaven, brightly robed, gay embroidered plush or velvet caps on the backs of their heads. One alleyway of the bazaar is devoted entirely to little open-fronted shops in which old men squat making these caps. There are stacks of caps of all colours piled up on shelves . . . with tassels and embroideries in gold or silver thread; others are very richly and cunningly embroidered in a multitude of coloured silks." —Ethel Mannin, *South to Samarkand*, 1937

"Disappearing too, are the national dress and national customs of the inhabitants. Only a very few old men wear the turban. Only a very few women wear the *paranja* . . . Even the *khalat*, the brightly striped many-coloured robe of Central Asia is rarely to be seen. Only the *tibiteika* survives universally, the little embroidered skullcap." —Fitzroy Maclean, *Back to Bokhara*, 1959

Самаркандъ. Общій видъ Биби-Хана
Samarkand. Ansicht von Bibi-Chan

1.

2.

3.

4.

5.

THE BAZAAR

Always teeming, the nineteenth- and early twentieth-century bazaar (*tim*) was the heartbeat of a city, the business and social center of an urban man's life. Here could be found just about any commodity that Central Asia (and Russia) produced. Men could get away from the crowds in one of the many teahouses, talk with friends, sip green tea, crack sunflower seeds, and perhaps be entertained by a troupe of dancing boys (*bacha*). If hungry, there were flatbread sellers, kebab and steamed dumpling (*manti*) stands, vendors of ice cream (often shaved ice with sweet raisin sauce), and other prepared foods.

1. BIBI-KHANUM MARKET. Samarkand, Uzbekistan, c. 1900. Russian period postcard. The ruins of Bibi-Khanum Mosque, the monumental building that Timur (Tamerlane) built in 1404, supposedly for his favorite wife (a Chinese princess), dominate the landscape. The bazaar in front of the mosque—one of the oldest bazaars in Central Asia—has been operating for more than five hundred years.

2. RUBLE PROVISIONAL NOTE. Russian note issued in 1918 specifically for use in Turkestan. It still bears the Tsarist double-headed eagle. 2.5 x 4.5"

3. 5,000-TENGA NOTE. Bukhara, 1918. Issued by the khanate of Bukhara during the reign of Emir Sayed Mir-Alim; printed by wooden blocks. It was worth about twenty-seven dollars at the time. 4.75 x 7.5"

4. SILVER TENGA COIN. Bukhara, 1901–02. Issued by the khanate of Bukhara during the reign of Emir Abd al-Ahad. .5" D.

5. SHIR-DAR *MADRASSAH* MARKET. Samarkand, c. 1903. Shir-Dar is one of the three imposing *madrassahs* that make up the Registan, the central square of Samarkand. Photograph by Annette Meakin.

6. MARKET BY THE ARK. Bukhara, Uzbekistan, 1895. The Ark, a massive mud-brick walled fortress, was the official residence and court of the rulers of Bukhara for more than a thousand years. Destroyed and rebuilt many times, it was like a small city, with artisan workshops, mosques, stables, jails, the state mint, and many other buildings. It was a rather gloomy place, and the last two emirs preferred to stay in their country palaces.

7. GRAIN BAZAAR. Samarkand, 1919. "A rainbow was shattered and the fragments fell in the grain market of Samarkand." Photograph and quotation by Maynard Owen Williams.

6.

7.

1.

2.

3.

4.

5.

6.

7.

THE BAZAAR Tea

Tea (*chai*, *choy*) was, and still is, an integral part of Central Asian daily life. Green tea (*kok chai*), imported from China, was preferred over black tea. It was sipped throughout the day, accompanied every meal, and sometimes became the meal itself—fortified with chunks of hard bread or pieces of mutton fat. The serving of tea was a gesture of hospitality, to friend and stranger alike.

The teahouse (*chaikhana*) provided a teapot (*chainik*) of hot water from a large samovar (sometimes called *Shaiton chainik*, or "Satan's teakettle"), a bowl (*piala*) to drink from, and maybe a little food. The chinaware was often imported Russian porcelain from the Gardner manufactory, located near Moscow. The men usually brought their own loose tea in small pouches, such as fig. 8.

1. TEA VENDORS. Samarkand, Uzbekistan, 1871–72. Russian Gardner porcelain lines the shelves. Russian printed scarves for sale hang above. Photograph from the Turkestan Album.

2, 3. GARDNER TEAPOT AND BOWL. Russia, late 19th–early 20th c. Imported porcelain was so highly valued that when broken, it was brought to the china mender to be repaired, as was this hand-painted teapot. The same teapot in different colors can be seen in the painting *Tea-House* (see fig. 1, page 31). (fig. 2) 6" H.; (fig. 3) 3 H. x 6" D.

4, 7. *CHAIKHANAS*. Tashkent, Uzbekistan. Russian period postcards. (fig. 4) 1906; (fig. 7) 1929; showing Russian samovars and porcelain teapots. Men would remove their shoes before entering a teahouse.

5. AMONG THE MENDERS IN SAMARKAND. Samarkand, 1919. The menders use bow drills, copper rivets, and metal cages. Photograph by Maynard Owen Williams.

6. TEAPOTS AND BOWLS. Uzbekistan, 2005. Niche in a private home. These porcelain teacups and bowls were made in Uzbekistan and feature a cotton-boll motif.

8. *CHAI KHALTA*. Ersari Turkmen, 1st quarter, 20th c. Embroidered tea bag. Silk lacing stitch on cotton; loop-manipulation trim, plain-cotton lining. 7 x 5"

9. DANCING BOYS (*bachas*). Uzbekistan, c. 1900. Traveling troupes of dancing boys and musicians would entertain men at the teahouses.

8.

9.

1.

2.

THE TEAHOUSE *Chaikhana*

Teahouses (*chaikhana*) were ubiquitous: on a dusty backstreet; by a roadside irrigation canal; tucked under a massive shade tree; in an urban park or grimy station house. Seating was traditionally on a raised, usually carpeted, wooden platform called a *takhta*. Often caged quails (*bedana*) would be softly singing. Women did not venture into a teahouse. The old men, or *aksakals* (whitebeards), could linger there all day sipping weak green tea. One disgruntled Russian in Soviet-era Samarkand complained, "Those old men take their tea as seriously as one does the Revolution!" As these photographs show, outwardly at least, little has changed in the Central Asian "way of tea," save for the three women patrons shown in fig. 4.

1. TEA IN MAIMANA. Maimana, Afghanistan, 1978. Photograph © Luke Powell.

2. TEAHOUSE. Tashkent, Uzbekistan, c. 1930s–40s. Photograph by Max Penson.

3. *CHAIKHANA.* Samarkand, Uzbekistan, 1911. Photograph by Prokudin-Gorskii.

4. *CHAIKHANA.* Tashkent, 2003. The *aksakals* (whitebeards) are wearing traditional Chust-style skullcaps.

3.

4.

1.

2.

3.

4.

5.

6.

FLATBREAD SELLERS

Flatbread (*non, lepeshka, lepyoshka*) is a staple in much of Central Asia—historically, more so among settled peoples where grain was grown and clay *tandoor* ovens were available. *Non* is treated with respect and special customs are part of its use. In Uzbekistan, when a family member departs on a long journey, he might bite off a small piece of bread and the rest will be kept until he returns (to finish it). *Non* is placed under the head of a newborn to wish it a long and problem-free life. And *non* should never be placed upside down, or cut with a knife.

Each region is proud of its own kind of *non*—from plain and flat to puffy ones studded with crushed nuts, raisins, onions, etc. *Non* served with the hearty rice, shredded carrot, and mutton dish (*plov, pillau, pilaf*) and endless cups of pale green tea is a traditional Uzbek meal.

1. A TREAT. Uzbekistan, c. 1930s–40s. Photograph by Max Penson.

2. *TANDOOR* OVEN MAKER. Samarkand, 1871–72. The flattened dough is slapped onto the inside walls of a hot clay *tandoor* oven to cook. Photograph from the Turkestan Album.

3. FLATBREAD VENDORS. Samarkand, 1911. Photograph by Prokudin-Gorskii.

4. FLATBREAD VENDOR. Samarkand, 1871–72. Photograph from the Turkestan Album.

5, 6. *NON* STAMPS and FLATBREAD. Uzbekistan, 2010. A wooden utensil embedded with iron "pins," called a *chekich,* is used to stamp a pattern in the center of the flattened dough (fig. 6) just before cooking; 5.5 x 3"; 5.5 x 2.5"

7. WOMAN SELLING FLATBREAD. Kamchik Pass, Uzbekistan. 2008.

8. UZBEK BREAD SELLERS. Ferghana Valley, Uzbekistan, 2008.

7.

8.

1.

Гор. Андижанъ. Торговцы дынями

2.

THE MELON BAZAAR

Melons (*kavun, qovun*) are the pride and joy of Central Asia, especially Uzbekistan, where more than 150 varieties are grown. Travelers past and present write that there are no sweeter melons anywhere. It was said that long ago, melons traveled the Silk Road, packed in straw and glacial ice for the pleasure of the Chinese emperor. Marco Polo wrote about dried melon slices that were "sweet as honey and sent for sale to other countries." When hung fresh in a cool place, or dried in slices, they can be enjoyed year-round.

1. MELON MERCHANT. Uzbekistan, c. 1910. Russian period postcard.

> *"Come and try*
> *Melons of mine,*
> *Sweeter than honey,*
> *Worth your money."*
> —Cry of the melon vendor

2. MELON MARKET. Andijan, Uzbekistan, c. 1910–15. Russian period postcard. These melons are tied with cords for ease of transport and storage.

3. BOY WITH MELON. Uzbekistan, c. 1920s. Russian period postcard.

4. MELON VENDOR. Samarkand, Uzbekistan, 1911. Photograph by Prokudin-Gorskii.

5. MELON GROWER. Uzbekistan, c. 1930s. Slices of melon dry in the sun. Photograph by Max Penson.

3.

4.

5.

1.

Кокандъ. Продажа мѣстныхъ издѣлій изъ хлопка/мата.

2.

THE CLOTH BAZAAR

In the nineteenth and early twentieth centuries, each vendor usually sold a specific type of cloth. There were stalls for *alacha* and *bekasab* (locally woven stripes), *karbos* (hand-loomed plain cotton), *chit* (block-printed *karbos*), imported Russian-printed chintz and calico (*sitetz*), etc. In the Soviet era, hand-produced fabrics were mostly replaced by factory-made silk ikat, faux-ikat, and other silk, cotton, and synthetic cloth from the Central Asian textile combines. After they closed in the early 1990s, much of the cloth was imported from China and South Korea.

1. VENDOR OF TURBANS. Samarkand, Uzbekistan, 1871–72. Long, narrow turban cloth of fine muslin was woven locally and also imported from India and England. Photograph from the Turkestan Album.

2. "*ALACHA/MATA* SELLERS." Kokand, Uzbekistan, c. 1910. Russian period postcard. Striped *alacha* is on the left, white homespun *mata* (*karbos*) is on the right.

3. FABRIC MERCHANT. Samarkand, 1911. This iconic image of a vendor wearing a robe of Russian printed cotton shows him enthroned on a carpeted platform surrounded by bolts of imported cloth. Photograph by Prokudin-Gorskii.

4. FABRIC BAZAAR. Tashkent, Uzbekistan, 2010. Many of these fabrics were probably imported, possibly from China and South Korea. Most appear to be printed on silk or synthetic material.

3.

4.

1.

2.

3.

4.

5.

RUSSIAN PRINTED CLOTH (*Sitetz*)

In 1863 the Hungarian traveler and Orientalist Arminius Vámbéry wrote that the cloth bazaar in Kokand "exposed for sale, at low prices, exclusively Russian merchandise." Ten years later, Eugene Schuyler, an American diplomat, noted this about the Tashkent fabric bazaar: "Whole rows are filled with cotton goods, among which it is impossible not to notice in every shop the large quantity on sale of Russian printed fabrics." In 1896 the English author-traveler Annette Meakin remarked, "Materials manufactured in Moscow . . . are quietly but surely usurping the place of those glorious silks that once charmed the eye of every European traveler." Twenty years later, English journalist Stephen Graham wrote, "The foreign goods in the bazaar are mostly cotton, and if you examine the splendidly gay prints that go to form the clothing of the natives you find it all marked Moscow manufacturer." The following are details of Russian cloth exported to Central Asia, most of which was printed in mills located in and around Moscow. The city of Ivanovo produced so much printed cotton that it became known as "the Manchester [England] of Russia." All of the examples below were printed with engraved copper rollers.[1]

1 For more information on Russian-trade cloth to Central Asia, see Krody, *Colors of the Oasis: Central Asian Ikats*, "The Russian Connection" by Susan Meller, and Meller, *Russian Textiles: Printed Cloth for the Bazaars of Central Asia*.

1, 7. RUSSIAN CLOTH. Late 19th–early 20th c. Cotton lining fabric of *shohi* ikat men's robes from Bukhara. The candelabras are similar to those seen in some Central Asian mosques. (figs. 1, 7) 19 x 15"

2, 5. RUSSIAN CLOTH. Early 20th c. Cotton linings of women's *banoras paranjas*. (fig. 2) 13 x 11"; (fig. 5) 23 x 18"

3. RUSSIAN CLOTH. c. 1900. Cotton lining of a man's *bekasab* robe. Art nouveau peacock-feather pattern. 18 x 14"

4. RUSSIAN CLOTH. Late 19th c. Cotton lining of a woman's *adras* ikat robe (see fig. 5, page 55). 11 x 8"

6. RUSSIAN CLOTH. Last 3rd, 19th c. Cotton lining of a man's imported wool broadcloth robe. 21 x 15"

6.

7.

9

SOVIET INFLUENCE

"In 1925 the First Soviet Congress of Uzbekistan was held. Now the brass bed of the Emir still stands in the summer palace, but the wives are free from the harem, the Emir is gone, and the whole estate is shortly to become a rest home for the workers of the sovkhozes [state farms]. Peasants will sleep where they could not enter before, and women will stroll unveiled beneath grape arbors where once they walked only in paranjas guarded by eunuchs. And the fountains will play for the workers." —Langston Hughes, *The Collected Works of Langston Hughes*, 1932

"I see no cause for rejoicing when the sun rises in the West, and the East, losing its leisure, learns to drink its tea with one lump or two of Stalinist propaganda." —Ethel Mannin, *South to Samarkand,* 1937

"One thing, therefore, is now placed beyond question: a new leaf has been turned in the history of the ancient continent of Asia, and half at least will be written by the awakening women of the Russian East." —Fannina W. Halle, *Women in the Soviet East,* 1938

"Central Asian peoples have not lost their sense of ethnic identity, nor are they likely to become merged with the Russian people. There has been an evolution of the traditional cultures, with selective borrowing of new elements and modifications congenial to the traditional patterns and interests of the area." —Elizabeth E. Bacon, *Central Asians Under Russian Rule: A Study in Culture Change,* 1966

Except for the Arab conquests that imposed Islam in the seventh and eighth centuries, no other occupiers of Central Asia came with such an ideological agenda as the Soviets. The new Bolshevik regime had an advantage, since thirty years earlier tsarist Russia had completed its conquest of what was then called Turkestan. Under the tsars, a governor-general was installed, military units positioned, and railroads built, setting the stage for the influx of millions of Russian settlers. Tariffs were enacted to exclude foreign goods and cotton was planted. The result was a huge captive market for Russia's exports, particularly cotton cloth made from imported Central Asian cotton in the mills of Ivanovo and other Russian cities. The tsars were interested in strategic and economic benefits, not the customs of the native people, who for the most part were allowed to go about their everyday lives as before. Even the khans of Khiva and Kokand and the emir of Bukhara were granted a degree of autonomy.

But all this changed in 1917 when Tsar Nicholas II was overthrown and the Bolsheviks came to power. After the Red Army defeated the White, attention began to focus on this vast eastern land. Here dwelled the "Peoples of the East," millions of new Soviet citizens, who needed to be brought into the fold of Marxist-Leninist believers and made participants in the building of a modern, industrialized society. The authority of the Muslim imans and mullahs and the

centuries-old ways of life they endorsed stood in the way of Soviet goals. When persuasion failed, mosques and *madrassahs* were shut down or destroyed and laws were passed against what the Soviets deemed "*byt* crimes," or crimes based on custom, such as the bride-price (*kalym*), polygamy, and forced veiling.

At that time, many women and girls from strict religious households were not allowed to leave the family compound and lived a totally secluded life. Those who did venture out were required to completely veil themselves. These widespread, restrictive customs encouraged the Soviets to embrace the idea that change would best be achieved by "liberating" the Central Asian woman. They focused on the *paranja* and veil (*chachvan*) as the most visual symbols of female repression. A massive campaign called the *hujum* ("assault" or "onslaught") was launched to unveil women and girls. However, it was met with widespread resistance by both men and women and created repercussions far beyond anything the Soviets had imagined. The *paranja* and veil became a symbol of defiance, a source of national pride, and for many women who had never veiled, a necessity worn to avoid the wrath of their husbands and neighbors. Many women who dared to throw off the veil were murdered by family members or strangers in the street. The campaign began in 1927, and it would take at least another thirty years for the *paranja* and veil to disappear.[1]

Under Stalin's first Five-Year Plan (1928–32), the Soviets built factories in Central Asia, including many textile combines. Farms were collectivized into *kolkhozy* and more cotton planted, to the exclusion of many food and fodder crops. The guilds were disbanded and artisans collectivized into artels where production was carefully controlled. Even traditional striped robes (*chapans*) were sewn by seamstresses in state-owned factories. Labor-intensive handwoven fabrics such as velvet ikat (*baghmal*) and *adras* ikat ceased to be made. Nomadic lifestyles, already negatively impacted by tsarist incursions and the huge influx of Russian settlers, began to rapidly disappear under the Soviets. Ironically, at the same time that traditional ways of life were under siege, Soviet propaganda highlighted women working the cotton fields in colorful ikat dresses, or men in striped robes and embroidered skullcaps casting ballots in a *suzani*-draped election room. When it served the greater Soviet agenda, Central Asian tradition and culture was approved and even glorified. When it ran counter to Soviet ideology, it was suppressed.

---

1 "In . . . districts of Tashkent, as well as in the cities of Samarqand and Farghona, it is possible to meet many [women] in a veiled state, wearing *paranjis*. In the rural districts and cities of Surkhondaryo, Qashqadaryo, Namangan, Bukhoro, and Andijon provinces there remains a general tendency for [women] to walk about while veiled with all sorts of outer cloaks, using things like a *dasturkhon*, a *yakhtak*, a *jelak*, or a *chopon* in place of a *paranji*." —Soviet propagandist M. Aliev, 1953, from Douglas Northrop, *Veiled Empire: Gender and Power in Stalinist Central Asia* (Ithica: Cornell University Press, 2004), 342. The *hujum* is extensively covered in this deeply researched book.

1.

2.

3.

4.

SOVIET INFLUENCE

Soviet culture permeated Central Asia far more than that of tsarist Russia. While the main objective of the Russians was to bring Central Asia under their control in order to thwart the English in the Great Game and thereby secure their position in the region, the Soviets set out to control the very lives of the "Peoples of the East."

Soon, practically all aspects of Central Asian life took place under the ever-present images of Lenin and Stalin, textiles included. Their portraits, Soviet five-pointed stars, hammers and sickles, and political slogans were embroidered on *suzanis* and skullcaps. Cloth printed with propaganda patterns was sent from Russian mills.[1] And *hujum*, the campaign to unveil women, began in earnest.

1 For examples of Soviet agitprop fabrics, see Pamela Jill Kachurin, *Soviet Textiles: Designing the Modern Utopia* (Boston: Museum of Fine Arts, 2006).

1–3, 5, 6. CARDS. Moscow, USSR, 1967. These cards show the state emblem and state flag of each Central Asian Soviet Socialist Republic, surrounded by representative textile patterns. (fig. 1) Turkmen SSR; (fig. 2) Tajik SSR; (fig. 3) Kirghiz SSR; (fig. 5) Kazakh SSR; (fig.6) Uzbek SSR. Each card 5.75 x 4"

4. ARTISTS. Uzbekistan, 2nd quarter, 20th c. The artists are painting panels with Soviet stars, hammers and sickles, cotton bolls, and *suzani* motifs. Photograph by Max Penson.

7. EMBROIDERED HANGING. Uzbekistan, c. 1970s. Silk couching on cotton; machine-embroidered cotton trim; unlined. The main motif is the Soviet-era state emblem of Uzbekistan. 30 x 34"

8. SUZANI. Uzbekistan, dated 1972. Silk couching on cotton; machine-embroidered trim; unlined. "CCCP [SSSR] 50 Years!" Underneath is the proper name "BOZOROI." Soviet-star variation in center of medallion. 74 x 59"

5.

6.

7.

8.

1.

2.

3.

4.

5.

6.

SOVIET INFLUENCE

Important Soviet-related events and their anniversaries created a wave of commemorative textiles. The 10th of October (the Bolshevik revolution of 1917), Lenin's birth (1870), the Turkestan-Siberia Railroad, the Moscow Olympics—all were celebrated and their representative motifs printed on scarves and yard goods, embroidered on hats and household items, and woven into carpets. Textile plants and embroidery artels were given Soviet-specific names, such as the *Hujum* (Struggle) cooperative of craftswomen in Shakhrisabz, the "10th of October" textile factory in Bukhara, and the sewing enterprise "N. Krupskaia" (Lenin's wife) in Leninabad.

1. COMMEMORATIVE SCARF. Russia, 1967. Printed cotton. The words in the center read "THE GREAT OCTOBER 50 Years." It was printed by the III International factory, in Karabanovo (about sixty miles northeast of Moscow). Scarves such as these were given as awards to workers. 30 x 30"

2, 3. CHEMISE (and detail). Uzbekistan, 1980s. Silk *khanatlas*; printed-cotton facing commemorating the 22nd Olympic Games held in Moscow in 1980. The USA boycotted these games in protest of the Soviet Union's invasion of Afghanistan. (fig. 2) 42" length; (fig. 3, facing detail) 5 x 4"

4. IKAT PANEL. Namangan, Uzbekistan, c. 1940s. Silk warp/cotton weft *atlas* ikat. "Artel Stalin" stamped on back. 106 x 17" selvedge to selvedge

5, 6. WOMEN'S HATS. Ferghana region, Uzbekistan, 1970–71. Silk cross-stitch on cotton; plain-cotton linings. (fig. 5) "KOSMOS" refers to the Soviet space program; 5.5" D.; (fig. 6) "100 YEARS" celebrates the birth of Lenin in 1870; 5.5" D.

7. PORTRAIT OF A WOMAN. Tashkent, Uzbekistan, c. 1930s. The young woman is wearing a Tashkent-style embroidered hat popular at that time. Quilts are stacked against the wall and Stalin is peering over her shoulder. Photograph by Max Penson.

8. HAT. Uzbekistan, Soviet era. Silk embroidery on cotton; printed-cotton lining. The Cyrillic letters "CCCP" [SSSR] stand for the "Union of Soviet Socialist Republics." 5" D.

7.

8.

1.

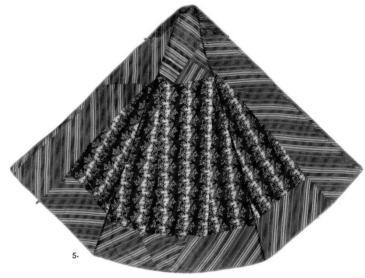

4.

2.

5.

3.

6.

7.

8.

HUJUM Unveiling Campaign

In their determination to convert the Central Asian people to the Soviet way of life, the Bolsheviks concentrated their efforts on women, particularly the women of Uzbekistan. They believed that if they could "liberate" the female population, wives, in turn, would spread the Soviet message to their husbands and families.

The first and most crucial step was to convince women to throw off their *paranjas* and *chachvans* (horsehair veils). In 1927 the official campaign called *hujum*, a Turkic word meaning "struggle," "attack," or "onslaught," began. The Bolsheviks sent hundreds of women members of the *Zhenotdel* (who were, in effect, "shock troops") to Uzbekistan, confident that they would complete their mission to unveil most, if not all, of the women in six months. Ironically, the campaign only succeeded in driving more women to don the *paranja* and veil as a sign of defiance as well as national identity. It was not until the 1950s that veiling gradually ceased.

1. WOMEN SELLING HATS. Uzbekistan, c. 1920s. Women in *paranjas* and veils. The few hats offered are Chust-style (see pages 140–41). Photograph by Max Penson.

2. MARRIAGE REGISTRATION. Tashkent Registry Office, 1930s. The bride wears a *paranja* and *chachvan*.

3. IN THE STREET OF TASHKENT. Old Tashkent, Uzbekistan, c. 1930s–early '50s. Two unveiled women in Western-cut coats (*kamzul*, fig. 6), among a group of veiled women in *paranjas*. Photograph by Max Penson.

4, 5. PARANJA (back and lining). Uzbekistan, 1st quarter, 20th c. Silk embroidery on *banoras*; silk tassels with glass beads; loop-manipulation trim; Russian printed- and woven-striped-cotton lining. 53" length

6. COAT (*kamzul*). Uzbekistan, c. 1930s–50s. This is the type of Western-style coat that Uzbek women might wear if they chose to throw off the *paranja*. Silk *banoras*, lined with Russian-printed cotton. *Banoras* was the same fabric used to make *paranjas*. 45" length

7. "SART WOMAN WITH VEIL LIFTED." Uzbekistan, c. 1903. The *chachvan* is thrown back over her head. A *tandoor* oven is in the background. Photograph by Annette Meakin.

8. *CHACHVAN*. Uzbekistan, 1st quarter, 20th c. Black horsehair veil with white horsehair pattern at bottom. Wide cotton border with silk machine-embroidery (probably added later). 47 x 26"

9. ARTIST AND PAINTING. Uzbekistan, c. 1930s. The artist Oganes Tatevosyan (1889–1974) lived in Tashkent from 1932 to 1966. The painting (most likely by Tatevosyan) depicts Uzbek women throwing their *paranjas* and veils into a bonfire. Scenes like this one were orchestrated by the Soviets at unveiling rallies. Though some women did participate, most did not—and those who did usually quickly re-veiled.[2] The speaker on the podium appears to be the famed Uzbek writer Hamza Niyazi (1889–1929), a strong proponent of women's rights. Photograph by Max Penson.

2 Other artists also painted this scene. The Swiss traveler Ella Maillart was in Samarkand in 1932. She wrote, "We find Benkof, the well-known artist, in the courtyard of the madrasah [Ulugh Beg] working on a striking canvas, the subject of which is The 8th of March in the Registan Square [International Women's Day], a date which celebrates the emancipation of the women, when the chedras [chachvans] were burnt in great heaps." Ella K. Maillart, *Turkestan Solo: One Woman's Expedition from the Tien Shan to the Kizil Kum* (New York: G. P. Putnam's Sons, 1935), 202.

9.

SOVIET INFLUENCE Lenin

Total control was the overriding objective of the Bolsheviks and it manifested itself in every aspect of Central Asian life. With mosques, *madrassahs*, synagogues, and churches either destroyed, boarded up, or appropriated for official use, the new gods became Lenin and Stalin. Their images were everywhere—from monumental statues to propaganda posters. Every home had a portrait of Stalin watching over it. As British author and traveler Ethel Mannin observed on her journey to Samarkand in 1936, "There are pictures of Stalin on the sunbaked walls of mud huts in the deserts, and on the white-washed walls of lonely farmhouses in the steppes."[3]

3 Ethel Mannin, *South to Samarkand* (New York: E. P. Dutton and Co., 1937), 253.

1. V. I. LENIN RUG. Uzbekistan, c. 1950s–70s. Hand-knotted wool pile: cotton weft and fringe. "Cult of Personality" rugs with larger-than-life portraits of Soviet leaders were popular during this period. Portrait rugs and tapestries were also machine-woven in Russian factories such as Karjakumsky Fabrika. They were used primarily as wall hangings. 78 x 66"

2. "GLORY TO OCTOBER!" Russian period postcard. 1962. This card bears a Soviet slogan that celebrates the October Revolution of 1917. Variations of this graphic profile of Lenin were often seen on posters, propaganda material, and textiles. "The name of Lenin has become a symbol of the new world, a banner of the struggle for freedom and social progress the world over."[4]

4 Lunin, *Lenin and the Peoples of the East.*

3. SUZANI. Uzbekistan, c. 1970s. Silk couching on cotton; cotton crocheted trim with metal spangles; unlined. *Suzanis* with variations of this particular pattern were probably sewn in a Soviet artel. They may have been made to commemorate the one-hundredth anniversary of Lenin's birth (1870), or the fiftieth anniversary of his death (1924). 41 x 44" as shown

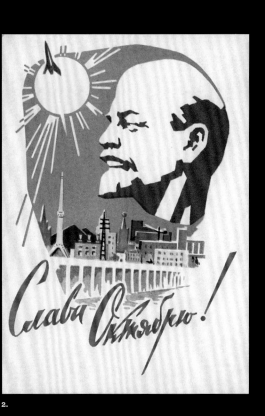

2.

3.

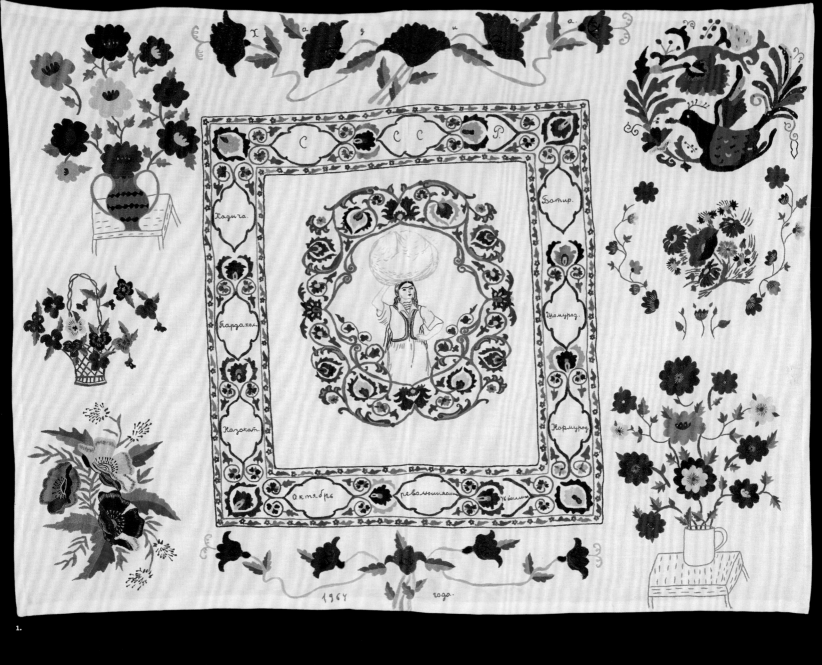

1.

2.

COMMEMORATIVE *SUZANI*

Three important and widely celebrated holidays introduced by the Soviets to Central Asia were International Workers' Day (May 1st), International Women's Day (March 8th), and Victory Day (May 9th). Victory Day marks the day Germany surrendered to the Soviet Union after four years of war (1941–45). During those years the USSR lost an estimated 25,000,000 people in what came to be called the Great Patriotic War. An estimated 850,000 Central Asian soldiers and 720,000 civilians from all five republics also died in this war.[5] Many *suzanis* and banners were embroidered to commemorate these dates. The October 1917 Bolshevik revolution was also commemorated with embroidered hangings.

5 Erlikman, *Poteri Narodonaseleniia v XX Veke*, 23-35.

1. "OCTOBER REVOLUTION 46 YEARS." Uzbekistan, dated 1964. Silk couching and stem stitch on cotton. "SSSR" (USSR) on top; "October Revolution 46 Years" on bottom; three women's names (left) and three men's names (right); iconic image of woman cotton harvester in center. 45 x 62"

2. BANNER. Uzbekistan, c. 1970s. Silk couching on cotton; cotton crochet trim with metal spangles. This banner commemorates International Women's Day, International Workers' Day, and Victory Day. The words translate as "Youth unlike a rose does not open each spring" (top) and "Friends, have fun—youth will not return" (bottom). 32 x 100" as shown

3. WOMAN PICKING COTTON. Uzbekistan, c. 1930s. *Kolkhoz* worker in cotton field with cotton boll tucked behind her ear. Photograph by Max Penson.

4. MARCH 8 (detail). Uzbekistan, dated 1974. Silk couching on cotton. Detail from a banner similar to fig. 2 commemorating International Women's Day. 27 x 29" as shown

3.

4.

10

ALBUM

This chapter presents images as seen through the lens of the photographer. These photographs are moments frozen in time and we can make of them what we will. The following quotations are the more fluid impressions left to us by long-ago travelers through the Central Asia that was.

"Personal observations are, however, the best materials; for, although some errors are inevitable, still the facts observed are stubborn things, and the deductions drawn from them must contain some truth." —Nikolai Khanikoff, *Bokhara: Its Amir and Its People,* 1845

"It seemed to me, when driving for the first time through the streets of Samarkand on a brilliant September morning in 1896, that Keats could not have chosen a more appropriate epithet for that city then 'Silken Samarkand'; almost every other man we met was clothed in silk. A gentle breeze filled their long wide sleeves till they looked like silken pillows, and spread out the folds of their ample garments, while the silk embroidery on the boys' caps shone in the direct rays of the midday sun." —Annette M. B. Meakin, *In Russian Turkestan,* 1903

"A wonderful calmness prevails at night, even the wind generally goes to sleep, and the complete silence . . . is only broken by the donkey who cannot, even at night, stop his dreary, loud braying . . . It is Satan crying into the ear of the mule donkey: 'All mares are dead!' And then he strikes up his sad cry which, however, always ends in a soft and more contented Haw! Or Naw! For Satan took pity on him and whispered: 'There is one mare left still!'" [old Bukharan legend] —Ole Olufsen, *The Emir of Bokhara and His Country,* 1911

"Then as night falls, we hasten through the deserted bazaars, barred and covered on both sides, where infrequent and dim electric lights can't quite spoil the fanciful effect, past great khans [*caravanserais*], in whose courtyard camels ponder . . . Here one old patriarch roars like

a lion while his turbaned master beats him to his wrinkled, calloused knees." —Maynard Owen Williams, "Russia's Orphan Races," *National Geographic,* October 1918

"In the autumn, if you step off the train almost anywhere in the fertile parts of Central Asia, you step into a cotton field, or into a city or town whose streets are filled with evidences of cotton nearby. On all the dusty roads, camels, carts, and trucks loaded with the white fibre go toward the gins and warehouses. Outside the towns, oft-times as far as the eye can see, the white balls lift their precious heads." —Langston Hughes, *A Negro Looks at Soviet Central Asia,* 1934

"It is a street that has all the intimacy of the market-place and the bazaar, a gay and heedless little street, full of eating-houses with unglazed windows open on to the pavement, a street of rickety wooden houses with overhanging balconies, a street in which twisted trees make shadow-patterns on the cobbles . . . the bright warm colours of Bokhara rugs on the wooden platforms of *chai-khanas* glow in the bright clear sunlight; turbans gleam and plush caps make brilliant splashes of colour; the Oriental crazy-patchwork of a street flowing between the Registan at one end and the broad boulevards of the new town at the other, the link between oldest Asia and newest Europe, between Tamerlane's Samarkand and Stalin's." —Ethel Mannin, *South to Samarkand,* 1937

"The [Alai] valley itself is a stretch of flowery alpine meadow of inconceivable beauty . . . rare flowers of every brilliant colour bloomed in profusion . . . Hundreds and hundreds of black Qirghiz yurts dotted the pastures, camels and yaks grazed peacefully side by side, flocks of innumerable sheep scrambled like chamois amongst the cliffs and rocks . . . Here is the last stronghold of Qirghiz freedom." —Gustav Krist, *Alone through the Forbidden Land,* 1938

1.

2.

PORTRAITS

1. BUKHARAN EMBASSY. Central Asia, early 20th c. Most of the men are wearing *bekasab* robes; three robes are ikat; two are printed cotton. (Note the shy little boy on the far left.)

2. DERVISHES. Central Asia, last 3rd, 19th c. Also called *kalandars*, these men were Sufi mendicants of various fraternal orders, each of which had its own costume. Some wore tall pointed hats and ragged patchwork robes that they might have pieced together themselves, or made into robes from old *caroq* quilts. They carried large hollow begging-bowl gourds and sang for alms. The Russian artist Vasily Vereshchagin (1842–1904) painted groups of dervishes in exquisite detail (see fig. 5, page 31).

3. MOUNTAIN TAJIK WOMEN. Tajikistan, c. 1935. *Kolkhoz* women from a collective farm, wearing printed cotton dresses, in front of their "School for the Liquidation of Illiteracy."

4. "SAMARKAND STREET TYPES." Uzbekistan, c. 1915. Russian period postcard. The man in the orange print robe is smoking a water pipe (*chillim*, *hookah*) that another man holds for him. Water pipes were often shared in this way by a group of men in a social setting such as a teahouse, or by strangers in the bazaar, who paid for a few puffs.

3.

САМАРКАНДЪ. Уличные типы.

4.

1.

2.

3.

4.

5.

6.

7.

PORTRAITS

1. KIRGHIZ DURING THE MEAL. Central Asia, c. 1910. Russian period postcard. Families (and guests) might eat with their hands from a large communal bowl with one tea bowl filled often and passed around. At this time, the Russians referred to the Kyrgyz as "Kara-Kirghiz" and Kazakhs as "Kirghiz." So these people may well be Kazakhs.

2. TAJIK WOMAN: SHARAFET-BIBI. Probably Samarkand, Uzbekistan, 1871–72. Sharafet-bibi wears an ikat robe over a printed dress and an embroidered skullcap. Photograph from the Turkestan Album.

3. FOUR WIVES OF A RICH KIRGHIZ. Central Asia, c. 1916. The date and title of this photograph suggest that these are Kazakh women. They wear wimplelike white *kimesheks* in the style worn by Kazakh women.

4. KARA-KIRGHIZ WOMAN: KYZLIAR-AI. Central Asia, 1871–72. Kyzliar-ai, a Kyrgyz, wears a fur hat (*tebetey*) and an ikat robe. Photograph from the Turkestan Album.

5. FATHER AND SON. Uzbekistan, 2nd quarter, 20th c. Photograph by Max Penson.

6. GRANDFATHER WITH HIS GRANDSON. Uzbekistan, 2nd quarter, 20th c. Photograph by Max Penson.

7. UZBEK WOMAN: IZET-AI. Uzbekistan, 1871–72. Izet-ai wears an elaborate headdress and ikat robe. Photograph from the Turkestan Album.

8. JEWISH WOMAN: SIPARA. Uzbekistan, 1871–72. Sipara wears a printed-cotton dress and headscarf. Photograph from the Turkestan Album.

9. JEWISH WOMEN AND GIRLS. Uzbekistan, c. 1916. The married women are wearing white headdresses similar to the *kimesheks* in fig. 3. Practically everyone is wearing a printed-cotton dress, and a few wear ikat robes.

8.

9.

1.

2.

3.

4.

5.

6.

PORTRAITS

1. **WATER CARRIER.** Jizzak, Uzbekistan, 1871–72. In summer, the bazaars were extremely dusty. Men were paid by the merchants to spray water from the necks of goatskin bags in order to keep down the dust. Water was also delivered in these bags. Photograph from the Turkestan Album.

2. **UZBEK FAMILY.** Probably Tashkent, Uzbekistan, c. 1940s. Family photograph of a man with a small boy and a young girl, who is wearing an ikat dress.

3. **"A BEK OF CHARDZHOU IN EMBROIDERED ROBE."** Chardzhou (Turkmenabat), c. 1887. Russian period postcard, printed c. 1910. Astanakul-bey dadha. Chardzhou was part of the emirate of Bukhara at this time. A *bek* (*bey, beg*) was the highest-ranking official of a region.

4. **YOUNG MAN OF TASHKENT.** Uzbekistan, 1906. *Bekasab* robe; belt with silver and/or gilt buckles and disk; elaborate turban. Obviously a well-to-do man of rank, he is posing in front of what appears to be carved plasterwork.

5. **A MAN FROM BUKHARA.** Uzbekistan, c. 1920s. German period postcard. *Bekasab* robe; Bactrian camel.

6. **BELLE OF OLD TASHKENT IN WEDDING COSTUME.** Uzbekistan, 1906. Russian printed-cotton dress; large Tashkent *suzani* in background.

7. **MAN WITH PIPE.** Samarkand, Uzbekistan, 1911. This water pipe (*chillim, hookah*) was made from a dried, hollowed gourd mounted with decorative brass. The brass bowl on top contained the lit tobacco, water was held in the gourd, and a long tube enabled the smoker to inhale the smoke as it bubbled through the water. The fabric of the man's robe is a combination stripe and ikat (for similar fabric, see fig. 6, page 55). Photograph by Prokudin-Gorskii.

8. **FAMILY OF BUKHARA.** Uzbekistan, c. 1890s. Russian period postcard, printed c. 1910. The woman holds a *chillim* similar to the one in fig. 7. Women enjoyed smoking the water pipe as much as men. The pose and props are evocative of an Orientalist painting. Photograph by A. Engel.

7.

8.

1.

2.

3.

4.

CHILDREN

"A house with children is a bazaar; a house without children is a mazar [tomb]."
—Old Kyrgyz proverb

1. THE IKAT CHAPAN. Aqcha, Afghanistan, 1975. This Uzbek boy and his father have come to town for market day. The boy's robe is *shohi* ikat in a pattern often found on robes from Afghanistan. Photograph © Luke Powell.

2. GIRL WITH A GREEN HAT. Between Taskhurghan and Balkh, Afghanistan, 1975. The girl's smock is block-printed on homespun cotton and her hat is made of factory-printed cloth. The horizontal cut of the neckline, with a tie at the shoulder, was worn by children and young girls; married women wore dresses with a vertical neckline to facilitate nursing. Photograph © Luke Powell.

3. A GIRL WITH BRAIDS. Uzbekistan, c. 1930s. The girl's dress is made from factory-printed cotton; her embroidered hat is in the Tashkent style. Photograph by Max Penson.

4. KIRGHIZ CHILDREN AT PLAY. Altai Mountains, c. 1920. There are lots of protective feathers (probably owl) in this girl's cap. Owl feathers were considered a very powerful amulet and Kyrgyz children often sported them in their hats.

5. MILK VENDOR. Probably Samarkand, Uzbekistan, 1871–72. The boy is wearing an *alacha* robe and most likely carrying yogurt in the clay pots. Photograph from the Turkestan Album.

6. SCHOOL. Uzbekistan, last third, 19th c. All boys, except for a baby sister and one girl (at the far left of the front row). The teacher is wearing a printed-cotton robe.

5.

6.

1.

2.

3.

TEATIME

Many of Max Penson's photographs show people drinking tea, some taken in what seem like improbable places—in the midst of a cotton field,[1] on a muddy construction site, in the open hull of a riverboat. And always with imported china teapots and bowls. Propaganda shots? Yes and no.

1 On visiting a cotton *kolkhoz* in 1932: "In the shade of large fig-trees stand samovars, and there is shelter for the workers who come to drink their tea here in the middle of the day." Maillart, *Turkestan Solo*, 162.

1. KHOREZM PEOPLE. Uzbekistan, 2nd quarter, 20th c. The men are wearing shaggy black sheepskin hats (*telpek*). The left banner reads: "Long Live German Hero Comrade Telman" (head of the German Communist party); and the right banner: "Long Live Socialist . . ." The portrait on the left is of M. Kalinin (chairman of the Congress of Soviets); and the one on the right, of L. Kaganovich (a close associate of Stalin). Photograph by Max Penson.

2. FERRYMEN FROM KHIVA. Amu Darya River, Uzbekistan, 2nd quarter, 20th c. The boat, a *kayuk*, is equipped with a *tandoor* oven. Photograph by Max Penson.

3. THE FARKHADSTROY. Farkhad, Uzbekistan, c. 1947. Workers taking a tea and flatbread break on the construction site of the Farkhad hydroelectric power station. Photograph by Max Penson.

4. PORTRAIT OF A MAN. Uzbekistan, 2nd quarter, 20th c. Printed-cotton robe and embroidered skullcap. The hard-edged, gearlike pattern on the man's robe is suggestive of Soviet agitprop prints. Photograph by Max Penson.

5. GRANDFATHER WITH GRANDDAUGHTER. Uzbekistan, 2nd quarter, 20th c. Young children often wore white crocheted caps. Photograph by Max Penson.

4.

5.

1.

2.

3.

4.

5.

6.

7.

ENTERTAINMENT

1. MUSICIANS. Kokand, Uzbekistan, c. 1910–15. Russian period postcard. Two men with traditional brass trumpets called *karnai*. These instruments were ten feet long and extremely loud . . . "lifting the roof of the sky."[2]

2 Graham, *Through Russian Central Asia*, 117.

2. CAROUSEL. Uzbekistan, c. 1940s. Photograph by Max Penson.

3, 4. *KURASH* (and detail). Uzbekistan, 1946. *Kurash* (wrestling) is the national Uzbek sport. Both men are wearing Chust-style hats and printed-cotton robes. The robe on the right is made from the same fabric as fig. 4.[3] Photograph by Max Penson. (fig. 4) 5.5 x 6"

3 This fabric can also be seen lining a Turkmen robe in Meller, *Russian Textiles*, 142.

5. TAMARA KHANUM. Uzbekistan, c. 1930s. Tamara Khanum (1906–91) was a highly acclaimed Uzbek dancer. In the 1920s, she became the first woman to perform unveiled on a public stage. Other dancers and actresses followed suit, and some were murdered by family members for daring to appear unveiled. She poses in front of a Tashkent *suzani* wearing a Western-style coat of Russian brocade over an ikat dress. Photograph by Max Penson.

6. ROPE WALKER (*dorvos*). Uzbekistan, 1895. Drawing throngs of people, the *dorvos* was once a regular sight in the public squares.

7. *BATCHAS*. Andijan, Uzbekistan, 1903. Wood engraving from "Journal des Voyages," Paris. *Batchas* were young boys or youths who usually belonged to a troupe of entertainers. The boys often assumed a feminine guise and danced either in public places such as teahouses, or at men's private gatherings. The khans and other wealthy men kept their own *batchas*.

8. *BUZKASHI*. Samarkand, Uzbekistan, 1911. *Buzkashi*, or *kok-boru*, is a traditional Central Asian sport. Played by scores of men on horseback in a large field, the goal is to grab the headless carcass of a goat, sheep, or calf; carry it around an end post; and drop it back into the center circle—all the while, being wildly pursued by the other horsemen. These men have gathered to watch and take part in the game. Photograph by Prokudin-Gorskii.

8.

1.

Самаркандъ. Дворъ богатаго сарта.
Samarcande. Cour de la maison d'un sarte. № 28.

2.

3.

4.

Самаркандъ.   Главная Улица.

5.

6.

7.

8.

STREET SCENES

1. HOUSE. Samarkand, Uzbekistan, 1911. Houses were built out of mud brick and surrounded by high walls. Numerous narrow canals (*arik*) ran alongside the roads and served for drinking, cooking, washing, and irrigation—"A most useful little trickle of water . . . One small stream could hardly do more for mankind!"[4] Photograph by Prokudin-Gorskii.

4 Wilson and Mitchell, *Vagabonding at Fifty*, 312.

2. "COURTYARD OF A SART HOUSE." Samarkand, c. 1910. Russian period postcard. As a rule, windows did not face the street. Doors and latticed windows opened onto an interior courtyard. "The little Eastern houses keep their secrets."[5]

5 Mannin, *South to Samarkand*, 259.

3. KEBAB RESTAURANT. Samarkand, 1911. Most of the men are wearing striped *bekasab* robes. Photograph by Prokudin-Gorskii.

4. KEBAB VENDOR. Samarkand, 1911. The boy wears a *bekasab* robe. Kebabs (*shashlik*) were made from pieces of fat-tailed sheep mutton roasted on skewers over charcoal. Photograph by Prokudin-Gorskii.

5. "MAIN STREET." Samarkand, c. 1910. Russian period postcard. Market stalls on a street alongside the Registan—the center and main public square of the city.

6. MIR-I ARAB *MADRASSAH*. Bukhara, Uzbekistan, 1919. Theological students and urn merchants in front of the sixteenth-century monument. Photograph by Maynard Owens Williams.

7. KYRGYZ MAN AND WOMEN. Samarkand, Uzbekistan, 1871–72. The man wears a traditional white felt hat (*kalpak*) and the women, traditional headdresses (*elechek*). Photograph from the Turkestan Album.

8. "*MEDRESE* DONOMI." Kokand, Uzbekistan, c. 1910. Russian period postcard. The dirt streets could be knee-deep in mud or dust depending on the season.

9. "SART WOMAN." Uzbekistan, 1911. Woman in *paranja* and veil. Photograph by Prokudin-Gorskii.

10. A DRIVER'S NIGHTMARE. Tajikistan, c. 1967. On the road to Dushanbe.

9.

10.

1.

2.

3.

TRANSPORT

No man would consider walking, even a short distance, if he could ride—it just wasn't done. A good horse was preferred, but if that was beyond one's means, then a donkey, camel, ox, or even a yak would do. Urban women rode in horse-drawn carts (*arbas*), nomad women on their sturdy little horses or Bactrian camels. As English journalist-traveler Stephen Graham noted in 1916, "In this country where wishes are horses, even the hawker of bootlaces in the bazaar has his nag tied to a poplar tree nearby."[6]

6 Graham, *Through Russian Central Asia*, 143.

1. *CARAVANSERAI.* Bukhara, c. 1920. Here, weary travelers and their animals could find shelter and fodder. Photograph by Maynard Owen Williams.

2. **MIGRATION.** Central Asia, early 20th c. Period photograph. Kazakhs or Kyrgyz.

3. **MAN ON OX.** Chimkent, Kazakhstan, 1871–72. If a man was too poor to own a horse, a saddled ox would do. Rather slow going, but better than walking. Photograph from the Turkestan Album.

4. **RUBY AND AMETHYST IN FERTILE FERGHANA.** Uzbekistan, 1919. Photograph by Maynard Owen Williams.

5. **MAN ON DONKEY.** Nurata region, Uzbekistan, c. 2000. The man is wearing a Chust-style hat. Donkeys were a common means of transport. It was not unusual to see a large man atop a small donkey with his feet practically dragging on the ground and the beast half hidden by his rider's voluminous robes.

4.

5.

1.

2.

3.

4.

TRANSPORT

"A Russian motor-car comes bounding over the cobbles, whooping and coughing its alarm signals; a score of dogs try to set on it and bite it as it passes, and the natives sit in their cupboard shops and laugh ... There was one Bokharian—a Sart, in full cloak and turban—who rode a bicycle, an astonishing exception." —Stephen Graham, 1916[7]

7 Graham, *Through Russian Central Asia*, 36.

1. THE OLD AND THE NEW WAY IN TURKESTAN. 1930. Two Kazakh women and a child beside the recently completed Turkestan-Siberian (Turk-Sib) railway that linked Ferghana, the cotton-producing center of Turkestan, with grain-rich Siberia. The slogan on the side of the train reads, "We will cover the vast plains of Kazakhstan with a network of railways." It was not unusual for Soviet trains to be used as traveling propaganda billboards.

2. STAMPS. Kazakhstan, 1992. One-ruble stamp commemorating the Turkestan-Siberian (Turk-Sib) railway begun in 1912 and completed in 1930. Painting by the much-esteemed Kazakh artist Abylkhan Kasteev. Each stamp: 1.5 x 2"

3. BUKHARAN WAGON. Bukhara, 1880s. This horse-drawn wooden cart (*arba, araba*) was the standard means of local transport for heavy goods, as well as people. The enormous wooden wheels (five to seven feet in diameter) enabled the cart to navigate through mud and water four feet deep without wetting the load. Photograph by F. Hordet.

4. *LA BICYCLETTE PÈNÈTRE À LA CAMPAGNE.* Uzbekistan, c. 1920s. French period postcard. In 1899 Englishman Robert L. Jefferson rode his bicycle across Europe and Russia to Khiva and back. His book, *A New Ride to Khiva*, chronicles this amazing feat.

5. CHILDREN IN CAR. Uzbekistan, c. 1930s. An appealing, but improbable picture. Cars were scarce at this time, even among Soviet officials. Photograph by Max Penson.

5.

1.

2.

3.

4.

ARCHITECTURE

Settled peoples' houses and the walls surrounding them were made of yellowish-gray sundried mud. Stone and heavy lumber would have had to be transported from afar but the claylike loess soil was readily available. Mixed with chaff and water from the canals, it was packed by hand inside a framework of poplar planks and narrow branches. Sun-baked mud bricks were also used. A few rafters supported the roof, which was covered with straw mats and a topcoat of mud mixed with chopped straw. When spring came, the roofs sprouted a profusion of poppies and other wild flowers.

Larger buildings such as palaces, mosques, and *madrassahs* were built entirely of plain and embossed kiln-baked mud bricks, more expensive, but far more durable. The grand ones were covered with a facade of brilliantly glazed tiles in shades of turquoise, cobalt, and emerald, some of which can still be seen today.

5.

1. THE AMEER'S HAREM. Shirbudin, Uzbekistan 1895. One of the Emir of Bukhara's country palaces. When the American author Langston Hughes visited Shirbudin in 1932, he wrote, "The women were always shut up in one place . . . or when, on occasions, he might allow them to bathe in the great square pool behind his summer house. There he would sit on a screened balcony and gaze down upon the beauty of a hundred wives in the water."[8] Photograph by F. Hordet.

8 Langston Hughes, *The Collected Works of Langston Hughes*, vol. 9 (Columbia: University of Missouri Press, 2002).

2. TILIA-KARI. Samarkand, Uzbekistan, 1911. One of the three imposing *madrassahs* that surround the Registan, the central square of the city. Tilia-Kari (Golden Mosque) was built in the seventeenth century. Photograph by Prokudin-Gorskii.

3. BIBI-KHANUM MOSQUE. Samarkand, 1911. Built by Timur supposedly in honor of his favorite wife, a Chinese princess, it was completed in 1404. Too massive in scale to support its design, the building began to crumble less than a hundred years later. A *caravanserai* is in the foreground. Photograph by Prokudin-Gorskii.

4. TAQI-ZARGARON BAZAAR. Bukhara, c. 1960s–70s. Soviet postcard. Cupolas of the covered jewelers' market, 16th century (see page 1).

5. WALL DECORATION. Uzbekistan, 1911. Painted plaster walls in a wealthy home. Photograph by Prokudin-Gorskii.

6. SHIRBUDIN. Uzbekistan, 1911. The emir of Bukhara's country palace. Photograph by Prokudin-Gorskii.

7. VIEW OF KHIVA. Uzbekistan, c. 1960s–70s. Soviet postcard. The Islam-Khodja minaret.

6.

7.

GLOSSARY

NOTE: The Central Asian words used in this book may be spelled in various ways, depending on region, dialect, time frame, and transliteration. If a textile is specific to a certain ethnic group, then whenever possible the term used by that group is given. However, inconsistencies are bound to occur.

ABR general term for ikat fabric; from the Persian word meaning "cloud"

ABRBANDI term for the ikat technique; *abrbandchi* is the master who draws the ikat pattern on the warp

ADRAS silk warp/cotton weft plain-weave fabric with fine horizontal ribbing; term usually refers to ikat

AINA KHALTA small embroidered wall hanging; also called a mirror-bag; also *oyna khalta, ainak push*

AKSAKAL "whitebeard"; the name given to older men, often respected elders of the community

ALACHA silk warp/cotton weft plain-weave striped fabric; also called *bekasab*; *alacha* may also be woven with a cotton warp/cotton weft

ALAMAN Turkmen raiding party

ARBA horse-drawn wooden cart with two very large wheels; also *araba*

ARIK irrigation canal

ARTEL Soviet artisans' collective

ATLAS silk warp/silk weft satin-weave fabric (usually ikat); may also be woven with a silk warp/cotton weft

AUL encampment of yurts

BACTRIAN Central Asian breed of camel with two humps (as opposed to the one-humped dromedary)

BAGHMAL velvet ikat; either all silk or silk warp/cotton weft; also *bakhmal*

BALAK loose-fitting trousers worn under a Turkmen woman's dress

BANORAS silk warp/cotton weft handwoven cloth; usually gray, green, or blue with narrow black stripes; most often used to make *paranjas*

BANOT imported wool broadcloth of English or Russian manufacture; also *bannot, sukno* (Russian), *ushiga* (Karakalpak)

BASMA type of laid and couched stitch; often used on *suzanis*; see fig. 3, page 173 for detail

BATCHA young dancing boy; also *bacha*

BEG highest official of a district

BEKASAB silk warp/cotton weft plain-weave, multicolored striped fabric with fine horizontal ribbing; also called *alacha*

BELBOG square scarf worn around the waist like a sash to secure a robe; also *belbew, belbo'o* (Kyrgyz)

BELDEMCHI embroidered Kyrgyz apronlike skirt

BESHIKPUSH embroidered cloth cradle cover (Uzbek); *gavaraposh* (Tajik); *beshik* (wooden cradle)

BIGIZ handheld hooked iron tool used for making fine chain stitch (*yurma, tambour*); also *daravsh*

BODUM Central Asian word for "almond"; the *bodum* motif looks like a paisley

BOKCHE flat, envelope-shaped bag (Turkmen)

BOLINPUSH square embroidered *suzani* held over the bride during the marriage ceremony; later it is placed over the pillows on the newlyweds' bed

BORIK Kazakh warm hat with rounded crown and fur trim

BOSH tall Kungrat headdress composed of many scarves wrapped around a woman's *kiygich*

BUGJAMA large cloth used to wrap and store clothing; also *bugzhoma*

BUZ handwoven, homespun, undyed cotton fabric; also *bo's, bo'z, baz, karbos, karbaz, beyz* (Kyrgyz), *mata* (Russian)

BUZGUNCH pistachio galls; used to make black dye

BUZKASHI horsemanship game played with a goat or calf carcass; *kok-boru* (Kyrgyz)

CAROQ patchwork; thought to have talismanic properties; also *kurok*

CHACHAK silk fringe

CHACH KEP Kyrgyz embroidered headdress with soft cap and long plait cover

CHACHVAN tightly woven horsehair veil worn with the *paranja*; also *chachvon*; also *chedra*

CHAI KHALTA Small embroidered bag used to carry tea and personal items; *chai, choi,* and *choy* (tea)

CHAIKHANA teahouse

CHAINIK teapot; also *choynak*

CHAKMATUR type of embroidery using tiny white stitches to create a pattern on skullcaps

CHALMA	turban; also *salla*, *selde* (Kyrgyz)
CHAPAN	general term for a robe; also *khalat*
CHARKH	spinning wheel
CHEKMEN	heavy outer robe usually made of sheep's wool or camel's hair, also *chepken*
CHIRIK	wooden cotton gin with rollers to separate the husks from the fibers
CHIT	woodblock-printed cotton fabric, often printed on handwoven *buz*
CHITAGAR	man who block-prints *chit*; also *chitkar*
CHODOR	a Turkmen tribe; also Chowdur
CHOISHAB	large embroidered cloth like a *ruijo*; formerly used as a wedding sheet
CHUK	stack of bedding quilts piled neatly against a wall in a yurt or house
CHUVAL	large Turkmen storage bag usually with a wool-pile face
CHYRPY	Turkmen woman's elaborately embroidered capelike robe; worn on top of the head with long false sleeves hanging down in back
DASTARKHAN	cloth on which food is served; the meal itself
DAURI	horse cover
DOGA	triangular cloth amulet; also *tumar*
DORPECH	long, narrow, horizontal embroidery hung at ceiling height; also *zardevor*
DUPPI	Uzbek skullcap; also *do'ppi*, *topu* (Kyrgyz), *toki* (Tajik)
DUYE BASHLYK	long patchwork camel trapping used in Turkmen wedding procession; *duye* (camel)
DUYE DIZLYK	camel knee trappings used in Turkmen bridal procession
ELECHEK	northern-style voluminous white cotton turban and cowl worn by Kyrgyz women
ELEK	Turkmen child's biblike garment; thought to have protective properties; also *kirlik*
ERSARI	a Turkmen tribe
FARANGI	imported European and Russian fabrics
GAVARAPOSH	cover for a baby's cradle (Tajik)
GÖL	a tribal geometric medallion, usually octagonal; often seen on Turkmen carpets
GUL	a flower
GYRMYZY DON	traditional Turkmen red, striped man's robe
GYRMYZY DONLYK	Turkmen red, striped cloth
HUJUM	Soviet unveiling campaign; Turkic word meaning "onslaught," "attack"
ICHIGI	soft leather boots with soft soles (worn indoors)
ICHKARI	inner courtyard; the women's part of the house
ILGICH	small square- and shield-shaped embroidered hangings
IKAT	fabric produced by binding the warp threads prior to dyeing in such a way as to create a distinctive pattern; the dyed warp threads are then strung on the loom and the weft threads woven in; *ikat* is an Indonesian term; also *abr* (Central Asian term)
ILEKI	southern-style large white cotton turban worn by Kyrgyz women; the neck and chin are uncovered
ILMOK	ladder stitch; open chain stitch; also *ilmoq*; see fig. 2, page 167 for detail
ILON	snake; protective of women and children
IPAK	silk; silk thread
IROKI	small cross-stitch embroidery; also *iroqi*; see fig. 6, page 217 for detail
ISHTON	men's baggy cotton trousers narrowing at the ankles; also *ichtan* (Kyrgyz)
ISPARAK	yellow dye made from the flowers of *Delphinium sulphureum* (a yellow larkspur)
JELAK	short capelike garment worn as a headdress in rural areas of Uzbekistan
JINN	evil spirit
JIYAK	handwoven narrow trim for skullcaps and robes (Tashkent term)
JOINOMOZ	embroidered prayer mat with *mihrab* in center; also *joinamaz, joynomoz*
KALAMKASH	draftswoman skilled at drawing *suzani* patterns
KALAMPIR	capsicum pepper; widely used talismanic motif; also *qalampir*
KALPAK	tall white-felt Kyrgyz or Kazakh man's hat with upturned brim
KALTACHA	woman's robe (Bukhara and Samarkand); also *munisak* (Tashkent and Ferghana), *misak* (Khorezm)
KALYM	bride price; also *kalin, qalin*
KAMARBAND	a belt; particularly an embroidered belt

KARA	the color black; *kyzyl* (red); *ak* (white)
KARAKALPAK	Turkic-speaking people (formerly from a confederation of Uzbek tribes), most of whom live in the Karalkalpakstan region of Uzbekistan; also *Qaraqalpaq*
KARA-KIRGHIZ	former Russian name for the people now known as Kyrgyz
KARBOS	homespun, handwoven, off-white, plain-weave cotton; often used as the foundation cloth of *suzanis*; also *karbaz, buz, boz, baz, mata*
KEJEBE	tentlike cloth that covers a Turkmen bride in her litter (*kedzheba*) atop a camel
KELIN	newly wedded girl; daughter-in-law
KESDI	type of lacing or double chain stitch; commonly used by Turkmen women; see figs. 7 and 8, page 103 for details
KETENI	handwoven silk cloth made by Turkmen women on narrow looms
KHALAT	general term for a robe; also *chapan*
KHALTA	a bag; usually embroidered, e.g., *chai khalta* (tea bag)
KHAN	ruler of a khanate; tribal chief
KHANATLAS	silk warp/silk weft satin-weave ikat; highest grade *atlas* fabric
KIBITKA	a felt tent or yurt
KIRGHIZ-KAISAK	former Russian name for the people now known as Kazakh
KIRLIK	Turkmen child's embroidered protective bib; also *elek*
KIRMIZ	tiny scale insects; when dried they make a bright, fast red dye similar to cochineal; also *kermes*
KIRPECH	long narrow embroidered panel used to cover wall niches
KIYGICH	soft rounded cap with long plait-cover extension in back; worn under a headdress of wrapped scarves; also *kulta*
KIYMESHEK	Karakalpak woman's elaborately embroidered headdress; also *kimeshek* (Kazakh, Kyrgyz)
KOLIB	carved wooden stamp for block-printing cloth; also *kolyb*
KOLKHOZ	Soviet collective farm; *kolkhozy* (plural)
KOYNEK	Turkmen woman's long shiftlike dress; also *kurta*
KUDUNG	process of glazing *adras* and *bekasab* fabrics
KULOKH	tall conical-shaped skullcap; also *kulox*
KUMISS	fermented mare's milk; also *koumiss, kymyss*
KUNDAL	brocaded cloth (usually refers to Russian brocade)
KUNGRAT	an Uzbek tribe
KUROK	patchwork; also *caroq*
KUROMA	patchwork camel flank trappings used in Turkmen bridal procession
KURPA	padded bedding quilt; serves as a mattress
KURPACHA	narrow quilt or long pillow to sit on
KURTA	dress; child's shirt; man's tuniclike shirt; also *kurte*
KUYLAK	dress; also *kuilak* (Uzbek), *koylek* (Karakalpak), *köynök* (Kyrgyz), *kurta* (Tajik)
LAKAI	an Uzbek tribe
LOZIM	woman's long pantaloonlike trousers; worn under a dress or robe; also *shalwars*, *balak* (Turkmen), *ichtan* (Kyrgyz)
MADDER	dye made from the powdered roots of *Rubia tinctoria*; shades of red, purple, and rust were obtained depending on the mordant used
MADRASSAH	Islamic school; also *madrasa, medrese*
MAHALLA	a neighborhood; a neighborhood's self-governing committee
MIHRAB	niche in an inner wall of a mosque indicating the direction to Mecca; the *mihrab* shape, as in a prayer mat; also *mehrab*
MUNISAK	a woman's robe that is lightly gathered under the armpits; also *mursak, kaltacha*
NAPRAMACH	large rectangular woven or embroidered storage bag; also *mapramach*
NIL	indigo; blue dye extracted from leaves of the plant family *Indigofera*
NINA	embroidery needle
NON	flatbread; also *lepeshka, lepyoshka*
OFTOBA	water jug, ewer; small ewer motifs often appear on *suzanis*; symbol of purity
OY	literally "moon" (Uzbek); *oy palyak* is a type of Tashkent *suzani*; also *oi*
PAKHTA	cotton; *pakhtagul* cotton flower
PARANJA	woman's long capelike robe worn over the head with false sleeves fastened in back; also *paranji, faranji*
PARDAH	wall hanging; often made from joined lengths of cloth
PATRAGAR	mender of crockery

PESHANABAND — headband worn across the forehead, usually with gold embroidery (Bukhara)

PESHKURTA — narrow embroidered strips along the neckline of a dress

PIAZY — brown handwoven camel's wool cloth (Kyrgyz)

PILTA — small cylinders of wadded cotton or paper inserted between rows of quilting to give skullcaps a ribbed appearance; *piltado-zi* is the technique

PIOLA — porcelain teacup like a small bowl without handles; also *piala*

POPUK MASHINA — sewing machine

PYOPYOK — tassels

QIZIL — the color red; *qizil-gul* red flower; also *kyzyl*

QO'CHQOR — ram; *qo'chqor muguz* ram's horn

RUIJO — sheet for the marriage bed that is embroidered on three sides around an unadorned center; also *ruydjo*

RUMOL — scarf; also *rumal*

RUYAN — madder; dye made from the roots of *Rubia tinctoria*, also *rujan*

SALLA — man's turban; also *chalma*, *selde* (Kyrgyz)

SANDALPUSH — embroidered cloth laid over a wooden frame on top of a brazier

SANDUK — storage chest, often with bedding quilts stacked on top

SART — former Russian term for city-dwelling Central Asians

SAUKELE — tall conical hat worn by a Kazakh bride

SAXAUL — scrubby, thorny low desert and steppe shrub used for fuel and fodder; also *saksaul*

SAYMA — Kyrgyz word for embroidery; *sayma topu* (embroidered skullcaps); also *keshte*

SEGUSHA — embroidered V-shaped or triangular decorations for the bedding stack (*chuk*); also *saye gosha*

SHALWARS — woman's baggy trousers; also called *lozim* (Kyrgyz)

SHEROZA — decorative trim along the edges of robes and skullcaps (Surkhandarya term)

SHOHI — silk warp/silk weft plain-weave cloth, particularly ikat; also *shahi*, *kanaous*

SHYRDAK — Kyrgyz wool felt "mosaic" rug

SITETZ — Russian word for printed cloth; chintz

SOVCHOK — long false sleeves of a *paranja*

SUZANI — embroidered hanging; from the Farsi word *suzan* (needle)

TAKHTA — raised outdoor seating platform at a teahouse

TAKHYA — Turkmen skullcap; *takiya* (Kyrgyz, Kazakh, Karakalpak, and Khivan)

TAMBOUR — fine chain stitching made with a handheld tool (*bigiz*, *daravsh*); also *yurma*

TEKKE — a Turkmen tribe

TELPEK — man's tall, shaggy lambskin hat; also *telpak*, *kurash*

TERMÉ — narrow woven wool tent bands

TIZMA — narrow woven trim; also *tesma*

TOKI — Tajik skullcap; also *topu* (Kyrgyz), *duppi* (Uzbek)

TON — heavy Kyrgyz and Kazakh sheepskin overcoat worn with the fur inside

TOPU — Kyrgyz skullcap; *sayma topu* (embroidered skullcap)

TOR — place of honor in a yurt, against the back wall facing the entrance

TUKHMAK — yellow dye obtained from buds of the Japanese pagoda tree, *Sophora japonica*

TUMAR — triangular amulet; also *tumor*; a small hollow tubular container, usually of silver, which held text from the Koran or other protective items and was worn as an amulet

TUS KIIZ — large Kazakh or Kyrgyz embroidered wall hanging; also *tush kiyiz* (Kyrgyz)

TYUBETEIKA — Uzbek embroidered skullcap; also *tubeteika*

USTO — master artisan; overseer of a workshop

YAHKTAK — lightweight unlined robe; also *yaktak*

YAKRUYA — silk warp/cotton weft satin-weave cloth

YOMUT — a Turkmen tribe; also Yomud

YURMA — chain stitch; also *yo'rma*; may be made with a needle or a hook (*bigaz*); see fig. 5, page 169 for detail

ZARCHAPAN — gold-embroidered robe; formerly only worn by khans and very high officials; embroidered in Bukhara

ZARDEVOR — long, narrow embroidery hung like a frieze at ceiling height; also *dorpech*

ZARDUZI — gold embroidery of Bukhara

ZEH — narrow patterned trim on skullcaps; wider trim used on robes (Bukhara term)

SELECTED BIBLIOGRAPHY

"And sunset steeps them in a golden haze. And they still move there whilst the traveler who has spell-bound them in his writing has gone on his way." —From a letter to British journalist Stephen Graham in response to his article "Towards Turkestan," published in the *Times* during the summer of 1913

Abazov, Rafis. *The Palgrave Concise Historical Atlas of Central Asia.* New York: Palgrave Macmillan, 2008.

Alexander, Christopher Aslan. *A Carpet Ride to Khiva: Seven Years on the Silk Road.* London: Icon Books, 2010.

Andrews, Mogul, and Peter Andrews. *Turkmen Needlework.* London: Central Asian Research Centre, 1976.

Antipina, Klavdiya. *Kyrgyzstan.* Milan: Skira, 2006.

Museum of the Applied Art of Uzbekistan. *Applied Art of Uzbekistan.* Tashkent, 2003.

Babanazaova, Marinika. *Igor Savitsky: Artist, Collector, Museum Founder.* London: Silk Road Publishing House, 2011.

Bacon, Elizabeth E. *Central Asians under Russian Rule: A Study in Culture Change.* Ithaca: Cornell University Press, 1966.

Baker, Patricia. *Islamic Textiles.* London: The British Museum Press, 1995.

Bausback, Franz. *SUSANI: Stickereien aus Mittelasien.* Auction catalog. Mannheim, Germany: April 1981.

Becker, Seymour. *Russia's Protectorates in Central Asia: Bukhara and Khiva, 1865–1924.* Cambridge: Harvard University Press, 1968.

Billeter, Erika. *Usbekistan: Documentary Photography 1925–1945 by Max Penson.* Bern: Benteli Verlag, 1996.

Black, David, and Clive Loveless. *Embroidered Flowers from Thrace to Tartary.* Exhibition catalog. London: David Black Oriental Carpets, 1981.

Bogoslovskaya, Irina, and Larisa Levteeva. *Skullcaps of Uzbekistan: 19th–20th Centuries.* Tashkent, 2006.

Burnaby, Frederick Gustavus. *A Ride to Khiva: My Travels and Adventures in Central Asia, 1875.* London: Cassell Petter & Galpin, 1876. The Narrative Press facsimile, 2003.

Burnes, Alexander. *Travels into Bokhara: Being the Account of a Journey from India to Cabool, Tartary and Persia.* London: John Murray, 1834. BiblioBazaar, LLC facsimile.

Christie, Ella. *Through Khiva to Golden Samarkand.* London: Seeley, Service & Co., 1925.

Curtis, William Eleroy. *Turkestan: The Heart of Asia.* New York: Hodder & Stoughton, 1911.

Erlikman, Vadim. *Poteri Narodonaseleniia v XX Veke: Spravochnik* [Population losses in the 20th century: Handbook]. Moscow, 2004.

Fell, Nelson E. *Russian and Nomad: Tales of the Kirghiz Steppes.* New York: Duffield and Company, 1916.

Figes, Orlando. *Natasha's Dance: A Cultural History of Russia.* New York: Picador, 2002.

Fihl, Esther. *Exploring Central Asia: From the Steppes to the High Pamirs 1896–1899,* 2 vols. Seattle: University of Washington Press, 2002.

Fitz Gibbon, Kate, and Andrew Hale. *The Guido Goldman Collection: Ikat Silks of Central Asia.* London: Lawrence King Publishing, 1997.

——. *Uzbek Embroidery in the Nomadic Tradition: The Jack A. and Aviva Robinson Collection.* Minneapolis: Minneapolis Institute of Arts, 2007.

Gibb, H. A. *Ibn Battuta: Travels in Asia and Africa 1325–1354.* New Delhi: Manohar facsimilie, 2006.

Glazebrook, Philip. *Journey to Khiva: A Writer's Search for Central Asia.* New York: Kodansha America, 1994.

Graham, Stephen. *Through Russian Central Asia.* New York: The Macmillan Company, 1916.

Halle, Fannina W. *Women in the Soviet East.* London: Martin Secker & Warburg, 1938.

Harvey, Janet. *Traditional Textiles of Central Asia.* London: Thames & Hudson, 1996.

Hedin, Sven. *Through Asia, Volume I and II.* New York: Harper & Brothers, 1899.

Hodgson, Barbara. *Dreaming of East: Western Women and the Exotic Allure of the Orient.* Vancouver: Greystone Books, 2005.

Hopkirk, Peter. *The Great Game: The Struggle for Empire in Central Asia.* New York: Kodansha America, 1994.

Hughes, Langston. "In an Emir's Harem." *Woman's Home Companion,* September 1934, 12 and 91–92.

——. *I Wonder as I Wander.* New York: Hill and Wang, 1999.

——. *The Collected Works of Langston Hughes.* Vol. 9. Columbia: University of Missouri Press, 2002.

Jackson, Peter. *The Mission of Friar William of Rubruck: His Journey to the Court of the Great Khan Möngke 1253–1255.* Indianapolis: Hackett Publishing Company, 2009.

Jefferson, Robert. *A New Ride to Khiva.* New York: New Amsterdam Book Co., 1900. General Books facsimile, 2010.

Kachurin, Pamela Jill. *Soviet Textiles: Designing the Modern Utopia.* Boston: The Museum of Fine Arts, 2006.

Kalter, Johannes. *The Arts and Crafts of Turkestan.* London: Thames & Hudson, 1984.

Kalter, Johannes, and Margareta Pavaloi. *Uzbekistan: Heirs to the Silk Road.* London: Thames & Hudson, 1997.

Khanikoff, Nikolai. *Bokhara: Its Amir and Its People.* London: James Madden, 1845. Elibron Classics facsimile, 2005.

King, David. *The Commissar Vanishes: The Falsification of Photographs and Art in Stalin's Russia.* New York: Metropolitan Books, 1997.

——. *Red Star over Russia: A Visual History of the Soviet Union from the Revolution to the Death of Stalin*. New York: Abrams, 2009.

Krist, Gustav. *Alone through the Forbidden Land: Journeys in Disguise through Soviet Central Asia*. London: Faber and Faber, 1938.

Krody, Sumru Belger. *Colors of the Oasis: Central Asian Ikats*. Washington, DC: The Textile Museum, 2010.

Lansdell, Henry. *Russian Central Asia, Including Kuldja, Bokhara, Khiva and Merv*. Vol. 1. London: Low, Marston, Searle, and Rivington, 1885. General Books facsimile.

Lunin, B. *Lenin and the Peoples of the East*. Moscow: Novosti Press Agency Publishing House, 1970.

Macintyre, Ben. *The Man Who Would Be King: The First American in Afghanistan*. New York: Farrar, Straus, and Giroux, 2004.

Maclean, Fitzroy. *Back to Bokhara*. New York: Harper & Brothers, 1959.

——. *To the Back of Beyond: An Illustrated Companion to Central Asia and Mongolia*. Boston: Little, Brown and Company, 1975.

Mahkamova, Sayora. *Old Silk Costumes of Uzbekistan*. Moscow: Tair Tairov, 2010.

Maillart, Ella K. *Forbidden Journey: From Peking to Kashmir*. London: William Heinemann, 1937.

——. *Turkestan Solo: One Woman's Expedition from the Tien Shan to the Kizil Kum*. New York: G. P. Putnam's Sons, 1935.

Mannin, Ethel. *South to Samarkand*. New York: E. P. Dutton and Co., 1937.

Markham, Charles R. *Narrative of the Embassy of Ruy Gonzalez de Clavijo to the Court of Timour, at Samarcand A.D. 1403-6*. London: The Hakluyt Society, 1859. Kessinger Publishing facsimile.

Marsden, William. *The Travels of Marco Polo (The Venetian)*. New York: Boni & Liveright, 1926.

Marvin, Charles. *Reconnoitring Central Asia: Pioneering Adventures in the Region Lying between Russia and India*. London: Swan Sonnenschein, Le Bas & Lowrey, 1886.

Max Penson: Soviet Uzbekistan 1920-1930s. Moscow: Moscow House of Photography, 2006.

Meakin, Annette M. B. *In Russian Turkestan: A Garden of Asia and Its People*. London: George Allen, 1903.

Meller, Susan. *Russian Textiles: Printed Cloth for the Bazaars of Central Asia*. New York: Abrams, 2007.

Murav'yov, Nikolay. *Journey to Khiva through the Turkoman Country*. Moscow: Avgust Semyon Printing House, 1822. London: Oguz Press, 1977.

Murray, Edward. "With the Nomads of Central Asia." *National Geographic*, January 1936.

Music for the Eyes: Textiles from the Peoples of Central Asia. Exhibition catalog. Antwerp: 1997.

Naumkin, Vitaly, ed. *Bukhara: Caught in Time*. Reading: Garnet Publishing, 1993.

Nazaroff, Paul S. *Hunted Through Central Asia*. Edinburgh: Wm. Blackwood & Sons, 1932.

Nodir, Binafsha. *San'at* magazine. Academy of Arts, Uzbekistan. Issue 2, 2005.

Norman, Henry. *All the Russias*. New York: Charles Scribner's Sons, 1902.

Northrop, Douglas. *Veiled Empire: Gender and Power in Stalinist Central Asia*. Ithica: Cornell University Press, 2004.

Olcott, Martha Brill. *The Kazakhs*. Stanford, CA: Hoover Institution Press, 1987.

Olufsen, Ole. *The Emir of Bokhara and His Country*. London: William Heinemann, 1911. Elibron Classics, 2005.

Richardson, David, and Sue Richardson. *Qaraqalpaqs of the Aral Delta*. Munich: Prestel Verlag, 2012.

Russia's Unknown Orient: Orientalist Paintings 1850-1920. Groningen: Groningen Museum exhibition catalog, 2010.

Sahadeo, Jeff. *Russian Colonial Society in Tashkent, 1865-1923*. Bloomington: Indiana University Press, 2010.

Schmidt, Emil. *The Russian Expedition to Khiva in 1873*. Calcutta: Foreign Department Press, 1876. Nabu facsimile.

Schuyler, Eugene. *Turkestan: Notes of a Journey in Russian Turkestan, Khokand, Bukhara and Kuldja*, 2 vols. London: Sampson Low, Marston, Searle, & Rivington, 1876. Elibron Classics, 2006.

Scott, Philippa. *The Book of Silk*. London: Thames and Hudson, 1993.

Sodikova, Naphisa. *National Uzbek Clothes (XIX-XX Centuries)*. Tashkent, 2003.

Strizhenova, Tatiana. *Soviet Costume and Textiles 1917-1945*. Paris: Flammarion, 1991.

Sumner, Christina, and Guy Petherbridge. *Bright Flowers: Textiles and Ceramics of Central Asia*. Sydney: Powerhouse Publishing, 2004.

Taylor, Bayard. *Central Asia: Travels in Cashmere, Little Tibet, and Central Asia*. New York: Charles Scribner's Sons, 1888.

Thompson, Jon. *Timbuktu to Tibet: Exotic Rugs & Textiles from New York Collections*. New York: The Haji Baba Club, 2008.

Turkmen Folk Art. Ashkhabad, 1990.

Vámbéry, Arminius. *Sketches of Central Asia*. London: Wm. H. Allen & Co., 1868. Google Books facsimile.

——. *Travels in Central Asia*. London: John Murray, 1864. Elibron Classics, 2005.

Vok, Ignazio, and Jakob Taube. *Vok Collection: Suzani A Textile Art from Central Asia*. Munich: Herold Verlagsauslieferung, 1994.

Wardell, J. W. *In the Kirghiz Steppes*. London: The Galley Press, 1961.

Williams, Maynard Owen. "Russia's Orphan Races." *National Geographic*, October 1918.

Wilson, Helen Calista, and Elsie Reed Mitchell. *Vagabonding at Fifty: From Siberia to Turkestan*. New York: Coward McCann, 1929.

INDEX

Note: Page numbers in *italics* refer to illustrations. Text pages pertaining to these illustrations have not been listed separately if the page numbers are the same as those of the illustrations, or the illustrations have accompanying captions.

CREDITS

ACKNOWLEDGMENTS

ИСТАРАУМКИ КЛЯБЛАРАЯ ДУСТЛИК, ЧАШМАДЕК ПОК ТУГАНМАС БУЛСА!

I would like to thank the following people for their help in making this book:

My husband, Frank Rubenfeld, for his unflagging interest, patience, and editorial assistance. His words "reality is an infinity of hidden worlds waiting to be seen" seem particularly apropos to the textiles in this book.

Don Tuttle for giving every photograph his best. From a small piece of printed cloth to a glorious *suzani*, Don took pride and pleasure in bringing out the full potential of each piece.

Marty Kelly and Sophia Tuttle, who assisted with close to six hundred studio shots with a keen eye and good humor.

Susan Homer, my editor, for her continually upbeat attitude, unfailing attention to detail, and willingness to go the extra mile through the long, and at times tedious, editing process. It was a privilege and pleasure to work with her.

Darilyn Carnes, Associate Art Director, Abrams Books. Over the past twenty-three years, Darilyn and I have worked together on all my books, *Textile Designs*, *Russian Textiles*, and *Silk and Cotton*. She has played a key role in making these books as beautiful as they are. Her support, enthusiasm, and dedication are very much appreciated.

Eric Himmel, Vice President and Editor in Chief, Abrams Books, who successfully championed *Silk and Cotton*.

Jutta Pakenis, Marti Malovany, and everyone at Abrams who did their part to help this book come to fruition and will continue to help make it a success after publication.

Robert Kushner, who contributed an artist's perspective on Central Asian *suzanis*, and whose view of the decorative arts as "the sincere and unabashed offering of pleasure and solace" I completely agree with!

Elizabeth Hewitt, my friend and Central Asian textile colleague, who was always there (in Istanbul) to answer the many questions that arose. She and her husband, Huseyin Kaplan, provided contemporary photographs and sent their beautiful Lakai textiles to be photographed for the book. Elizabeth combed the bazaars for my special requests and even came through with Uzbek "pampers"—a baby's clay "pee pot."

Vyacheslav Purgalin graciously translated the Russian and Uzbek words embroidered on *suzanis* and hats; printed on scarves; and emblazoned across banners and railroad cars in Soviet-era photographs. He was always willing and available to help answer questions.

Alex Schaub, Tashkent textile historian, teacher, and collector, who gave most generously of his time and knowledge.

Andrew Hale, Kate Fitz Gibbon, Thomas Cole, Irina Bogoslovskaya, Gail Martin, Michael Frances, Clive Loveless, Seref Ozen, who shared their expertise with me—it was very much appreciated!

Laurel Victoria Gray, artistic director and founder of the Silk Road Dance Company, for her generous help with Uzbek translations and clarifying certain cultural customs.

Samuel Omans, Fulbright scholar to Kazakhstan, for volunteering to review my manuscript; for his enthusiastic support; and for many pleasurable conversations.

The following people also contributed in various ways to help this project come to fruition:

Peter and Claire Koepke, The Design Library; Malcolm Margolin, Publisher, Heyday Books; Lucy Kelaart, Editor, *Steppe* magazine; Max Penson's daughter Dina Khojaeva and his grandson Maxime Penson, Tashkent; Adam Smith Albion, Tashkent; Anna Motorina, Tashkent; German Abramov, Tashkent; Marina Ivanova, Permissions, State Tretyakov Gallery; Marinika Babanazarova, Director, Nukus Museum of Art; David Pearce, Friends of Nukus Museum; Jill D'Alessandro, Curator, Textile Department, de Young Fine Arts Museum; Ashley Morton, *National Geographic*; Claude English; Judy Brick Freedman; Cam Knuckey; Luke Powell, photographer; A. Yohann de Silva, Vicarious Eye Photography; Murod Nararov, Advantour Travel Agency, Tashkent; Jonathan Tyrrell, Retrospective Traveler; Exodus Travels, UK; Jean-Paul Rodrigue, Hofstra University.

And, of course, my family and friends.

Vor Samarkand. Samarkand, 1926. Camel caravan approaching the ruins of Tamerlane's Bibi-Khanum mosque.
Photograph by Countess Carmen Finkenstein.

Project Manager: Eric Himmel
Editor: Susan Homer
Design: Susan Meller and Darilyn Lowe Carnes
Production Manager: Anet Sirna-Bruder

Library of Congress Control Number: 2013935978

ISBN: 978-1-4197-0674-5

Printed and bound in China
10 9 8 7 6 5 4 3 2 1

Abrams books are available at special discounts when purchased in quantity
for premiums and promotions as well as fundraising or educational use. Special
editions can also be created to specification. For details, contact specialsales@
abramsbooks.com or the address below.

THE ART OF BOOKS SINCE 1949

115 West 18th Street
New York, NY 10011
www.abramsbooks.com